UNITED STATES POSTAL SERVICE

The Postal Service Guide to U.S. Stamps

10th Edition
U.S. Stamps in Full Color
1984 Stamp Values

Y0-CBG-139

United States Postal Service
Washington, D.C.   20260-6355
Item No. 820

IMPORTANT INFORMATION

The United States Postal Service sells only the commemoratives released during the past few years and current regular and special stamps and postal stationery.

Prices listed in this book are called "catalog prices" by collectors and serve only as a guide to market prices for Fine specimens when offered by an informed dealer to an informed buyer.

Prices in regular type for single unused and used stamps are taken from the latest Brookman Price List (© 1983), whose editors have based these values on the current stamp market. Prices quoted for unused and used stamps are for "Fine condition, except where Fine is not available. Prices in italics for single unused and used stamps are taken from Scott's Standard Postage Stamp Catalogue, Vol. 1, 1984 Edition, © 1983. If no value is assigned, market value is individually determined by condition of the stamp, scarcity and other factors.

Prices for Plate Blocks and First Day Covers are taken from Scott's Specialized Catalogue of U.S. Stamps, 1984 Edition, © 1983. The Scott numbering system for stamps is used in this book.

Prices for Souvenir Cards have been taken from the Catalog of United States Souvenir Cards, by Franklin R. Bruns, Jr., and James H. Bruns, published by Washington Press.

Prices for American Commemorative Panels are from Frank Riolo, Delray Beach, Florida. Souvenir Pages prices are from Charles D. Simmons of Buena Park, California.

Prices of actual stamp sales are dependent upon supply and demand, changes in popularity, local custom, quality of the stamp itself and many other factors.

Library of Congress Catalogue Card Number 83-050369.
ISBN: 0-9604756-3-X
Printed in the United States of America

Photo Credits: pages 32-43, all color photos courtesy of SPORTS ILLUSTRATED; page 41, Bettmann Archive.

Editorial and Design: Mobium Corporation for Design and Communication, Chicago, IL
Printing: R.R. Donnelley and Sons Co., Crawfordsville, IN

TABLE OF CONTENTS

HOW TO USE THE POSTAL SERVICE GUIDE TO U.S. STAMPS

The Postal Service Guide to U.S. Stamps is a color catalog of postage stamps of the United States, designed to put all the vital information you need in one handy reference line.

Each line listing contains the following information:

	Un	U	PB	#	FDC	Q
1710 13¢ Spirit of St. Louis, May 20	.00	.00	0.00	(6)	0.00	000,000,000

| ↑ Scott Catalog Number | ↑ Denomination | ↑ Description First Day of Issue | ↑ Unused Catalog Price | ↑ Plate Block Price Used Catalog Price | ↑ First Day Cover Price # in Plate Block* | ↑ Quantity Issued |

1710

*All Plate Blocks are blocks of four unless otherwise indicated in parentheses.

The Postal Service Guide to U.S. Stamps also lists philatelic details such as watermarks, perforations and years of issue. These will aid you in identifying stamps of similar design. Watermarks (Wmk.) are designs incorporated in the paper on which certain stamps are printed. Perforations are the number of small holes in a two centimeter space on the edge of the stamp. A stamp which has 12 such holes is listed as Perf. 12 (perforated 12), while a stamp with no perforations is listed as Imperf. (imperforate). Coil stamps are perforated on two sides only, either horizontally or vertically. **When a perforation, year of issue, or watermark is mentioned, the description applies to all succeeding issues until a change is noted.**

Illustration Numbers. Some of the stamps cataloged in this book are not shown. The illustrations for such stamps are identified by a number in parentheses. For example, in the listings which appear below, Scott No. 247 has the same illustration as Scott No. 246.

246   1¢ Franklin
247   1¢ blue Franklin (246)

How to Order Stamps. When ordering stamps from a dealer, identify items wanted by country of issue, Scott No., and condition (unused or used).

Condition is an important factor of price. Prices are for stamps in fine condition. Off center, heavily cancelled, faded or stained stamps usually sell at large discounts. Values in italics indicate latest auction prices, infrequent sales or fluctuating market values.

Suppose someone asked you, "What is the most popular hobby in the world?" Since you're reading this book, you can probably guess the answer. That's right. It's stamp collecting. In the United States alone, about 20 million people are stamp collectors. And there are millions more around the world.

What makes stamps so fascinating? Some people think of stamps as tiny windows on the world. Most countries have stamps that show people or things or events that their citizens think are very important, or valuable, or beautiful. So when you look at a postage stamp, you learn something about the country it comes from.

Another reason people like to collect stamps is that many stamps are really works of art. Talented artists and photographers design the stamps. They are printed with great care and skill. Having a collection of beautiful stamps is like having an art gallery of your own.

Another thing that makes stamp collecting so popular is that there is no special age for it. You can enjoy stamp collecting just as much when you're 70 years old as when you're 10. In stamp collecting, you never run out of something to do. If you started now, and collected stamps for the rest of your life, you'd probably not be able to collect all the stamps in the world. The first postage stamp was issued in 1840. Since then, hundreds of thousands of different stamps have been issued by the countries of the world. But rather than trying to collect as many different kinds of stamps from as many places as you can, you'll probably find some types of stamps that are particularly interesting to you—and concentrate on collecting those.

Stamps can help with schoolwork. They can be used in special projects in classes like history, geography, and science. Also, stamp collecting is a merit badge activity for Scouts.

Stamp collecting doesn't have to be an expensive hobby. Of course, you could spend many thousands of dollars on stamps, but you can also be a collector without spending much money at all.

You can start out by asking your family and your friends to save used stamps for you. Just ask them to save the used stamps on envelopes they receive in the mail at their homes or businesses. As you gather stamps, you'll want to put them in order so you can show them to other people. A ring binder with loose leaf paper can be your first stamp album. But don't paste or tape your stamps into the album! That would destroy their value.

You'll find out how to handle your stamps throughout this section. But first, look at the next page. There you'll see some stamps that are very famous or very rare. At the bottom of the page are descriptions of the stamps, but they are not in order. How many stamps can you match up with their descriptions? Beside each description, there is a box. You can write in the box the *letter* of the stamp that matches the description. The answers are on page 9.

George Washington
1732-1982
USA 20c

A

B

PROJECT MERCURY

C

D

FIRST MAN ON THE MOON

E

BRITISH
Patana Petimum
One Vicissim
GUIANA.

G

POSTAGE
ONE PENNY

H

1. The first postage stamp ever issued that had a gummed b
printed in England and had a picture of Queen Victoria. It was
"Penny Black."

2. One of the most valuable U.S. stamps. Issued in 1918, it wa
airmail stamp. By mistake, 100 were printed with the airplan
upside down! See page 239 for its current catalog value.

3. A recent stamp that honors the 250th anniversary of the b
famous American. This person has been pictured on more U
postage stamps than any other individual.

4. A stamp made from a master steel die that had been carr
round-trip journey to the moon.

5. The first U.S. postage stamp to honor an American woma
Martha Washington, the wife of the first President of the Uni
This stamp was issued in 1923.

6. The first U.S. postage stamp. The person featured is calle
"father of the U.S. postal system." The date of the stamp wa
July 1, 1847.

7. The "secret stamp." Designed and printed in secrecy, this :
issued in 1962. The event it honored was astronaut John Gl
successful flight around the earth in a spaceship.

8. In 1980, this stamp was sold for $850,000! It is the only one
of a special printing in a British colony in 1856.

TYPES OF STAMPS

Many people who know about stamp collecting suggest that you shouldn't decide right away what kind of stamps you are going to collect. At first, they say, just get together as many different stamps as you can. United States stamps. Stamps from some other countries. Stamps that feature special subjects—birds, dogs, famous women, or Scouts, for example. (Stamps of this type are called *topicals,* because they are about one *topic*.) Then, after you've been collecting for a while, you'll have a better idea about what kind of stamps you want to specialize in. Just be sure to pick a type that has a lot of stamps, so you'll be able to get enough for a good-sized collection. U.S. commemoratives are an easy way to start.

Regular or Definitive Stamps These are the stamps you'll find on most mail. They are printed in unlimited quantities and sold by the Postal Service for long periods of time— several years, usually.

Regular or Definitive

Commemorative Stamps These stamps are issued to honor an important event, person, or special subject. They are usually larger and more colorful than definitives. They are sold for only a certain length of time—a few months, maybe, and are printed in limited quantities.

Coil Stamps These stamps are issued in rolls. Each stamp has two straight edges and two perforated edges.

Coil

Commemorative

Airmail Stamps U.S. airmail stamps are used for sending mail overseas.

Postage Due Stamps Postage due stamps are put on mail at the post office to show that the postage already paid was not enough. The amount shown on the stamp must be paid by the receiver of the mail.

Airmail   Postage Due

Special Delivery Stamps These stamps were sold to the sender for extra-fast delivery of the letter or package. They are not currently being produced by the Postal Service.

Special Delivery

EQUIPMENT FOR STAMP COLLECTING

Tongs for moving a stamp from one place to another, especially when handling unused stamps, to prevent damage.

Hinges for attaching stamps to the pages of your album. Hinges come either folded or unfolded.

Stamp catalog to help you identify stamps and give you other information about them, including their value, used and unused. This book is one of the best U.S. stamp catalogs.

Mounts are small plastic envelopes. They cost more money than hinges, but are necessary to protect unused stamps.

A package of glassine (glass-ene) **envelopes** to hold different kinds of stamps until you are ready to put them in an album. Glassine is a special kind of thin paper that keeps grease and air from damaging stamps.

Magnifying glass, four- or six-power, to help you distinguish stamps that seem to be the same.

Perforation gauge to help you identify stamps. It is used to measure the size and number of perforations (cuts or holes along the edges) on stamps.

Watermark fluid and a watermark tray of black glass or plastic. The stamp is placed face down in the tray and covered with a few drops of the watermark fluid. Then the watermark shows up. Watermark fluid can be dangerous, so be careful in following the directions.

You can buy all these supplies at any stamp store or by mail through advertisements in stamp collecting publications.

WHAT KIND OF ALBUM?

A simple ring binder with loose-leaf pages will do very nicely for your first album. But after a while you may want to buy a special stamp album. It's usually best to buy an album with loose-leaf pages. Then you can add more pages as your collection grows.

There is a kind of album that does not have pictures of the stamps that are to go on the pages. It just has plastic pockets on the pages. This type of album is called a *stock book*. The pages can be placed in a binder. You can buy as many pages as you need to hold your stamps. Or you may decide to buy an album just for the stamps of the United States or another country. This type of album has places for all stamps issued in that country within a certain time period. Album supplements are printed for recent years.

Putting Stamps in Albums
To get stamps off paper, you'll need a small pan with some warm (not hot) water in it, some newspapers or paper towels, and your tongs. Place a few stamps face down in the water. Wait a little while, until the stamps float off the paper. The stamps will sink to the bottom. The paper will float. As soon as the stamps are free, lift them out with the tongs, one by one. Place them face down on the newspaper or paper towel. If they dry flat, you can put them in your album. Follow carefully the next directions. If the stamps are curled up when they are dry, put them between the pages of a telephone directory or another big, heavy book. Put another heavy book or some other kind of weight on top. Leave the stamps overnight. The next day they should be flat and ready to place in your album.

You can use either folded or unfolded hinges to put stamps in your album. The shiny side is the gummed side. If you are using a folded hinge, lightly touch your tongue to the short side. Then, press the short side to the back of the stamp. Next, while holding the stamp with your tongs, touch your tongue to the long side of the hinge. Now put the stamp in its place on the album page, pressing it down with a blotter. (*Never* handle stamps with your fingers. Even if your hands are clean, oil from your skin may damage the stamps.) Finally, gently lift the corners of the stamp with the tongs to be sure it has not stuck to the page.

If you are using an unfolded hinge, follow the same steps, but first fold the hinge yourself. Fold one-third of the hinge down, and attach that to the stamp. Be sure the shiny side is out when you fold it.

If you are collecting unused (called *uncancelled or mint*) stamps, you should use plastic mounts to put them in your album. Mounts will protect your stamps better than hinges. A mount is a small envelope that covers the whole stamp. It keeps air, grease, and dirt from damaging the stamp.

Answers to quiz on page 6:

1. H   2. D   3. A   4. F

5. B   6. E   7. C   8. G

Adhesive A gummed stamp made to be attached to mail.

Aerophilately The hobby of collecting airmail stamps, covers and other postal materials that are delivered by balloon, airplane, or other types of aircraft.

APS Abbreviation for American Philatelic Society.

Approvals Stamps sent by a dealer to a collector for examination. Approvals must either be bought or returned to the dealer within a certain time.

ATA Abbreviation for American Topical Association.

Autographed Cover A cover sheet or envelope signed by a person who had something to do with the event that is being commemorated—for example, the pilot of the plane that carried the material. Or an envelope addressed to a famous person, and signed by that person.

Block An attached group of stamps at least two stamps high and two stamps wide.

Booklet Pane A small sheet of stamps especially cut and printed to be sold in booklets.

Cachet (ka-shay') A design on a first day cover (envelope).

Cancellation A mark placed on a stamp to show that the stamp has been used.

Centering The position of the design on a postage stamp. On perfectly centered stamps the design is exactly in the middle of the stamp.

Coils Stamps issued in rolls for use in dispensers, affixers or vending machines.

Commemoratives Stamps that honor anniversaries, important people, or special events. Commemoratives are usually sold for only a certain length of time.

Condition The state of a stamp in regard to such things as centering, freshness, color, gum, and hinge marks.

Cover The envelope or wrapping in which a letter has been sent through the mail.

Definitives Regular issues of stamps—not commemoratives. Regular issues are usually sold over long periods of time.

Face Value The value of a stamp as printed on the stamp.

First Day Cover An envelope with a new stamp and a cancellation showing the date the stamp was first sold.

Gum The adhesive on the back of a stamp.

Hinges Small strips of paper gummed on one side and used by collectors to put their stamps in albums.

Imperforate Stamps Stamps printed in sheets without perforations or other means of separating them. Users had to cut the stamps apart with scissors or a knife. These stamps were usually early issues. They were printed before machines to make perforations had been invented.

Mint Sheet A sheet of unused stamps.

Mint Stamp A postage stamp that is in the same condition as when it was purchased from a post office.

Overprint A regular issue stamp that has some printing on top of the original design. Sometimes stamps are overprinted when there has been a change of government or when one country takes over another in a war.

Pane Part of an original large printed sheet of stamps. Sheets are cut into panes so that they are easier to handle and sell at post offices.

Pen Cancellation A cancellation made before modern post office equipment was used. Postmasters drew a line in ink across stamps, initialed them, or wrote their names on them.

Perforations Lines of small cuts or holes between two rows of stamps so that the stamps are easy to separate.

Philately (fi-lat'-el-lee) The collecting and study of postage stamps and other postal material.

Plate The metal base from which stamps are printed.

Plate Block (or number plate block) A block of stamps with the plate number or numbers in the margin.

Postal Stationery Envelopes, postal cards, aerogrammes, and wrappers with stamps printed or embossed on them.

Postmark A mark put on envelopes and other mailing pieces, showing the date and the name of the post office where it was mailed.

Postmaster Provisionals Stamps made by local postmasters. They were used before the government of the country began issuing stamps, or when the post office ran out of regular stamps.

Precancels Stamps with cancellations applied before the material was mailed.

Reissue An official reprinting of a stamp that was no longer being printed.

Revenue Stamps Stamps issued for use in collecting taxes on special papers or products. Not used for postage.

Selvage The paper around panes of stamps. Sometimes called the margin.

Se-tenant An attached pair, strip or block of stamps which differ in value, design or surcharge.

Surcharge An overprint which alters or restates the face value or denomination of the stamp to which it is applied.

Tagging Marking stamps with chemicals to be read by machines that sort mail and turn letters face-up for cancellation.

Thin Spot A thinning of the paper on the back of a stamp where a hinge was carelessly removed.

Tied On A stamp is "tied on" when the cancellation or postmark goes across the stamp to the envelope.

Topicals A group of stamps all with the same subject—space travel, for example.

Unused A stamp with or without original gum that has no cancellation or other sign of use.

Used A stamp that has been cancelled.

Want List A list of stamp numbers or philatelic items needed by a collector.

Watermark A design or pattern pressed into paper during its manufacture.

Overprint

Precancel

Perforate

Imperforate

Se-tenant

First Day Cover

Coils

Surcharge

11

Specialty collecting hasn't anything to do with the subject matter of the stamps you collect. (Collecting stamps that have a particular subject is called **topical** collecting.) A specialty collection is a particular form of stamps, such as:

Blocks of Four A square block of four unused (mint), unseparated stamps, with two stamps above and two below. A block can come from anywhere on a sheet of stamps. This is the easiest block to collect.

Plate Blocks Usually plate blocks are four corner stamps with the printing plate number in the margin (selvage) of the sheet. On January 1, 1981, the Postal Service started a new plate number system. Each color plate first used in the production of a stamp is represented by a number 1 in the group of numbers in the margin. Whenever a plate is worn out and replaced during the printing process, a number 2 replaces the number 1. The color of the number is the same as the color of the plate it stands for.

Copyright Blocks The U.S. Postal Service now copyrights all new stamp designs. The copyright C in a circle, followed by "United States Postal Service" or "USPS" and the year, appears in the margin of each sheet of stamps. The first copyright notice appeared January 6, 1978, in the margin of sheets of the Carl Sandburg stamp. Most copyrights are collected in blocks of four.

Booklet Panes Stamp booklets were first issued in 1898. Usually six or more of the same stamps are on a page, called a pane. Several pages of stamps are stapled in a cover. Most collections are of an entire pane.

Covers Covers (envelopes) stamped and postmarked with the date of the stamp's first day of issue are collected by a large number of people. On page 20 you'll find more information about first day covers and how to order them.

Souvenir Cards These 6″ x 8″ cards are issued as souvenirs of the philatelic (stamp collecting) events. They are distributed by the United States Postal Service, or the Bureau of Engraving and Printing. Some are available cancelled. They cannot be used for postage. Of special interest to American stamp collectors is the annual souvenir card for National Stamp Collecting Month each October, first issued in 1981.

Mr. ZIP Blocks The Zoning Improvement Plan—better known as ZIP Code—helps the Postal Service handle and deliver mail quickly. A Mr. ZIP cartoon and slogan were first printed on the Sam Houston stamp of 1964. Mr. ZIP blocks have become quite popular with collectors.

The U.S. Postal Service encourages people to collect stamps and helps them with their hobby. One of the ways it does this is through the Benjamin Franklin Stamp Clubs. These are clubs that are sponsored by the U.S. Postal Service in schools and libraries across the country. They are for students in third through seventh grade.

Benjamin Franklin Stamp Clubs were first started in 1974. Since then more than 5 million students have been introduced to stamp collecting through these clubs. There are about 50,000 Ben Franklin Stamp Clubs now. Why are these clubs named after Benjamin Franklin? Because he was a leader in organizing our postal system. He was the first Postmaster General, in 1775.

1474

How does a Benjamin Franklin Stamp Club get started?

At the beginning of the school year, a person who works for the U.S. Postal Service in your area telephones schools and libraries to see if they are interested in having a stamp club. If the answer is yes, the person goes to the school or library to tell the teachers, librarians, and students about the Ben Franklin clubs. Sometimes a film about stamp collecting is shown. Usually a teacher, librarian, or parent agrees to be the club's advisor.

The U.S. Postal Service gives some materials to the Benjamin Franklin Stamp Clubs. Each of the members gets a free Treasury of Stamps album every year. This album has places for most of the new U.S. postage stamps that will be issued during the school year. Each member also gets a membership card. And every month during the school year, a newsletter called *Stamp Fun* is sent to the club. The advisor gets other free materials to help get the club started and keep it going. Films, slide-tape programs, and filmstrips are also available free from the Postal Service. The Postal Service representative will give other help to the club as it needs it.

What are some activities of the Ben Franklin Stamp Clubs?

If possible, the club meets every week. One of the most important activities, of course, is collecting, showing, and trading stamps. The club might arrange to have a stamp show. There might be a trip to visit a post office. Older stamp collectors in the community might visit the club, show their collections, and talk about them. Stamp dealers are often invited to meet with the clubs.

A new activity of the Benjamin Franklin Stamp Clubs is the Pen Pal Program. Clubs that want to write letters to other Ben Franklin clubs send their club names, addresses, and identification numbers to the Benjamin Franklin Stamp Club headquarters in Washington, D.C. A club can say in which states it wants Ben Franklin club pen pals. Then headquarters will send to the club addresses of pen pals in those states. Clubs write letters to their pen pal clubs about their activities. They also exchange "want lists" of stamps members need for their collections. Stamps can be traded or even bought this way.

Around the Nation-Around the World
World Communications Year 1983

© USPS 1982

USA 30c

AEROGRAMME · VIA AIRMAIL · P. ON

② Second fold

③ Seal top flap last

The Great Seal
of the United States
1782-1982

USA 20c

USA
13c

Old Post Office, Washington, D.C.

© USPS 1983

Three items of postal stationery are popular with stamp collectors. These are embossed stamped envelopes, postal cards, and aerogrammes. You can buy these items at post offices.

Stamped Envelopes On stamped envelopes, the stamp is not printed separately. It is printed and embossed (made with a raised design) right on the envelope. Stamped envelopes are made for the Postal Service by a private contractor. They are made in several sizes and styles, including the window type. The embossed designs are sometimes commemoratives in more than one color.

Stamped envelopes were first issued in 1853. Today the average issue of stamped envelopes in one year is more than 1 million.

Postal Cards Postal cards are made of a heavier paper than envelopes. Plain and simple one-color postal cards were first issued in 1873. They stayed plain and simple until 1956. Then the first U.S. commemorative postal card came out. Usually several different postal cards are issued during a year. About 800 million are printed each year.

Aerogrammes An aerogramme (air letter) is a flat sheet of paper that's made to be a letter and an envelope in one. It's specially stamped, marked for folding, and gummed. After you write your letter, fold up the aerogramme and seal it. It's meant for foreign air mail only. An aerogramme will carry your message anywhere in the world at a lower postage rate than regular airmail.

Just as is the case with stamped envelopes and postal cards, the Postal Service has in recent years increased the use of commemorative designs on aerogrammes. The 1983 commemorative aerogramme is the 30¢ World Communications Year. It shows some modern methods of communication.

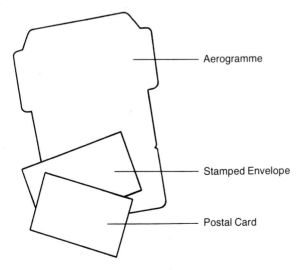

Aerogramme

Stamped Envelope

Postal Card

The value of a stamp depends mostly on two things: how rare it is—that is, how few of them there are—and what condition it's in. You can get an idea of how rare a stamp is by the price listed for it in a catalog. But a stamp may sell for more or less than the catalog price, depending on its condition. A very rare stamp may be quite expensive even though it's in poor condition. For a while anyway, you'll probably be collecting stamps that aren't very expensive. But still, you should try to get stamps that are in the best condition you can.

Here are some of the things to look for when you are judging the condition of a stamp. Look at the front of the stamp. Are the colors bright? Or is the stamp dirty, stained, or faded? Is the design in the center of the paper, or is it a little crooked or off to the side? Are the edges in good condition? Or are some of the perforations missing? A stamp with a light cancellation mark is in better condition than one with heavy marks across it.

Now look at the back of the stamp. Is there a thin spot in the paper? It may have been caused by careless removal of paper or a hinge. Can you see marks from hinges? Stamps that have the original gum and have never been hinged are more valuable.

Stamp dealers put stamps into categories according to their condition. The worst is "Poor" or "Spacefiller." Most stamps you see will be in the categories "Superb," "Fine," and "Good." You can look at the examples on the next page to see the differences among stamps in these big categories.

Catalog prices listed in *The Postal Service Guide to U.S. Stamps* are for used and unused stamps in Fine condition that have been hinged. A stamp that has not been hinged and has excellent centering and color will cost more. A stamp in less than Fine condition that has been heavily cancelled will cost less than the catalog price.

You may see a stamp listed as mint. A mint stamp is one that is in the same condition as it was when purchased from the post office. An unused stamp is one that has not been cancelled. It may not have any gum on it or it may be damaged in some way. Stamps in mint condition are usually more valuable than in unused condition.

Light Cancel-Very Fine   Medium Cancel-Fine   Heavy Cancel

Superb   Very Fine

Fine   Good

Most stamp catalogs are printed only in black and white, not colors. That makes it hard to imagine what the stamps really look like, because most of them are in colors. Sometimes, to help you, the catalogs give the names of the colors on the stamps shown.

On these pages are some popular names for stamp colors, along with examples of stamps that are printed in those colors. The stamp colors shown here are not 100% accurate because printing processes such as the one used for this **Guide** don't use the same kinds of inks and paper as the original stamps. So the colors here may not look quite the same.

When you become an experienced stamp collector, you'll be able to recognize a stamp whose color makes it rare and valuable. In the meantime, you can use this guide to get a better idea of what stamps in a catalog really look like.

Blue

Dark Blue

Ultramarine

Bright Blue

Purple

Violet

Carmine

Rose Lake

Peach Blossom

Henna Brown

Brown

Bistre Brown

Red

Sepia

Gray Brown

Dark Gray

Black

Light Green

Green

Olive

Light Olive Green

Blue Green

Yellow Gold

Orange

Deep Orange

Yellow-Black-Green

A first day cover is an envelope that has a new stamp cancelled with the date of the first day it was issued. For each new postal stamp or stationery issue, the Postal Service names one post office that is related in some way to the subject of the stamp. Each first day cover is cancelled at the post office that conducts the first day ceremonies.

Here's how you can get a first day cover through the Postal Service. You will get faster service if you buy the stamp yourself, and then send it to the first day post office for cancellation. When a new stamp goes on sale at your post office (usually the next day after the first day of issue), you can buy one and put it on your own envelope. Put the address in the lower right-hand corner. Leave plenty of room for the stamp and the cancellation. You can use a peelable address label if you don't want the address to remain on the envelope. Put your first day envelope inside another envelope. Mail it to "Customer Affixed Envelopes" in care of the postmaster of the first day city. The post office will cancel your envelope and return it to you through the mail. You may do this for 30 days after the issue date of the stamp.

Or, you can send an envelope addressed to yourself, but without a stamp. Put the addressed envelope into another envelope. Address the outside envelope to the name of the stamp, in care of the postmaster of the first day city. You must also include payment for the stamp or stamps that are to be put on your envelope. Do not send cash. You may send a check, a bank draft, or a U.S. Postal money order. Make it out to the U.S. Postal Service.

Do not send requests more than 60 days prior to the issue date. Usually you will receive your cancelled cover within three weeks after the first day of issue. If you don't, write to the postmaster of the first day city. Tell how the envelope was addressed, what kind of design or cachet it had, and how many stamps were ordered. If you ever get a first day cover that is damaged, send it back to the postmaster. A new one will be sent to you.

The U.S. Postal Service tries to get the first day covers into the mail just as soon as possible. To do this, it sends a special team of workers to a first day post office. Their job is just to work on first day covers. Of course, they can't do all that work on one day. Often it takes weeks. When there's an especially popular stamp issue, it may take even longer than usual to get all the first day covers out. For example, for the 1982 State Birds and Flowers issue 12,070,206 first day covers were cancelled.

The Bureau of Engraving and Printing in Washington, D.C. prints U.S. stamps and money. The Bureau has tours for visitors, and is a popular spot with tourists. To see the printing presses in operation can be very interesting, especially for stamp collectors. Stamps produced in the United States are the most carefully made and inspected in the world.

Several types of printing are used in the production of stamps.

Typography, or letterpress In this process, the design that is to appear on the stamp is raised above the metal printing plate. It is coated with ink and then pressed against the paper to print the design.

Intaglio (in-tal´-yo) In this type of printing, the design is cut into the metal printing plate. The ink flows down into the lines. Then damp paper is forced onto the plate to pick up the ink.

Gravure This process is a form of intaglio. The design is photographed through a very fine screen. The screen breaks the image up into patterns of small dots. The photograph is then cut into a metal plate. The tiny dots made by the screen become holes that catch and hold the ink. The deeper the holes are, the more ink they will hold. When paper is pressed against the printing plate, it collects the ink from the holes. In this way, the design is printed on the paper.

Offset This printing process is based on the fact that water and grease do not mix. The stamp design is put on a metal printing plate by a photographic process. The part of the design that is to print (the image area) is made so that it will accept the greasy ink. The plate is wet with acid and water. When the plate is inked, the greasy ink sticks only to the image area. If paper were pressed against the plate at this point, the design would print backward. So the design is first "offset" onto a rubber blanket, and then onto the paper.

In all these processes, a separate printing plate is made for each color in the stamp.

Sometimes when a stamp is complicated, different printing processes are combined. For example, the International Peace Garden commemorative of 1982 was printed by a combination of offset and intaglio presses. The offset colors in this stamp are yellow, red, green, and black. The intaglio colors are black, brown, and green. Each pane (sheet) of 50 stamps has two groups of plate numbers. The four-number group is for the offset plates. The three-number group is for the intaglio plates.

2014

These four colorful stamps were issued in 1975 to celebrate the 200th birthday of the U.S. Postal Service. They show an early stagecoach and a modern trailer truck, old and new locomotives, an early mail plane and a jet, and a satellite for sending mailgrams. All have been carriers of the mail in this country during the past 200 years.

1572–1575

But, of course, people had been sending and receiving mail long before Ben Franklin became this country's first Postmaster General. About 4,000 years ago, a system of writing was first developed in countries around the Mediterranean Sea. The writing was cut into soft clay tablets. Then the tablets were baked and hardened. Sometimes the writing was a message to someone, and the tablets were carried by runners. The messengers' job became a little easier after the Egyptians began making a kind of paper out of the papyrus plant about 2400 B.C. Papyrus was easier to write on—and easier to carry. It was the most common writing material for 3,000 years.

The Romans developed some of the best methods of travel and correspondence in ancient times. Their mail system was so good that they had messenger stations every five to twelve miles. Sometimes the messengers rode one horse and had another to carry letter bags. Ships, too, carried mail across the Mediterranean to other parts of the Roman empire.

The Chinese emperor Kublai Khan built a postal system with 10,000 stations that were connected by good roads. The unusual thing about the Khan's system was that it could be used for private letters as well as for government mail. Most other systems of that time could be used only to carry mail sent by rulers, military commanders, and government officials. Of course, if you were an ordinary citizen, your letter went by slow-moving camel, while the Khan's went by swift horses. But at least the mail was delivered.

The Aztec and Inca Indians also had a delivery service that was used by the public. They didn't have horses, so runners carried the knotted cords that had the message in a kind of code.

In 1533 in England, King Henry VIII established regular postal routes and schedules. Private citizens could send letters by this service, but only if there was room in the bag after all the government mail was put in. And then the official mail went free. The private letters had to pay for the entire postal service. This made sending a letter very costly.

When colonists first settled in North America, there was no regular mail service. What little communication there was went between the new settlements and the countries the colonists had come from. That meant mail ad to be carried by ships across the Atlantic Ocean. Government mail was carried by warships. Private citizens sent letters and packages with captains of trading ships. In 1639, Fairbank's Tavern in Boston was named as the place in Massachusetts where the transatlantic mail was to be collected.

The need for transportation of mail grew as the colonies grew. Several colonial governments set up postal services in cooperation with the British government. But these early postal services were not dependable. Sometimes the mail ships sailed when they were supposed to. Sometimes they didn't. Riders and mail coaches faced many dangers and delays.

As new types of transportation were developed, the mail services used them. Steamboats carried mail on the big rivers. By the 1830s, railroads began carrying mail.

About this time, back in England, Rowland Hill had an idea about the postal service. He was an inventor and teacher. His idea was that letters should be charged for by how much they weighed, not by the distance they were carried. For two years he argued for the "penny post." A fee of one penny would take a half-ounce letter to any part of the kingdom. And the person who sent the letter would pay the penny, not the person who received it. Finally, Hill's program was made into law. He was appointed to be in charge of the new service. So the first gummed postage stamp came into being. It was the "Penny Black," called that because it cost a penny, and it was black in color.

Five years later, in 1845, the Congress of the United States set new postal rates that were much like those in England. And on July 1, 1847, there was the first issue of U.S. postage stamps. The brown 5-cent stamp had a picture of Benjamin Franklin. The black 10-cent stamp showed George Washington. These stamps were not perforated. This means they did not have lines of holes between the rows of stamps. The user had to cut them apart. Before the U.S. stamps were issued, postmasters in some places had their own stamps printed. These stamps are called "postmasters' provisionals," and they are very valuable.

As settlers moved westward across the United States, attempts were made to set up a regular mail service from the Atlantic coast to the Pacific coast. The most famous overland mail service was the Pony Express. Relay stations were set up every 15 miles. There the riders got fresh horses.

The first western Pony Express trip was in April, 1860. A rider left St. Joseph, Missouri, on April 3, and the mail arrived in San Francisco, California, eleven days later. This service lasted only a year and a half. When the telegraph line across the country was completed, the Pony Express stopped.

1154

After the Civil War there were several improvements in mail service. In large cities, letter carriers began delivering mail to people's homes and businesses. Before that, a person had to go to the post office to pick up mail. Also, letter boxes were placed on street corners so that people could easily mail letters.

A new fast railroad mail service carried mail by train even to small towns. The mail went from St. Louis, Missouri, to San Francisco in five days—half as long as it took the Pony Express. Even if the train didn't stop at a town, mail was exchanged. A letter bag was handed by a postal worker to another postal worker on the train. And a letter bag was handed off the train to the postal worker standing beside the track. The train slowed, but didn't stop. Later, cranes were developed to help in the exchanging of mail with a moving train. The Fast Mail trains began in 1875 and continued in service until the United States entered World War I in 1917. These trains actually had post office cars.

One of the problems the postal service has had is keeping costs down while continuing to give dependable, fast service. In an effort to keep the price of stamps down, the federal government's Bureau of Engraving and Printing began printing all stamps in 1893. Before that, stamps were printed by private companies.

During the 1890s rural free delivery of mail was started. Until that time, people who did not live in cities, but on farms and in the countryside, had to go to the post office for their mail. In those days, more than half the American people lived in these rural areas. At first the rural carriers delivered mail with a horse and wagon. But beginning in 1902, automobiles were used more and more.

For city mail service, many kinds of transportation have been used. There have been postal street cars, in which the mail was collected and sorted. Some big cities had pneumatic tube lines. Mail was moved by air pressure through the tubes between main post offices and smaller ones. In New York and San Francisco postal boats picked up foreign mail from mail steamers in the harbor and took it to a nearby railroad. And there have been a few postal subway systems, in which mail was moved through underground passages. But since the 1950s, trucks have been the most popular way to move mail on the ground.

After the automobile, the next great advance in carrying the mail was the airplane. During World War I the airplane proved that it could be a means of transportation. After the war, airmail service was started. The planes used for the first airmail service were military training planes called Curtiss Jennies. The 24-cent airmail stamp issued in 1918 shows a Curtiss Jenny in flight. This stamp became one of the most famous because of a mistake. One sheet of the stamps was printed with the plane flying upside down. A recent catalog priced one of these stamps (#C3a) at $145,000!

The first airmail pilots had to have been daredevils. They often had engine trouble or ran into bad weather. The landing fields didn't have lights, and they had only road maps to fly by. Charles A. Lindbergh was one of these first airmail pilots. He flew a route between Springfield, Illinois,

C10

and St. Louis, Missouri. In 1927 he became famous for a private flight he made —the first nonstop flight from New York to Paris, made by a person flying alone. Other airmail-carrying craft shown on stamps include a dirigible, a "flying boat," propeller airplanes, and a jet. In 1977, airplanes became the standard way to move mail from city to city. Since then, it has not been necessary to buy a special airmail stamp to have your letter carried by this super-fast transportation. Today, machines, computers, and electronics help postal workers handle and carry mail.

A First for the USPS

The Date: April 8, 1983.
The Place: Los Angeles, California.
The Occasion: The U.S. Postal Service entered the Maximum Card field for the first time in American history.

A Maximum Card is a pictorial postcard to which a stamp can be affixed on the view side, and then appropriately cancelled for philatelic purposes. The picture, stamp and cancellation are usually related to a common theme, most often the subject of the stamp.

Maximum Cards originated in Europe over 40 years ago and have become increasingly popular among philatelists. The name derives from the fact that the illustration on the picture side of the card and the stamp affixed to it should have the maximum relationship and that the size of the card is the maximum allowed to be mailed at the postal card rate by the Universal Postal Convention. The U.S. Maximum Cards measure 4⅛" x 5⅞" as compared with the standard postal card of 3½" x 5½".

This new philatelic venture, currently a market test, is a promising area of specialization for the stamp collecting community. The cards are available by mail order from the Philatelic Sales Division for 50¢ each. Customers also may purchase individual cards with the appropriate Olympics stamp affixed and cancelled for 50¢ plus the value of the stamp affixed. For additional information, use the postal card following page 272.

This original artwork by Robert Peak was used for the design of the weight-lifting stamp from the 40-cent international airmail block of four honoring the 1984 Summer Olympics. This stamp was issued in Los Angeles, California, on April 8, 1983.

A Promising Philatelic Revival

January 12, 1983, marked a philatelic milestone when the U.S. Postal Service released its Official Mail Stamps and Stationery for the first time in over half a century. Therefore, the 1983 issue is regarded as a rare and historic event in the annals of philately.

Looking back, the story of the first Officials is brief but certainly worthy of note: During the mid-19th century, government mail was delivered free by means of franking (the use of a signature or symbol of a person entitled to send letters postage-free). In the years immediately following the Civil War, the Government grew by leaps and bounds, and with it, franking became so abused that the privilege had to be abolished. In its place, Official Stamps were issued to nine government departments, each with its own stamp design and denomination. However, that program, too, proved to have its drawbacks and was superceded by the penalty envelope in 1879. Official stamps were last issued in 1911. Thus, the revival of Official Mail Stamps and Stationery in 1983 has sparked great curiosity among students and collectors of stamps.

The 1983 Officials are part of a U.S. Postal Service test to develop procedures for the possible future introduction of an Official Mail stamp system. The nationwide test involves only branch offices of the Departments of Agriculture and the Air Force.

The collection is comprised of seven different denominational stamps to provide a full range of services for single-piece mailings: 1¢, 4¢, 13¢, 17¢, 20¢, $1, and $5. There is a 13¢ postal card, as well as two No. 10 20¢ embossed stamped envelopes—one with a window, the other without. The 20¢ stamps are issued in coils of 100 with the plate number appearing at intervals of 52 stamps. All other stamps are distributed in panes of 100 and bear one single-digit plate number. The only other marginal marking is the copyright notice.

Because the stamps and postal stationery are restricted to Official Government mail, and may not be employed for private use, the U.S. Postal Service waived the minimum purchase requirements that normally apply: to accommodate collectors, plate blocks are sold as plate blocks and coil pairs are available as pairs.

The design, by veteran stamp artist, Bradbury Thompson, is similar for all items except that the embossing process slightly alters its appearance on the envelope. The Official design was unveiled on September 14, 1983, at the National Postal Forum in Washington, D.C. Thompson was assisted by modeler Peter Cocci and engravers Gary J. Slaught (lettering and numerals) and Edward P. Archer (vignette).

Collectors can purchase the new Official Stamps and Stationery only through the Philatelic Sales Division, Washington, D.C. 20265-9997. For additional information, send the postal card following page 272.

0127

0128

0129

0130

0132

0133

0135

Germany and Sweden: Partners with the U.S. in 1983

At times, world governments have acted as partners in joint stamp issues commemorating an event of historical importance to the two countries. The United States has participated in several such issues since 1959 (see pages 30 and 31 for more information on these joint issues), as well as two joint issues during 1983.

U.S./Germany

A 20-cent commemorative marking the 300th anniversary of the arrival of the first German immigrants in the United States was issued in Germantown, Pennsylvania, on April 29, 1983. On May 5th, the Federal Republic of Germany issued a stamp with the same design. More than seven million immigrants have come to the U.S. since 1683 when the ship, *Concord,* brought 13 families to the New World in search of religious freedom. Since no pictures of the *Concord* existed, the designer based his drawing on written descriptions of the vessel.

U.S. #2040   Germany #1397

U.S. #2036   Sweden #1453

U.S./Sweden

A stamp commemorating the 200th anniversary of the signing of the Treaty of Amity and Commerce between the United States and Sweden was issued in both countries on March 24, 1983. The treaty, a pledge of lasting peace and friendship between the two nations, was the first treaty entered into by the United States and a friendly foreign nation. Since 1783, when Gustav Philip Creutz, a representative of King Gustavus III, and Benjamin Franklin signed the document in Paris, the friendship between the two nations has flourished. The designer of both stamps was Dan Jonsson, a well-known Swedish artist and graphic designer. The stamps were engraved by Czeslaw Slania, also of Sweden. Slania is Sweden's court engraver and the creator of more than 500 stamps for countries around the world.

By agreement between the two governments, the Swedish stamps were sold in America by the U.S. Postal Service and the U.S. stamps were sold in Sweden for a limited period of time.

JOINT ISSUES

Issued in 1960 to commemorate the 150th anniversary of Mexican Independence.

U.S. #1157   Mexico #910

Part of the 400th anniversary in 1965 of the first continuous permanent European settlement in the New World, which was located in Florida.

U.S. #1271   Spain #1312

The St. Lawrence Seaway Opening stamp was issued in 1959 in New York State and at Ottawa, Canada.

U.S. #1131   Canada #387

U.S. #1569-70

U.S.S.R. #4339-40

The historic U.S./U.S.S.R. joint space mission was celebrated as both nations issued pairs of stamps in 1975.

U.S. #1721

Canada #737

These stamps, issued in 1977, commemorate the 50th anniversary of the construction of the Peace Bridge between the United States and Canada.

U.S. #1935

U.S. #1936

Ireland #504

Issued in 1981, this joint issue depicted the Irish-American who was the architect for the White House, James Hoban.

U.S. #1690

Canada #691

Benjamin Franklin, the first Postmaster General of both the United States *and* Canada, was the subject of nearly identical stamps in 1976.

U.S. #2003

Netherlands #640

Netherlands #641

These stamps marked the 200th anniversary in 1982 of diplomatic recognition of the U.S. by the Netherlands, the longest continuously peaceful diplomatic association of the U.S. with any foreign power.

Men's Hurdles

It's 1864 and ordinary sheep hurdles, measuring 3½ feet high, are set up on the grounds of England's Oxford University. Students are competing against each other by jumping over the cumbersome hurdles with both legs tucked under their bodies. That's what the sport was like a century ago.

It wasn't until the 1900 Olympic Games in Paris that this awkward form of jumping was revolutionized. It took the talents and imagination of America's Alvin Kraenzlein, a 23-year-old athlete from the University of Pennsylvania, to devise a unique method of jumping, and it paid off. Much to the astonishment of Olympic spectators, he cleared each barrier with the now-familiar one leg extended position while his contemporaries trailed behind, tucking their legs and skimming the hurdles.

Among the four Gold Medals awarded to Kraenzlein in the 1900 track and field events, two were for hurdle races (the 110-meter and 200-meter races). Those two victories inspired future hurdlers to imitate Kraenzlein's style and form.

Hurdling might well be thought of as an American specialty sport. When the 110-meter race was featured at the first modern Olympics of 1896 in Athens, it was won by American Tom Curtis. Four years later, the 400-meter was introduced in Paris, and again an American—Walter Tewkesbury—crossed the finish line to win the Gold. Tewkesbury joined Kraenzlein to assure an American sweep in the 1900 hurdles.

Since those first two victories, Americans have established almost total dominance in the 110 and 400-meter events. The number of Gold Medals bestowed on Americans best tells the story: 15 out of 19 in the 110-meter hurdles; and 12 of 17 in the 400-meter hurdles.

Issued June 17, 1983, in San Antonio, Texas. International Airmail rate.

33

Men's Diving

Diving entered the Olympic arena at St. Louis in 1904. Since then, there have been many highlights in this challenging event. A look at the Olympic records show us:

• For the greatest feat in men's Olympic diving history, honors go to Klaus Dibiasi. This talented Italian won three consecutive Golds for his highboard victories in 1968, 1972 and 1976. To add to that record, Dibiasi also won two Silver Medals—one for the highboard in 1964; the other for springboard in 1968.

• Two other divers have gained fame for consecutive Olympic wins, but they were only to accomplish this twice. Sammy Lee, the small but powerful American of Korean ancestry (and an M.D.) won the Gold in 1948 and 1952 for his highboard performances; and Robert Webster dove from the highboard to victory in 1960 and 1964. That Webster was Dr. Lee's student adds an interesting note of Olympic continuity.

Scheduled to be issued in the spring of 1984 in Los Angeles, California (may be issued as single stamps rather than a block of four).

In earlier Olympic competitions, American divers twice won both the springboard and highboard Gold Medals. Albert White was the first in 1924, and Peter Desjardins did the same in 1928. When Desjardins accomplished his "double," he electrified the Amsterdam crowds by executing dives never before attempted in competition. On one of his springboard performances, he received the first perfect score of 10 ever awarded for Olympic diving. In over half a century, no one has been able to match the double Gold wins of White and Desjardins. Recently, divers have occasionally reached the finals in both events but the increased intensity and high quality of competition has prevented anyone from winning Golds in each of the two events.

• Another outstanding accomplishment was the springboard victory of Phil Boggs of the U.S.A. in 1976 at Montreal. Boggs had the highest score of any contestant on eight of his ten dives; and took first place by an unprecedented margin of 49 points.

• No other nation has dominated an Olympic sport as completely as has the United States in diving. This tally of Olympic results is sufficient testimony: 12 of the 16 springboard champions have been Americans while 10 out of 17 Gold Medals have been presented to Americans for the highboard!

Women's Volleyball

Few events have been so enthusiastically greeted on the Olympic scene as was women's volleyball when it made a debut at the 1964 Tokyo Games. The Japanese women's team had already gained wide popularity. For their match in the finals against the Soviet Union, the Japanese television networks exceeded a staggering 90 percent viewership. As one writer said at the time: "People cling to their television sets to watch the game, leaving the public bathhouses almost deserted, the Ginza nearly empty and the toll switchboard out of action." Spectators intensely watched a very competitive Japanese women's team overwhelm a taller, heavier Soviet team to win the Gold Medal.

Ever since, these two countries have dominated the Olympic volleyball competition. The Soviet Union has a reputation for showing strength and power while the Japanese are known for exhibiting incredible speed and skill. High standards of play have also been demonstrated by Czechoslovakia, Poland, East Germany, Cuba and Korea.

The name of the United States, however, is noticeably absent from the roster of Olympic volleyball winners. And that is somewhat ironic. The sport was invented in Holyoke, Massachusetts, in 1895 and became a popular indoor-outdoor activity for men and women of all ages.

Years later, the game spread overseas during World War II when United States servicemen introduced it to many areas including the Orient, where it flourished and was perfected.

While the U.S. can take credit for making volleyball an international favorite, it is the Japanese and Russians who deserve applause for taking the sport out of the backyard and placing it in the spotlight of the Olympic arena.

Scheduled to be issued November 4, 1983, in Colorado Springs, Colorado. International Airmail rate.

Men's Hockey

The American spirit was flagging as the 1980 Winter Olympics opened at Lake Placid, New York. There were frustrations at home and abroad; the political climate was tense. The country needed a boost and it certainly got it when the U.S. hockey team defeated the top-seeded Russians and went on to capture the Gold.

In February 1980, there was not a glimmer of hope for the U.S. team. They were virtually a group of unknowns and considered rookies compared to their competition: the Soviet Union, Czechoslovakia, Sweden, Norway and Finland. But one by one, each of these "greats" was trounced by the U.S.A. as they picked up their hockey sticks and pushed the puck to Olympic victory.

Behind these odds-against triumphs is a story of iron leadership, fierce team effort and relentless training. No one knew that Coach Herb Brooks had rigorously conditioned his 20 men to the hilt—mentally and physically. He pushed them to the limit and beyond. He treated each man equally and without compassion. As the ruthless coach doled out orders, the boys gritted their teeth, gave their all and banded together to form a team.

Few sports enthusiasts will forget the night the U.S.A. upset the U.S.S.R. with a score of 4-3. When the final buzzer went off, it sounded a patriotic chant from coast to coast. People danced in the streets, honked their car horns and fireworks skyrocketed. American optimism had been restored.

To conquer the Gold, the U.S.A. still had to face Finland but that, of course, is Olympic history. The final score: U.S.A., 4; Finland, 2. With that Gold Medal victory, everyone was reminded of a national trait as deeply rooted as our American heritage: commitment to a common cause.

Sportswriter Peter Michelmore describes that final night: "At game's end, the Americans came together in a jubilant mass of arms and sticks and red-white-and-blue. At the dawn of a fresh decade, our youngsters had a new set of heroes, for these hockey players brought back the surpassing thrill of team victory. Their lesson, so vigorously taught on the Olympic ice, was that young men pulling together and drawing strength from one another could prevail against any adversary."

Scheduled to be issued January 1984 in Lake Placid, New York.

39

Issued July 28, 1983, in South Bend, Indiana. Domestic postal card rate.

Women's High Jump

When Los Angeles last hosted the Olympics in 1932, an 18-year-old woman from Texas went to California as a first-time competitor and came back an Olympic star. That person was Mildred "Babe" Didrickson and her claim to fame—four world records (although one was not officially recognized).

"The Babe," as Didrickson was always called by her friends and fans, set her first record for the '32 Olympics in the javelin competition, and two more followed in the 80-meter hurdles.

When she entered the high jump event, the world record stood at 5 feet 3⅛ inches. Didrickson topped it by going 5 feet 5 inches. But so did her teammate Jean Shiley. As the bar was set higher, tension mounted. The event became a fierce competition between teammates. In the final

40

Babe Didrickson Zaharias, all around athlete and Olympian, was honored by a commemorative stamp in 1981.

round, Didrickson and Shiley tied for the new world record with the high jump at 5 feet 5¼ inches. But the honors and Gold were awarded to Jean Shiley because The Babe went head first over the bar, a practice not recognized at the time.

It's ironic to note that only one year later, the "no diving" regulation was scratched from the high jump rule book.

There were, however, other moments of glory in store for Babe Didrickson. After the 1932 Games, she went on to unofficially match or break every woman's Olympic track and field record that existed at the time. Then, too, she later gained fame and fortune as a great golfer by consecutively winning 17 tournaments.

Men's Gymnastics

When Shun Fujimoto, a member of Japan's gymnastic team, arrived in Montreal for the 1976 Olympic Games, it was his personal dream come true. After years of rigorous training, conditioning and discipline, he had finally arrived at the peak of sports competition.

Then fate played a cruel trick on Fujimoto—he broke his leg during the team floor exercise, the first in a series of six gymnastic events. It seemed as if his dream had been shattered. But no, the young gymnast was not going to let a broken bone get in his way. After all, it had been a long road to Montreal and he was going to see it to the end.

He was fitted with a plastic cast from hip to toe, and insisted on continuing the competition. Because of the cast, Fujimoto had to be assisted up to the rings, but once in motion, he put on a stellar performance that was awarded a 9.70—the best score of his life! In front of a stunned crowd of spectators, Shun Fujimoto finished the ring exercise with a triple somersault and a twist that forced him to land heavily on both feet.

Upon seeing this incredible performance, the Olympic doctor who had treated Fujimoto exclaimed: "It is beyond my comprehension how he could land without collapsing in screams." Fujimoto candidly responded, "Yes, the pain shot through like a knife. It brought tears to my eyes. But now I have the medal, the pain has gone."

Because of Shun Fujimoto's determination to continue despite all odds, Japan won the Team Gymnastic Gold Medal in the 1976 Olympics.

Japanese teammates, including Shun Fujimoto, were recipients of the 1976 Team Gymnastic Gold Medal.

Issued April 8, 1983, in Los Angeles, California. International Airmail rate.

1¢ Franklin Types I-IV of 1851-56

5

Bust of **5**

Detail of **7** Type II
Lower scrollwork incomplete
(lacks little balls).
Side ornaments are complete.

11

Bust of **5**

Detail of **6** Type Ia
Top ornaments and outer line
partly cut away.
Lower scrollwork is complete.

Bust of **5**

Detail of **8** Type III
Outer lines broken in the
middle.
Side ornaments are complete.

Detail of **8A** Type IIIa
Outer lines broken top or
bottom but not both.

Detail of **11**
THREE CENTS.
Type I. There is an outer frame
line at top and bottom.

Bust of **5**

Detail of **5** Type I
Has curved, unbroken lines
outside labels.
Scrollwork is complete, forms
little balls at bottom.

Detail of **5A** Type Ib
Lower scrollwork is incomplete,
the little balls are not so clear.

Bust of **5**

Detail of **9** Type IV
Outer lines recut top, bottom,
or both.

12

Detail of **12**
FIVE CENTS.
Type I. There are projections on
all four sides.

Washington Types I-IV
1855

15

Bust of **15**

Detail of **13**
Type I. The "shells" at the lower corners are practically complete. The outer line below the label is very nearly complete. The outer lines are broken above the middle of the top label and the "X" in each upper corner.

Bust of **15**

Detail of **14**
Type II. The design is complete at the top. The outer line at the bottom is broken in the middle. The shells are partly cut away.

Detail of **15**
Type III. The outer lines are broken above the top label and the "X" numerals. The outer line at the bottom and the shells are partly cut away, as in Type II.

Bust of **15**

Detail of **16**
Type IV. The outer lines have been recut at top or bottom or both.
Types I, II, III and IV have complete ornaments at the sides of the stamps and three pearls at each outer edge of the bottom panel.

Bust of **5**

Detail of **24**
ONE CENT FRANKLIN
Type V. Similar to Type III of 1851-56 but with side ornaments partly cut away.

Bust of **11**

Detail of **26**
THREE CENTS WASHINGTON
Type II. The outer frame line has been removed at top and bottom. The side frame lines were recut so as to be continuous from the top to the bottom of the plate.

30A

Detail of **30A**
FIVE CENTS JEFFERSON
Type II. The projections at top and bottom are partly cut away.

Detail of **35**
TEN CENTS WASHINGTON
(Two typical examples).
Type V. Side ornaments slightly cut away. Outer lines complete except over right X.

45

55   **57**

Detail of **67**
5¢. A leaflet has been added to the foliated ornaments at each corner.

Detail of **64**
3¢. Ornaments at corners have been enlarged and end in a small ball.

Issue of 1861

Detail of **55**

56   **58**   **68**   **69**

Detail of **57**

63   **67**

Detail of **56**

Detail of **68**
10¢. A heavy curved line has been cut below the stars and an outer line has been added to the ornaments above them.

Detail of **58**

Issue of 1861-62

Detail of **63**
1¢. A dash has been added under the tip of the ornament at right of the numeral in upper left corner.

62   **64**

Detail of **69**
12¢. Ovals and scrolls have been added to the corners.

72

Detail of **62**

46

Detail of **72**
90¢. Parallel lines from an angle above the ribbon with "U.S. Postage"; between these lines a row of dashes has been added and a point of color to the apex of the lower pair.

Detail of **134**

Detail of **138**

118

135   136   139   140

Detail of **118**
FIFTEEN CENTS.
Type I. Picture unframed.

Detail of **135**

Detail of **139**

Detail of **119**
Type II. Picture framed.
Type III. Same as Type I but without fringe of brown shading lines around central vignette.

Detail of **136**

Detail of **140**

Issue of 1870-71:
Printed by the National Bank Note Company.
Issued without secret marks (see Nos. 156-163).

134

137   138   141

Detail of **137**

Detail of **141**

1873: Printed by the Continental Bank Note Co.

Designs of the 1870-71 Issue with secret marks on the values from 1¢ to 15¢ as described and illustrated below.

159   **160**

Detail of **159**
6¢. The first four vertical lines of the shading in the lower part of the left ribbon have been strengthened.

Detail of **160**
7¢. Two small semi-circles are drawn around the ends of the lines which outline the ball in the lower right hand corner.

161   **162**

Detail of **161**
10¢. There is a small semi-circle in the scroll, at the right end of the upper label.

Detail of **162**
12¢. The balls of the figure "2" are crescent shaped.

163

Detail of **163**
15¢. In the lower part of the triangle in the upper left corner two lines have been made heavier forming a "V". This mark can be found on some of the Continental and American (1879) printings, but not all stamps show it.

Secret marks were added to the dies of the 24¢, 30¢ and 90¢ but new plates were not made from them. The various printings of these stamps can be distinguished only by the shades and paper.

206   **207**

Detail of **206**
1¢. Upper vertical lines have been deepened, creating a solid effect in parts of background. Upper arabesques have lines of shading.

Detail of **207**
3¢. Shading at sides of central oval is half its previous width. A short horizontal dash has been cut below the "TS" of "CENTS".

208   **209**

Detail of **208**
6¢. Has three vertical lines instead of four between the edge of the panel and the outside of the stamp.

48

Detail of **209**
10¢. Has four vertical lines instead of five between left side of oval and edge of the shield. Horizontal lines in lower part of background have been strengthened.

$1 Perry
Types of 1894

261

283

2¢ Washington
Types I-III of 1894

Triangle of **248-250**
Type I. Horizontal lines of uniform thickness run across the triangle.

Detail of **261**
Type I. The circles enclosing $1 are broken.

Detail of **283**
Type II. The lips of the ornaments break the curved line below the "E" of "TEN" and the "T" of "CENTS."

Detail of **261A**
Type II. The circles enclosing $1 are complete.

251

282C

Watermark **191**

Triangle of **251**
Type II. Horizontal lines cross the triangle, but are thinner within than without.

USPS

Watermark **190**

Detail of **282C**
TEN CENTS
Type I. The tips of the foliate ornaments do not impinge on the white curved line below "TEN CENTS."

USPS

Watermark **191**

Triangle of **252**
Type III. The horizontal lines do not cross the double frame lines of the triangle.

1847-1875

1 2 3 4 5 11

12 15 17 30A 38 39

	Un	U

**Issues of 1847 to 1894 are Unwatermarked,
Issue of 1847, Imperf.**

		Un	U
1	5¢ Benjamin		
	Franklin, July 1	3,750.00	950.00
2	10¢ George		
	Washington,		
	July 1	16,500.00	2,750.00

Issue of 1875, Reproductions of 1 & 2

3	5¢ Franklin	2,175.00	—
4	10¢ Washington	2,750.00	—

Reproductions. The letters R. W. H. & E. at the bottom of each stamp are less distinct on the reproductions than on the originals.

5¢. On the original the left side of the white shirt frill touches the oval on a level with the top of the "F" of "Five." On the reproduction it touches the oval about on a level with the top of the figure "5."

10¢. On the reproduction, line of coat at left points to right of "X" and line of coat at right points to center of "S" of CENTS. On the original, line of coat points to "T" of TEN and between "T" and "S" of CENTS.

On the reproduction the eyes have a sleepy look, the line of the mouth is straighter, and in the curl of hair near the left cheek is a strong black dot, while the original has only a faint one.

Issue of 1851-56, Imperf.

5	1¢ Franklin, type I	100,000.00	18,500.00
5A	1¢ Same, type Ib	10,500.00	3,000.00

Nos. 6-9: Franklin (5)

6	1¢ dark blue,		
	type Ia	13,000.00	4,000.00
7	1¢ blue, type II	500.00	100.00
8	1¢ blue, type III	4,500.00	1,300.00
8A	1¢ pale blue,		
	type IIIA	1,500.00	550.00
9	1¢ blue, type IV	335.00	85.00
10	3¢ orange brown Washington,		
	type I (11)	1,350.00	70.00
11	3¢ Washington, type I	120.00	7.50

		Un	U
12	5¢ Jefferson, type I	8,500.00	1,350.00
13	10¢ green Washington,		
	type I (15)	7,000.00	725.00
14	10¢ green, type II (15)	1,350.00	300.00
15	10¢ Washington, type III	1,450.00	300.00
16	10¢ green, type IV (15)	9,500.00	1,500.00
17	12¢ Washington	1,750.00	275.00

	Un	U

Issue of 1857-61, Perf. 15

Nos. 18-24: Franklin (5)

18	1¢ blue, type I	750.00	350.00
19	1¢ blue, type Ia	8,500.00	1,250.00
20	1¢ blue, type II	475.00	135.00
21	1¢ blue, type III	3,000.00	1,000.00
22	1¢ blue, type IIIa	600.00	200.00
23	1¢ blue, type IV	1,400.00	250.00
24	1¢ blue, type V	135.00	27.50

		Un	U
	Nos. 25-26: Washington (11)		
25	3¢ rose, type I	675.00	30.00
26	3¢ dull red, type II	55.00	3.25
	Nos. 27-29: Jefferson (12)		
27	5¢ brick red, type I	6,500.00	975.00
28	5¢ red brown, type I	1,350.00	295.00
28A	5¢ Indian red, type I	7,500.00	1,175.00
29	5¢ brown, type I	775.00	200.00
30	5¢ orange brown		
	Jefferson, type II (30A)	800.00	900.00
30A	5¢ Jefferson, type II	425.00	180.00
	Nos 31-35: Washington (15)		
31	10¢ green type I	4,250.00	525.00
32	10¢ green, type II	1,475.00	150.00
33	10¢ green, type III	1,475.00	150.00
34	10¢ green, type IV	11,500.00	1,250.00
35	10¢ green type V	190.00	75.00
36	12¢ black Washington		
	(17)	340.00	85.00
37	24¢ Washington	700.00	225.00
38	30¢ Franklin	900.00	300.00
39	90¢ Washington	1,500.00	2,750.00
	90¢ Same, with pen cancel	—	1,000.00

Note: Beware of forged cancellations of No. 39. Genuine cancellations are rare.

1875: Government Reprints, Perf. 12, White Paper, Without Gum

40	1¢ bright blue Franklin (5)	500.00	—
41	3¢ scarlet Washington (11)	2,750.00	—
42	5¢ orange brown		
	Jefferson (30A)	900.00	—
43	10¢ blue green		
	Washington (15)	2,250.00	—

		Un	U
1875 continued			
44	12¢ greenish black		
	Washington (17)	*2,450.00*	—
45	24¢ blackish violet		
	Washington (37)	*2,750.00*	—
46	30¢ yel. org. Franklin		
	(38)	*2,850.00*	—
47	90¢ deep blue		
	Washington (39)	*4,000.00*	—

Issue of 1861, Perf. 12

Following the outbreak of the Civil War, the U.S. Government demonetized all previous issues.

55	1¢ Franklin	*16,000.00*	—
56	3¢ Washington	750.00	—
57	5¢ brown Jefferson	*11,000.00*	—
58	10¢ Washington	*4,500.00*	—
59	12¢ Washington	*35,000.00*	—
60	24¢ dk. vio. Washington		
	(70)	4,750.00	—
61	30¢ red org. Franklin		
	(71)	14,000.00	—
62	90¢ dull blue		
	Washington (72)	18,000.00	—
62B	10¢ dark green		
	Washington (58)	*4,500.00*	500.00

Nos. 55-62 were not used for postage and do not exist in a cancelled state. The paper they were printed on is thin and semi-transparent, that of the following issues is more opaque.

Issue of 1861-62, Perf. 12

63	1¢ Franklin	110.00	21.50
64	3¢ Washington	*3,000.00*	275.00
65	3¢ rose Washington (64)	52.50	1.40
66	3¢ lake Washington (64)	*1,350.00*	—
67	5¢ Jefferson	*3,850.00*	400.00
68	10¢ Washington	240.00	23.50
69	12¢ Washington	475.00	45.00
70	24¢ Washington	500.00	60.00
71	30¢ Franklin	515.00	65.00
72	90¢ Washington	1,100.00	225.00

Issue of 1861-66, Perf. 12

73	2¢ Andrew Jackson		
	("Black Jack")	130.00	25.00

		Un	
74	3¢ scarlet Washington		
	(64)	*3,500.00*	—
75	5¢ red brown Jefferson		
	(67)	1,250.00	200.00
76	5¢ brn. Jefferson (67)	275.00	45.00
77	15¢ Abraham Lincoln	550.00	67.50
78	24¢ lilac Washington (70)	250.00	40.00

No. 74 was not regularly issued.

Grills on U.S. Stamps

Between 1867 and 1870, postage stamps were embossed with grills to prevent people from re-using cancelled stamps. The pyramid-shaped grills absorbed cancellation ink, making it virtually impossible to remove a postmark chemically.

Issue of 1867, With Grills, Perf. 12

Grills A, B, C: Points Up

A. Grill Covers Entire Stamp

79	3¢ rose Washington		
	(64)	*1,650.00*	500.00
80	5¢ brn. Jefferson (67)	*40,000.00*	—
81	30¢ org. Franklin (71)	—	*32,500.00*

B. Grill about 18x15 mm.

82	3¢ rose Washington (64)	—	*35,000.00*

C. Grill about 13x16 mm.

83	3¢ rose Washington (64)	1,500.00	335.00

Grills, D, Z, E, F: Points Down

D. Grill about 12x14 mm.

84	2¢ blk. Jackson (73)	*2,300.00*	800.00
85	3¢ rose Washington (64)	1,100.00	300.00

Z. Grill about 11x14 mm.

85A	1¢ bl. Franklin (63)	—	*110,000.00*
85B	2¢ blk. Jackson (73)	1,100.00	300.00
85C	3¢ rose Washington (64)	*2,500.00*	750.00
85D	10¢ green Washington		
	(68)	—	*23,500.00*
85E	12¢ black Washington		
	(69)	1,600.00	500.00
85F	15¢ blk. Lincoln (77)	—	*35,000.00*

E. Grill about 11x13 mm.

86	1¢ blue Franklin (63)	635.00	200.00
87	2¢ black Jackson (73)	300.00	70.00
88	3¢ rose Washington (64)	225.00	9.00
89	10¢ grn. Washington (68)	1,150.00	145.00
90	12¢ blk. Washington (69)	1,250.00	145.00

5

55

56

57

58

59

2

63

64

67

68

69

12
113
114
115
116

17
118
120
121
122

34
135
136
137
138

1867 continued	Un	U
91	15¢ black Lincoln (77)	2,350.00	335.00
	F. Grill about 9x13 mm.		
92	1¢ blue Franklin (63)	250.00	75.00
93	2¢ black Jackson (73)	150.00	25.00
94	3¢ red Washington (64)	85.00	3.50
95	5¢ brown Jefferson (67)	875.00	200.00
96	10¢ yellow green		
	Washington (68)	600.00	85.00
97	12¢ black Washington		
	(69)	635.00	85.00
98	15¢ black Lincoln (77)	675.00	97.50
99	24¢ gray lilac		
	Washington (70)	1,250.00	475.00
100	30¢ orange Franklin (71)	1,450.00	365.00
101	90¢ blue Washington		
	(72)	3,350.00	900.00

Reissues of 1861-66 in 1875, Without Grill, Perf. 12

102	1¢ blue Franklin (63)	475.00	650.00
103	2¢ black Jackson (73)	2,500.00	3,250.00
104	3¢ brown red		
	Washington (64)	2,850.00	3,500.00
105	5¢ brown Jefferson (67)	1,600.00	1,850.00
106	10¢ grn. Washington (68)	2,100.00	2,500.00
107	12¢ blk. Washington (69)	2,850.00	3,350.00
108	15¢ black Lincoln (77)	2,850.00	3,500.00
109	24¢ deep violet		
	Washington (70)	3,500.00	5,000.00
110	30¢ brownish orange		
	Franklin (71)	4,250.00	6,000.00
111	90¢ blue Washington (72)	5,500.00	8,500.00

Issue of 1869, With Grill Measuring 9½x9 mm., Perf. 12

112	1¢ Franklin	250.00	67.50
113	2¢ Post Horse & Rider	190.00	30.00
114	3¢ Locomotive	150.00	5.50
115	6¢ Washington	875.00	100.00
116	10¢ Shield and Eagle	975.00	115.00
117	12¢ S.S. Adriatic	850.00	100.00
118	15¢ Columbus		
	Landing, type I	2,000.00	300.00
119	15¢ brown and blue		
	Columbus Landing,		
	type II (118)	1,000.00	135.00

		Un	U
119b	Center		
	inverted	130,000.00	17,000.00
120	24¢ Declaration of		
	Independence	2,750.00	585.00
120b	Center		
	inverted	100,000.00	16,500.00
121	30¢ Shield, Eagle		
	and Flags	2,500.00	300.00
121b	Flags inverted	115,000.00	45,000.00
122	90¢ Lincoln	7,500.00	1,250.00

Reissues of 1869 in 1875, Without Grill, Hard White Paper, Perf. 12

123	1¢ Buff (112)	375.00	250.00
124	2¢ brown (113)	415.00	375.00
125	3¢ blue (114)	2,750.00	1,250.00
126	6¢ blue (115)	850.00	500.00
127	10¢ yellow (116)	1,400.00	1,000.00
128	12¢ green (117)	1,500.00	1,000.00
129	15¢ brown and blue		
	Columbus Landing,		
	type III (118)	1,300.00	500.00
130	24¢ grn. & vio. (120)	1,250.00	500.00
131	30¢ bl. & car. (121)	1,750.00	1,000.00
132	90¢ car. & blk. (122)	5,500.00	10,000.00

Reissues of 1869 in 1880, Soft, Porous Paper, Perf. 12

133	1¢ buff (112)	225.00	175.00

Issue of 1870-71, With Grill, White Wove Paper, Perf. 12

134	1¢ Franklin	500.00	60.00
135	2¢ Jackson	335.00	33.50
136	3¢ Washington	250.00	8.50
137	6¢ Lincoln	1,350.00	250.00
138	7¢ Edwin M. Stanton	1,100.00	235.00
139	10¢ Jefferson	1,500.00	375.00
140	12¢ Henry Clay	11,500.00	1,400.00
141	15¢ Daniel Webster	1,500.00	675.00
142	24¢ General Winfield		
	Scott	—	10,500.00

It is generally accepted as fact that the Continental Bank Note Co. printed and delivered a quantity of 24¢ stamps. They are impossible to distinguish from those printed by the National Bank Note Co.

		Un	U
	1870-71 continued		
143	30¢ Alexander		
	Hamilton	3,750.00	900.00
144	90¢ Commodore Perry	5,000.00	675.00
	Without Grill, White Wove Paper, Perf. 12		
145	1¢ ultra. Franklin (134)	150.00	7.50
146	2¢ red brn. Jackson		
	(135)	50.00	4.25
147	3¢ green Washington		
	(136)	100.00	.50
148	6¢ carmine Lincoln (137)	185.00	10.00
149	7¢ verm. Stanton (138)	335.00	50.00
150	10¢ brown Jefferson (139)	185.00	11.50
151	12¢ dull violet Clay (140)	550.00	45.00
152	15¢ bright orange Webster		
	(141)	500.00	45.00
153	24¢ purple W. Scott (142)	575.00	67.50
154	30¢ black Hamilton (143)	1,000.00	95.00
155	90¢ carmine Perry (144)	1,150.00	165.00
	Issue of 1873, Without Grill, Perf. 12, White Wove Paper, Thin to Thick		
156	1¢ Franklin	47.50	2.00
157	2¢ Jackson	135.00	6.50
158	3¢ Washington	37.50	.17
159	6¢ Lincoln	185.00	8.50
160	7¢ Stanton	395.00	57.50
161	10¢ Jefferson	180.00	9.50
162	12¢ Clay	625.00	57.50
163	15¢ Webster	525.00	45.00
165	30¢ Hamilton (143)	525.00	45.00
166	90¢ Perry (144)	1,150.00	165.00
	Issue of 1875, Special Printing, Hard, White Wove Paper, Without Gum		
167	1¢ ultra. Franklin (156)	5,500.00	—
168	2¢ dark brown		
	Jackson (157)	3,000.00	—
169	3¢ blue green		
	Washington (158)	8,500.00	—
170	6¢ dull rose Lincoln		
	(159)	7,000.00	—
171	7¢ reddish vermilion		
	Stanton (160)	1,850.00	—
172	10¢ pale brown		
	Jefferson (161)	6,000.00	—

		Un	
173	12¢ dark violet Clay		
	(162)	2,350.00	—
174	15¢ bright orange		
	Webster (163)	6,500.00	—
175	24¢ dull purple		
	W. Scott (142)	1,650.00	—
176	30¢ greenish black		
	Hamilton (143)	6,000.00	—
177	90¢ violet car. Perry		
	(144)	6,000.00	—
	Although perforated, these stamps were usually cut apart with scissors. As a result, the perforations are often much mutilated and the design is frequently damaged.		
	Yellowish Wove Paper		
178	2¢ vermilion Jackson		
	(157), June 21	150.00	3.75
179	5¢ Zachary Taylor,		
	June 21	150.00	8.50
	Special Printing, Hard, White Wove Paper, Without Gum		
180	2¢ carmine verm.		
	Jackson (157)	16,500.00	—
181	5¢ bright blue Taylor		
	(179)	30,000.00	—
	Issue of 1879. Printed by the American Bank Note Company. Soft, Porous Paper Varying from Thin to Thick.		
182	1¢ dark ultramarine		
	Franklin (156)	100.00	1.35
183	2¢ vermilion Jackson		
	(157)	60.00	1.35
184	3¢ green Washington		
	(158)	45.00	.15
185	5¢ blue Taylor (179)	185.00	8.50
186	6¢ pink Lincoln (159)	425.00	9.75
187	10¢ brown Jefferson (139)		
	(no secret mark)	675.00	12.75
188	10¢ brown Jefferson (161)		
	(with secret mark)	450.00	14.50
189	15¢ red orange		
	Webster (163)	165.00	15.00
190	30¢ full black Hamilton		
	(143)	500.00	22.50
191	30¢ carmine Perry (144)	1,050.00	165.00

43

144

156

157

158

159

205

206

207

208

209

	Un	U
Issue of 1880, Special Printing, Soft, Porous Paper, Without Gum		
192 1¢ dark ultramarine		
Franklin (156)	*8,000.00*	—
193 2¢ black brown		
Jackson (157)	*4,500.00*	—
194 3¢ blue green		
Washington (158)	*11,500.00*	—
195 6¢ dull rose Lincoln		
(159)	*8,500.00*	—
196 7¢ scarlet vermilion		
Stanton (160)	*2,250.00*	—
197 10¢ deep brown		
Jefferson (161)	*7,500.00*	—
198 12¢ blackish purple		
Clay (162)	*4,250.00*	—
199 15¢ orange Webster		
(163)	*7,000.00*	—
200 24¢ dark violet		
W. Scott (142)	*2,350.00*	—
201 30¢ greenish black		
Hamilton (143)	*6,250.00*	—
202 90¢ dull car. Perry (144)	*6,250.00*	—
203 2¢ scarlet vermilion		
Jackson (157)	*15,000.00*	—
204 5¢ deep blue Taylor		
(179)	*25,000.00*	—
Issue of 1882		
205 5¢ Garfield, Apr. 10	115.00	4.25
Special Printing. Soft, Porous Paper, Without Gum		
205C 5¢ gray brown (205)	*16,500.00*	—
Issue of 1881-82, Designs of 1873 Re-engraved.		
206 1¢ Franklin	32.50	.60
207 3¢ Washington	37.50	.20
208 6¢ Lincoln	250.00	43.50
209 10¢ Jefferson	80.00	2.25
Issue of 1883		
210 2¢ Washington, Oct. 1	33.50	.12
211 4¢ Jackson, Oct. 1	155.00	7.50
Special Printing. Soft, Porous Paper.		
211B 2¢ pale red brown		
Washington (210)	*675.00*	—

	Un	U
211D 4¢ deep blue green		
Jackson (211) no gum	*13,000.00*	—
Issue of 1887		
212 1¢ Franklin	56.50	.75
213 2¢ green Washington		
(210)	25.00	.9
214 3¢ vermilion		
Washington (207)	55.00	36.50
Issue of 1888, Perf. 12		
215 4¢ carmine Jackson		
(211)	165.00	11.00
216 5¢ indigo Garfield (205)	150.00	6.50
217 30¢ orange brown		
Hamilton (143)	400.00	75.00
218 90¢ purple Perry (144)	800.00	165.00
Issue of 1890-93, Perf. 12		
219 1¢ Franklin	23.50	.12
219D 2¢ Washington	150.00	.50
220 2¢ carmine (219D)	21.00	.9
1890-93 continued		
221 3¢ Jackson	70.00	4.65
222 4¢ Lincoln	75.00	1.65
223 5¢ Ulysses S. Grant	70.00	1.65
224 6¢ Garfield	70.00	13.75
225 8¢ William T. Sherman	50.00	10.00
226 10¢ Webster	140.00	1.85
227 15¢ Clay	185.00	18.75
228 30¢ Jefferson	295.00	21.50
229 90¢ Perry	450.00	115.00

		Un	U	PB	#	FDC	
Columbian Exposition Issue, 1893, Perf. 12							
230	1¢ Columbus Sights Land	32.50	.35	500.00	(6)	*2,600.00*	449,195,550
231	2¢ Landing of Columbus	30.00	.10	450.00	(6)	*2,000.00*	1,464,588,750
232	3¢ The Santa Maria	65.00	18.00	850.00	(6)	*6,000.00*	11,501,250
233	4¢ Fleet of Columbus ultramarine	90.00	.7.00	1,100.00	(6)	*6,000.00*	19,181,550
233a	4¢ blue (error) (233)	*6,500.00*	*2,500.00*				
234	5¢ Columbus Seeking Aid	110.00	7.00	1,600.00	(6)	*6,250.00*	35,248,250
235	6¢ Columbus at Barcelona	110.00	30.00	1,300.00	(6)	*6,750.00*	4,707,550
236	8¢ Columbus Restored to Favor	75.00	8.75	850.00	(6)		10,656,550
237	10¢ Columbus Presenting Indians	160.00	7.00	*3,500.00*	(6)	*7,500.00*	16,516,950
238	15¢ Columbus Announcing						
	His Discovery	285.00	75.00	*5,750.00*	(6)		1,576,950
239	30¢ Columbus at La Rabida	395.00	110.00	*8,500.00*	(6)		617,250
240	50¢ Recall of Columbus	500.00	165.00	*12,000.00*	(6)		243,750
241	$1 Isabella Pledging Her Jewels	1,500.00	650.00	*23,000.00*	(6)		55,050
242	$2 Columbus in Chains	1,600.00	550.00	*25,000.00*	(6)	*14,000.00*	45,550
243	$3 Columbus Describing His						
	Third Voyage	3,000.00	1,150.00	*55,000.00*	(6)		27,650
244	$4 Isabella and Columbus	4,000.00	1,600.00	*110,000.00*	(6)		26,350
245	$5 Portrait of Columbus	4,500.00	1,750.00	*120,000.00*	(6)		27,350

A Nation Speaks Through Its Postage

Whether knowingly or unknowingly, governments say a lot about themselves by what they choose to put on their stamps. U.S. postage seems to be saying that America is maturing from a proud, scrappy young republic to a nation with other interests, such as history, the arts, wildlife and human achievement.

America's early philatelic history is a display of American political and military heroes. Benjamin Franklin and George Washington were on our first stamps, and Washington, our first military hero, has appeared on more U.S. stamps than anybody else. Early Americans, one might suppose, needed to be reassured that their young nation had founding fathers and heroes just like any other country.

The Columbian Exposition set of 1893 was the first U.S. commemorative issue and seemed to coincide with America's acceptance worldwide as something more than just an experiment in government. Since then, U.S. commemoratives have come to include a multitude of subjects, such as ecology, international history and space travel, reflecting our nation's concern with the overall human condition as opposed to just our own national welfare.

230

231

232

233

234

235

236

237

238

239

240

241

242

243

244

245

246   251   253   254   255   256

257   258   259   260   261   262

85

Bureau Issues

Starting in 1894, the Bureau of Engraving and Printing at Washington has produced all U.S. postage stamps except Nos. 909-921 (Overrun Countries), 1335 (Eakins painting), 1355 (Disney), 1410-1413 (Anti-Pollution), 1414-1418 (Christmas, 1970), 1789 (John Paul Jones), 1804 (Benjamin Banneker), 1825 (Veterans Administration), 1833 (American Education), 2023 (Francis of Assisi), 2038 (Joseph Priestley) and 2065 (Martin Luther).

Issue of 1894, Perf. 12, Unwmkd.

		Un	U	PB	#	FDC	Q
246	1¢ Franklin	22.50	3.25	325.00	(6)		
247	1¢ blue Franklin (246)	55.00	1.75	650.00	(6)		
248	2¢ Washington, type I	19.50	2.00	225.00	(6)		
	Nos. 249-252; Washington (251)						
249	2¢ carmine lake, type I	135.00	1.35	1,250.00	(6)		
250	2¢ carmine, type I	25.00	.22	325.00	(6)		
251	2¢ carmine, type II	190.00	3.00	2,500.00	(6)		
252	2¢ carmine, type III	100.00	3.35	1,200.00	(6)		
253	3¢ Jackson	95.00	7.00	1,000.00	(6)		
254	4¢ Lincoln	100.00	2.65	1,250.00	(6)		
255	5¢ Grant	67.50	3.85	875.00	(6)		
256	6¢ Garfield	150.00	16.50	1,600.00	(6)		
257	8¢ Sherman	115.00	11.00	1,000.00	(6)		
258	10¢ Webster	210.00	7.50	2,750.00	(6)		
259	15¢ Clay	300.00	50.00	4,250.00	(6)		
260	50¢ Jefferson	400.00	85.00	7,000.00	(6)		
261	$1 Commodore Perry, type I	1,100.00	250.00	*16,500.00*	(6)		
261A	$1 black Perry, type II (261)	2,000.00	485.00	*27,500.00*	(6)		
262	$2 James Madison	2,500.00	600.00	*40,000.00*	(6)		
263	$5 John Marshall	4,250.00	1,100.00	—	(6)		
	Issue of 1895, Perf. 12, Wmkd. 191						
264	1¢ blue Franklin (264)	6.75	.10	185.00	(6)		
	Nos. 265-267; Washington (251)						
265	2¢ carmine, type I	30.00	.75	375.00	(6)		
266	2¢ carmine, type II	32.50	3.15	425.00	(6)		
267	2¢ carmine, type III	5.00	.09	135.00	(6)		
268	3¢ purple Jackson (253)	42.50	1.10	650.00	(6)		
269	4¢ dk. brown Lincoln (254)	45.00	1.25	650.00	(6)		
270	5¢ chocolate Grant (255)	33.50	1.95	650.00	(6)		
271	6¢ dull brn. Garfield (256)	85.00	4.00	1,250.00	(6)		
272	8¢ vio. brn. Sherman (257)	33.50	1.10	700.00	(6)		
273	10¢ dk. green Webster (258)	67.50	1.35	1,300.00	(6)		
274	15¢ dark blue Clay (259)	210.00	8.50	3,500.00	(6)		
275	50¢ orange Jefferson (260)	325.00	22.50	6,750.00	(6)		
276	$1 black Perry, type I (261)	750.00	67.50	*11,500.00*	(6)		
276A	$1 blk. Perry, type II (261)	1,700.00	150.00	*23,500.00*	(6)		
277	$2 brt. blue Madison (262)	1,100.00	310.00	*21,000.00*	(6)		
278	$5 dk. grn. Marshall (263)	2,250.00	435.00	*60,000.00*	(6)		

Issue of 1898, Perf. 12	Un	U	PB	#	FDC	
279	1¢ dp. green Franklin (246)	11.50	.10	185.00	(6)		
279B	2¢ red Washington, type III (251)	11.00	.09	175.00	(6)		
280	4¢ rose brn. Lincoln (254)	33.50	.75	700.00	(6)		
281	5¢ dark blue Grant (255)	37.50	.75	800.00	(6)		
282	6¢ lake Garfield (256)	50.00	2.25	1,200.00	(6)		
282C	10¢ Webster, type I	170.00	2.35	3,250.00	(6)		
283	10¢ Webster, type II	110.00	1.85	1,800.00	(6)		
284	15¢ olive green Clay (259)	125.00	7.50	2,750.00	(6)		
Trans-Mississippi Exposition Issue, June 17, Perf. 12						
285	1¢ Marquette on the Mississippi	33.50	6.00	265.00		5,250.00	70,993,400
286	2¢ Farming in the West	33.50	1.50	250.00		4,500.00	159,720,800
287	4¢ Indian Hunting Buffalo	150.00	25.00	1,500.00			4,924,500
288	5¢ Frémont on the Rocky Mts.	150.00	20.00	1,400.00		5,500.00	7,694,180
289	8¢ Troops Guarding Train	200.00	42.50	2,400.00		8,000.00	2,927,200
290	10¢ Hardships of Emigration	240.00	22.50	3,000.00			4,629,760
291	50¢ Western Mining Prospector	950.00	180.00	18,500.00		9,250.00	530,400
292	$1 Western Cattle in Storm	2,250.00	650.00	45,000.00			56,900
293	$2 Mississippi River Bridge						
	at St. Louis	3,500.00	950.00	90,000.00			56,200
Pan-American Exposition Issue, 1901, May 1, Wmkd. 191						
294	1¢ Great Lakes Steamer	27.50	4.95	325.00	(6)	3,500.00	91,401,500
294a	Center inverted	11,000.00	3,000.00	48,500.00			
295	2¢ An Early Locomotive	25.00	1.10	325.00	(6)	3,000.00	209,759,700
295a	Center inverted	50,000.00	12,000.00				
296	4¢ Closed Coach Automobile	130.00	18.75	3,000.00	(6)	4,250.00	5,737,100
296a	Center inverted	14,000.00	—	75,000.00			
297	5¢ Bridge at Niagara Falls	135.00	20.00	3,250.00	(6)	4,500.00	7,201,300
298	8¢ Sault Ste. Marie Canal Locks	175.00	77.50	6,000.00	(6)		4,921,700
299	10¢ American Line Steamship	265.00	37.50	8,750.00	(6)		5,043,700

Western Cattle in Storm?

As part of their issue commemorating the Trans-Mississippi Exposition of 1898, The United States Postal Service printed, on the $1 denomination, a stirring picture they thought was entitled "Western Cattle in Storm" (#292). It was then being used as the trademark of an American cattle company who willingly gave permission for its use without informing the USPS that it was actually a copy of a painting called "The Vanguard." Scotsman James MacWhirter had in fact painted a scene of Scottish cows, not American. When the truth became known, the Postal Service sent profuse apologies to the owner of the painting, Lord Blythsword. Unfortunately, the stamp has never lost its original name and MacWhirter remains unacknowledged as the artist.

282C

283

285

286

287

288

289

290

291

292

293

294

294a

295

295a

296

296a

297

298

299

300

301

302

303

304

305

306

307

308

309

310

311

312

313

319

323

324

325

326

	Issue of 1902-03, Perf. 12, Wmkd. 191	Un	U	PB	#	FDC	Q
300	1¢ Franklin, 1903	12.00	.09	185.00	(6)		
301	2¢ Washington, 1903	13.50	.10	200.00	(6)	*2,750.00*	
302	3¢ Jackson, 1903	75.00	3.00	1,100.00	(6)		
303	4¢ Grant, 1903	75.00	1.10	1,100.00	(6)		
304	5¢ Lincoln, 1903	80.00	1.00	1,250.00	(6)		
305	6¢ Garfield, 1903	85.00	2.65	1,250.00	(6)		
306	8¢ Martha Washington, 1902	47.50	2.25	875.00	(6)		
307	10¢ Webster, 1903	85.00	1.40	1,500.00	(6)		
308	13¢ Benjamin Harrison, 1902	46.50	10.00	700.00	(6)		
309	15¢ Clay, 1903	225.00	6.50	*4,500.00*	(6)		
310	50¢ Jefferson, 1903	675.00	30.00	*9,500.00*	(6)		
311	$1 David G. Farragut, 1903	1,200.00	57.50	*18,500.00*	(6)		
312	$2 Madison, 1903	1,500.00	200.00	*27,500.00*	(6)		
313	$5 Marshall, 1903	3,250.00	750.00	*70,000.00*	(6)		

For listings of 312 and 313 with Perf. 10, see Nos. 479 and 480.

Issues of 1906-08, Imperf.

		Un	U	PB	#		
314	1¢ blue green Franklin (300),-06	35.00	22.50	300.00	(6)		
314A	4¢ brown Grant (303), 1908	*17,500.00*	*9,000.00*				
315	5¢ blue Lincoln (304), 1908	900.00	375.00	5,750.00	(6)		

No. 314A was issued imperforate, but all copies were privately perforated with large oblong perforations at the sides. (Schermack type III).

Coil Stamps, Perf. 12 Horizontally

316	1¢ blue green pair						
	Franklin (300), 1908	*22,500.00*					
317	5¢ blue pair Lincoln (304),-08	*4,500.00*					

Perf. 12 Vertically

318	1¢ blue green pair Franklin						
	(300), 1908	*3,500.00*	—				

Issue of 1903, Perf. 12, Shield-shaped Background

319	2¢ Washington, Nov. 12	8.50	.09	125.00	(6)		

Issue of 1906, Nos. 320-322; Washington (319), Imperf.

320	2¢ carmine, Oct 2	33.50	19.50	350.00	(6)		

Issue of 1908, Coil Stamps, Perf. 12, Horizontally

321	2¢ carmine pair	*35,000.00*	—				

Perf. 12 Vertically

322	2¢ carmine pair	*4,750.00*	—				

Issue of 1904, Perf. 12, Louisiana Purchase Exposition Issue, Apr. 30

323	1¢ Robert R. Livingston	40.00	5.00	225.00	*3,500.00*	79,779,200
324	2¢ Thomas Jefferson	35.00	1.65	250.00	*3,250.00*	192,732,400
325	3¢ James Monroe	105.00	40.00	750.00	*3,750.00*	4,542,600
326	5¢ William McKinley	135.00	25.00	900.00	*4,750.00*	6,926,700

	1904 continued	Un	U	PB	#	FDC	
327	10¢ Map of Louisiana Purchase	250.00	40.00	2,400.00		*7,000.00*	4,011,200
	Issue of 1907, Perf. 12, Jamestown Exposition Issue						
328	1¢ Captain John Smith	30.00	6.00	325.00	(6)	*2,500.00*	77,728,794
329	2¢ Founding of Jamestown	35.00	4.00	475.00	(6)	*2,750.00*	149,497,994
330	5¢ Pocahontas	160.00	35.00	3,500.00	(6)		7,980,594
	Regular Issues of 1908-09, Perf. 12, Wmkd. 191						
331	1¢ Franklin, 1908	9.50	.09	90.00	(6)		
331a	Booklet pane of 6	165.00	*35.00*				
332	2¢ Washington, 1908	8.50	.09	80.00	(6)		
332a	Booklet pane of 6	130.00	*35.00*				
333	3¢ Washington, type I, 1908	33.50	3.35	350.00	(6)		
	Nos. 334-342; Washington (333)						
334	4¢ orange brown, 1908	33.50	1.25	400.00	(6)		
335	5¢ blue, 1908	45.00	2.25	650.00	(6)		
336	6¢ red orange, 1908	57.50	4.75	1,000.00	(6)		
337	8¢ olive green, 1908	37.50	2.65	550.00	(6)		
338	10¢ yellow, 1909	75.00	1.50	1,150.00	(6)		
339	13¢ blue green, 1909	41.50	32.50	550.00	(6)		
340	15¢ pale ultramarine, 1909	67.50	6.00	750.00	(6)		
341	50¢ violet, 1909	335.00	16.50	*8,000.00*	(6)		
342	$1 violet brown, 1909	525.00	95.00	*12,000.00*	(6)		
	Imperf.						
343	1¢ green Franklin (331), 1908	11.00	3.75	90.00	(6)		
344	2¢ car, Washington (332), 1908	13.50	3.35	160.00	(6)		
	Nos. 345-347; Washington (333)						
345	3¢ deep violet, type I, 1909	26.50	16.50	300.00	(6)		
346	4¢ orange brown, 1909	55.00	21.75	450.00	(6)		
347	5¢ blue, 1909	85.00	40.00	750.00	(6)		
	Coil Stamps of 1908-10						
	Nos. 350-351, 354-356: Washington (333), Perf. 12 Horizontally						
348	1¢ green Franklin (331), 1908	27.50	15.00				
349	2¢ car. Washington (332), 1909	60.00	6.50				
350	4¢ orange brown, 1910	125.00	65.00				
351	5¢ blue, 1909	150.00	80.00				
	1909, Perf. 12 Vertically						
352	1¢ green Franklin (331), 1909	60.00	17.50				
353	2¢ car. Washington (332), 1909	55.00	6.75				
354	4¢ orange brown, 1909	150.00	45.00				
355	5¢ blue, 1909	150.00	67.50				
356	10¢ yellow, 1909	1,350.00	375.00				
	Issues of 1909, Bluish Paper, Perf. 12						
	Nos. 359-366: Washington (333)						
357	1¢ green Franklin (331)	125.00	100.00	1,250.00	(6)		
358	2¢ car. Washington (332)	110.00	75.00	1,250.00	(6)		

328

329

330

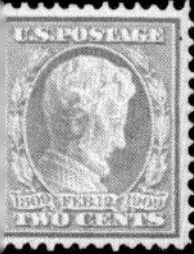

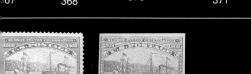

67

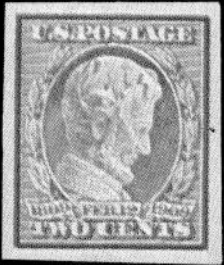

368

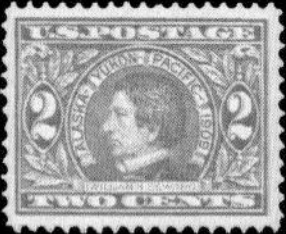

370

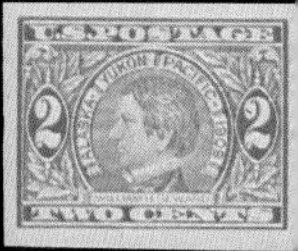

371

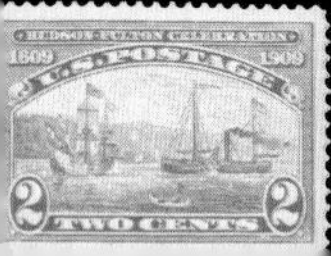

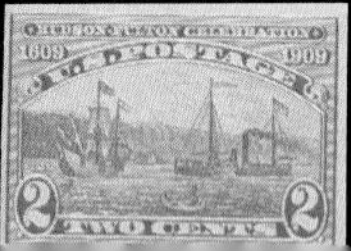

	1909 continued	Un	U	PB	#	FDC	Q
359	3¢ deep violet, type I	1,650.00	1,100.00	16,500.00	(6)		
360	4¢ orange brown	14,000.00	—	60,000.00			
361	5¢ blue	3,750.00	—	35,000.00	(6)		
362	6¢ red orange	1,110.00	575.00	11,000.00	(6)		
363	8¢ olive green	14,000.00	—	55,000.00	(6)		
364	10¢ yellow	1,150.00	650.00	12,000.00	(6)		
365	13¢ blue green	2,250.00	1,100.00	18,500.00	(6)		
366	15¢ pale ultramarine	1,000.00	675.00	10,000.00	(6)		
	Lincoln Memorial Issue, Feb. 12						
367	2¢ Lincoln, Perf. 12	8.75	3.00	200.00	(6)	350.00	148,387,191
368	2¢ Lincoln, Imperf.	57.50	30.00	375.00	(6)	1,900.00	1,273,900
369	2¢ Lincoln, Perf. 12, Bluish Paper	350.00	185.00	4,750.00	(6)		637,000
	Alaska-Yukon Exposition Issue						
370	2¢ William Seward, Perf. 12	13.50	2.50	325.00	(6)	1,800.00	152,887,311
371	2¢ William Seward, Imperf.	75.00	37.50	450.00	(6)		525,400
	Hudson-Fulton Celebration Issue, Sep. 25						
372	2¢ Half Moon and Clermont, Perf. 12	15.00	4.25	375.00	(6)	950.00	72,634,631
373	2¢ Half Moon and Clermont, Imperf.	90.00	40.00	500.00	(6)	2,350.00	216,480
	Issues of 1910-13, Perf. 12, Wmkd. 190						
	Nos. 376-382: Washington (333)						
374	1¢ green Franklin (331), 1910	8.25	.10	95.00	(6)		
374a	Booklet pane of 6	150.00	30.00				
375	2¢ car. Washington (332), 1910	7.50	.09	85.00	(6)		
375a	Booklet pane of 6	120.00	25.00				
376	3¢ deep violet, type I, 1911	16.75	1.75	185.00	(6)		
377	4¢ brown, 1911	25.00	.60	250.00	(6)		
378	5¢ blue, 1911	22.50	.60	285.00	(6)		
379	6¢ red orange, 1911	41.50	.80	525.00	(6)		
380	8¢ olive green, 1911	135.00	12.75	1,500.00	(6)		
381	10¢ yellow, 1911	130.00	4.75	1,450.00	(6)		
382	15¢ pale ultramarine, 1911	325.00	15.00	3,000.00	(6)		
	Imperf.						
383	1¢ green Franklin (331), 1911	5.75	3.75	85.00	(6)		
384	2¢ car. Washington (332), 1911	8.25	2.25	250.00	(6)		
	Coil Stamps, Perf. 12 Horizontally						
385	1¢ green Franklin (331), 1910	29.50	12.00				
386	2¢ car. Washington (332), 1910	41.50	10.75				
	Perf. 12 Vertically						
387	1¢ green Franklin (331), 1910	85.00	25.00				
388	2¢ car. Washington (332), 1910	625.00	85.00				
389	3¢ dp. vio. Washington,						
	type I (333), 1911	13,000.00	4,250.00				
	Perf. 8½ Horizontally						
390	1¢ green Franklin (331), 1910	5.75	2.95				

	1910-13 continued	Un	U	PB	#	FDC	
391	2¢ car. Washington (332), 1910	48.50	8.00				
	Perf. 8½ Vertically, Nos. 394-396; Washington (333)						
392	1¢ green Franklin (331), 1910	25.00	17.50				
393	2¢ car. Washington (332), 1910	56.50	5.50				
394	3¢ deep violet, type I, 1911	65.00	30.00				
395	4¢ brown, 1912	65.00	30.00				
396	5¢ blue, 1913	65.00	32.50				
	Panama Pacific Exposition Issue, 1913, Perf. 12						
397	1¢ Balboa	22.50	1.85	190.00	(6)	3,500.00	167,398,463
398	2¢ Locks, Panama Canal	26.50	.60	375,00	(6)		251,856,543
399	5¢ Golden Gate	115.00	12.75	2,900.00	(6)	4,500.00	14,544, 363
400	10¢ Discovery						
	of San Francisco Bay	225.00	27.50	4,000.00	(6)		8,484,182
400A	10¢ orange (400)	325.00	19.50	11,500.00	(6)		
	1914-15, Perf. 10						
401	1¢ green Balboa (397), 1914	37.50	7.00	450.00	(6)		167,398,463
402	2¢ carmine Canal Locks (398),-15	115.00	1.75	2,500.00	(6)		251,856,543
403	5¢ blue Golden Gate (399),-15	275.00	21.75	5,750.00	(6)		14,544,363
404	10¢ orange Discovery of						
	San Francisco Bay (400), 1915	1,850.00	80.00	19,000.00	(6)		8,484,182
	Issues of 1912-14						
	Nos. 405-413: Washington (333), Perf. 12						
405	1¢ green, 1912	8.50	.09	115.00	(6)		
405b	Booklet pane of 6	75.00	7.50				
406	2¢ carmine, type I, 1912	7.50	.09	140.00	(6)		
406a	Booklet pane of 6	78.50	17.50				
407	7¢ black, 1914	120.00	7.00	1,500.00	(6)		
408	1¢ green, Imperf., 1912	1.75	.85	30.00	(6)		
409	2¢ carmine, type I, Imperf., 1912	2.15	.85	60.00	(6)		
	Coil Stamps, Perf. 8½ Horizontally						
410	1¢ green, 1912	7.50	3.50				
411	2¢ carmine, type I, 1912	10.00	3.50				
	Perf. 8½ Vertically						
412	1¢ green, 1912	29.00	5.50				
413	2¢ carmine, type I, 1912	50.00	.55				
	Perf. 12, Nos. 415-421; Franklin (414)						
414	8¢ Franklin, 1912	45.00	1.50	575.00	(6)		
415	9¢ salmon red, 1914	57.50	14.50	850.00	(6)		
416	10¢ orange yellow, 1912	45.00	.25	650.00	(6)		
417	12¢ claret brown, 1914	40.00	4.25	550.00	(6)		
418	15¢ gray, 1912	85.00	3.25	825.00	(6)		
419	20¢ ultramarine, 1914	215.00	15.00	2,350.00	(6)		
420	30¢ orange red, 1914	150.00	15.00	2,150.00	(6)		

397

398

399

400

405

406

414

420

	1912-14 continued	Un	U	PB	#	FDC		Q
421	50¢ violet, 1914	625.00	15.00	10,000.00	(6)			
	Nos. 422-423: Franklin (414), Perf. 12							
422	50¢ violet, Feb. 12, 1912	335.00	16.50	6,750.00	(6)			
423	$1 violet brown, Feb. 12, 1912							
	Wmkd. 191	665.00	80.00	12,500.00	(6)			
	Issues of 1914-15, Perf. 10, Wmkd. 190							
	Nos. 424-430: Washington (333)							
424	1¢ green, 1914	4.00	.10	60.00	(6)			
424d	Booklet pane of 6	6.50	.75					
425	2¢ rose red, type I, 1914	2.95	.09	40.00	(6)			
425e	Booklet pane of 6	17.50	3.00					
426	3¢ deep violet, type I, 1914	15.00	1.70	150.00	(6)			
427	4¢ brown, 1914	33.50	.40	450.00	(6)			
428	5¢ blue, 1914	31.50	.40	350.00	(6)			
429	6¢ red orange, 1914	42.50	1.35	325.00	(6)			
430	7¢ black, 1914	100.00	4.50	1,050.00	(6)			
	Nos. 431-440: Franklin (414)							
431	8¢ pale olive green, 1914	40.00	1.60	400.00	(6)			
432	9¢ salmon red, 1914	55.00	8.75	575.00	(6)			
433	10¢ orange yellow, 1914	55.00	.27	625.00	(6)			
434	11¢ dark green, 1915	30.00	6.75	200.00	(6)			
435	12¢ claret brown, 1914	27.50	4.00	250.00	(6)			
437	15¢ gray, 1914	145.00	6.85	900.00	(6)			
438	20¢ ultramarine, 1914	265.00	4.25	3,200.00	(6)			
439	30¢ orange red, 1914	350.00	12.75	4,850.00	(6)			
440	50¢ violet, 1914	950.00	18.50	11,500.00	(6)			
	Coil Stamps, Perf. 10, 1914							
441	1¢ green	1.25	.90					
442	2¢ carmine, type I	11.00	7.50					
443	1¢ green	27.50	5.85					
444	2¢ carmine, type I	43.50	1.30					
445	3¢ violet, type I	300.00	120.00					
446	4¢ brown	175.00	37.50					
447	5¢ blue	65.00	20.00					
	Coil Stamps, Washington (333), 1915-16, Perf. 10 Horizontally							
448	1¢ green, 1915	7.25	3.25					
449	2¢ red, type I, 1915	1,500.00	150.00					
450	2¢ carmine, type III, 1916	13.00	3.25					
	1914-16, Perf. 10 Vertically							
452	1¢ green, 1914	10.50	1.75					
453	2¢ red, type I, 1914	150.00	4.00					

		Un	U	PB	#	FDC		Q
	Coil Stamps, 1914-16 Issues, continued							
454	2¢ carmine, type II, 1915	165.00	12.50					
455	2¢ carmine, type III, 1915	14.00	.95					
456	3¢ violet, type I, 1916	325.00	87.50					
457	4¢ brown	37.50	16.00					
458	5¢ blue	37.50	16.00					
	Issue of 1914 Washington (333), Imperf., Coil							
459	2¢ carmine, type I, June 30	550.00	*600.00*					
	Issues of 1915, Perf. 10, Wmkd. 191							
460	$1 violet black Franklin							
	(414), Feb. 8	1,100.00	*85.00*	13,500.00	(6)			
	Perf. 11							
461	2¢ pale carmine red, type I.							
	Washington (333), June 17	110.00	*75.00*	1,000.00	(6)			
	Privately perforated copies of No. 409 have been made to resemble No. 461.							
	From 1916 all postage stamps except Nos. 519 and 832b are on unwatermarked paper.							
	Issues of 1916-17, Perf. 10							
	Nos. 462-469: Washington (333)							
462	1¢ green, 1916	8.00	.30	160.00	(6)			
462a	Booklet pane of 6	12.50	*1.00*					
463	2¢ carmine, type I, 1916	5.50	.15	110.00	(6)			
463a	Booklet pane of 6	90.00	*15.00*					
464	3¢ violet, type I, 1916	95.00	12.00	1,600.00	(6)			
465	4¢ orange brown, 1916	55.00	1.80	850.00	(6)			
466	5¢ blue, 1916	95.00	1.80	1,100.00	(6)			
467	5¢ car. (error in plate of 2¢), 1917	1,000.00	*525.00*					
468	6¢ red orange, 1916	110.00	7.50	1,150.00	(6)			
469	7¢ black, 1916	125.00	13.50	1,500.00	(6)			
470	8¢ olive green, 1916	56.50	5.75	600.00	(6)			
471	9¢ salmon red, 1916	56.50	14.50	700.00	(6)			
472	10¢ orange yellow, 1916	125.00	1.10	1,600.00	(6)			
473	11¢ dark green, 1916	31.50	16.50	325.00	(6)			
474	12¢ claret brown, 1916	50.00	6.00	600.00	(6)			
475	15¢ gray, 1916	195.00	11.00	2,500.00	(6)			
476	20¢ light ultramarine, 1916	295.00	12.50	3,750.00	(6)			
477	50¢ light violet, 1917	1,500.00	75.00	25,000.00	(6)			
478	$1 violet black, 1916	1,000.00	16.50	*13,500.00*	(6)			
	Issues of 1917, Perf. 10, Mar. 22							
479	$2 dark blue Madison (312), 1917	715.00	45.00	6,500.00	(6)			
480	$5 light green Marshall (313), 1917	585.00	60.00	5,250.00	(6)			

		Un	U	PB	#	FDC	Q
	Issues of 1916-17, Washington (333), Imperf.						
481	1¢ green, 1916	1.30	.85	16.50	(6)		
482	2¢ carmine, type I, 1916	2.00	1.60	32.50	(6)		
483	3¢ violet, type I, 1917	24.50	8.75	200.00	(6)		
484	3¢ violet, type II, 1917	15.00	5.00	150.00	(6)		
	Coil Stamps, Washington (333), 1916-19, Perf. 10 Horizontally						
486	1¢ green, 1918	1.00	.18				
487	2¢ carmine, type II, 1919	24.50	3.00				
488	2¢ carmine, type III, 1917	4.65	1.70				
489	3¢ violet, type I, 1917	6.00	1.25				
	1916-22, Perf. 10 Vertically						
490	1¢ green, 1916	.80	.17				
491	2¢ carmine, type II, 1916	*1,450.00*	200.00				
492	2¢ carmine, type III, 1916	11.50	.15				
493	3¢ violet, type I, 1917	36.50	2.50				
494	3¢ violet, type II,1918	19.75	.65				
495	4¢ orange brown, 1917	18.50	3.75				
496	5¢ blue, 1919	4.50	.75				
497	10¢ or. yel. Franklin (414), 1912	32.50	10.00			*1,250.00*	
	Issues of 1917-19, Perf. 11						
	Nos. 498-507: Washington (333)						
498	1¢ green, 1917	.70	.09	18.00	(6)		
498e	Booklet pane of 6	2.75	*.35*				
499	2¢ rose, type I, 1917	.70	.09	14.00	(6)		
499e	Booklet pane of 6	3.35	*.50*				
500	2¢ deep rose, type Ia, 1917	335.00	130.00	2,500.00	(6)		
501	3¢ light violet, type I, 1917	16.50	.13	190.00	(6)		
501b	Booklet pane of 6	95.00	*15.00*				
502	3¢ dark violet, type II, 1917	20.00	.30	250.00	(6)		
502b	Booklet pane of 6, 1918	62.50	*10.00*				
503	4¢ brown, 1917	15.00	.22	200.00	(6)		
504	5¢ blue, 1917	11.00	.13	165.00	(6)		
505	5¢ rose (error in plate of 2¢),-17	675.00	*400.00*	40.00			
506	6¢ red orange, 1917	18.50	.30	250.00	(6)		
507	7¢ black, 1917	32.50	1.10	375.00	(6)		
	Nos. 508-518: Franklin (414)						
508	8¢ olive bistre, 1917	16.50	.80	250.00	(6)		
509	9¢ salmon red, 1917	18.75	2.50	250.00	(6)		

	1917-19 continued	Un	U	PB	#	FDC	Q
510	10¢ orange yellow, 1917	22.50	.15	300.00	(6)		
511	11¢ light green, 1917	10.75	3.65	150.00	(6)		
512	12¢ claret brown, 1917	11.75	.60	150.00	(6)		
513	13¢ apple green, 1919	15.00	7.50	150.00	(6)		
514	15¢ gray, 1917	62.50	1.00	800.00	(6)		
515	20¢ light ultramarine, 1917	75.00	.30	875.00	(6)		
516	30¢ orange red, 1917	65.00	1.05	750.00	(6)		
517	50¢ red violet, 1917	125.00	.75	1,750.00	(6)		
518	$1 violet brown, 1917	125.00	1.85	1,300.00	(6)		
	Issue of 1917, Perf. 11, Wmkd. 191						
519	2¢ carmine Washington						
	(332), Oct. 10	225.00	200.00	2,500.00	(6)		
	Privately perforated copies of No. 344 have been made to resemble No. 519.						
	Issues of 1918, Unwmkd., Perf. 11						
523	$2 orange red and black						
	Franklin (547), Aug. 19	1,750.00	200.00	*22,500.00*	(8)		
524	$5 deep green and black						
	Franklin (547), Aug. 19	675.00	29.50	*8,500.00*	(8)		
	Issues of 1918-20, Washington (333)						
	Perf. 11						
525	1¢ gray green, 1918	2.65	.75	35.00	(6)		
526	2¢ carmine, type IV, 1920	32.50	3.75	250.00	(6)	*825.00*	
527	2¢ carmine, type V, 1920	20.00	.95	160.00	(6)		
528	2¢ carmine, type Va, 1920	10.50	.18	65.00	(6)		
528A	2¢ carmine, type VI, 1920	55.00	1.00	375.00	(6)		
528B	2¢ carmine, type VII, 1920	22.50	.15	170.00	(6)		
529	3¢ violet, type III, 1918	2.85	.13	60.00	(6)		
530	3¢ purple, type IV, 1918	1.10	.10	15.00	(6)		
	Imperf.						
531	1¢ green, 1919	14.00	8.75	100.00	(6)		
532	2¢ car. rose, type IV, 1919	45.00	26.50	350.00	(6)		
533	2¢ carmine, type V, 1919	325.00	70.00	2,500.00	(6)		
534	2¢ carmine, type Va, 1919	20.00	10.00	130.00	(6)		
534A	2¢ carmine, type VI, 1919	45.00	25.00	400.00	(6)		
534B	2¢ carmine, type VII, 1919	1,875.00	450.00	*14,500.00*	(6)		
535	3¢ violet, type IV, 1918	13.50	7.50	90.00	(6)		
	Issues of 1919						
	Perf. 12½						
536	1¢ gray green Washington						
	(333), Aug. 15	16.50	13.50	200.00	(6)		

	1919 continued	Un	U	PB	#	FDC	
	Perf. 11						
537	3¢ Allied Victory, Mar. 3	13.50	4.50	175.00	(6)	*700.00*	99,585,200
	Nos. 538-546: Washington (333), 1919, Perf. 11x10						
538	1¢ green	11.50	10.00	100.00			
539	2¢ carmine rose, type II	*2,150.00*	800.00	*15,000.00*			
540	2¢ carmine rose, type III	11.50	10.50	110.00			
541	3¢ violet, type II	45.00	40.00	450.00			
	1920, Perf. 10x11						
542	1¢ green, May 26	8.00	1.10	135.00	(6)	*525.00*	
	1921, Perf. 10						
543	1¢ green	.70	.11	20.00			
	1921, Perf. 11						
544	1¢ green, 19x22½mm	6,500.00	1,500.00				
545	1¢ green, 19½—20mmx22mm	180.00	110.00	1,100.00			
546	2¢ carmine rose, type III	120.00	80.00	900.00			
	Issues of 1920, Perf. 11						
547	$2 Franklin	600.00	36.50	*9,500.00*	(8)		
	Pilgrims 300th Anniv. Issue, Dec. 21						
548	1¢ Mayflower	7.75	3.00	80.00	(6)	*700.00*	137,978,207
549	2¢ Pilgrims Landing	12.50	2.25	110.00	(6)	*625.00*	196,037,327
550	5¢ Signing of Compact	75.00	20.00	900.00	(6)		11,321,607
	Issues of 1922-25, Perf. 11						
551	½¢ Nathan Hale, 1925	.25	.10	8.50	(6)	25.00	
552	1¢ Franklin (19x22mm), 1923	2.95	.10	35.00	(6)	37.50	
552a	Booklet pane of 6	6.75	.50				
553	1½¢ Harding, 1925	4.50	.25	55.00	(6)	40.00	
554	2¢ Washington, 1923	2.50	.09	35.00	(6)	50.00	
554c	Booklet pane of 6	8.00	*1.00*				
555	3¢ Lincoln, 1923	30.00	1.15	300.00	(6)	42.50	
556	4¢ Martha Washington, 1923	26.50	.20	300.00	(6)	55.00	
557	5¢ Theodore Roosevelt, 1922	25.00	.13	325.00	(6)	110.00	
558	6¢ Garfield, 1922	47.50	.95	600.00	(6)	200.00	
559	7¢ McKinley, 1923	12.50	.75	95.00	(6)	110.00	
560	8¢ Grant, 1923	65.00	.80	1,100.00	(6)	110.00	
561	9¢ Jefferson, 1923	18.75	1.15	250.00	(6)	110.00	
562	10¢ Monroe, 1923	28.50	.13	425.00	(6)	110.00	
563	11¢ Rutherford B. Hayes, 1922	2.50	.30	60.00	(6)	550.00	
564	12¢ Grover Cleveland, 1923	10.00	.13	100.00	(6)	150.00	
565	14¢ American Indian, 1923	7.50	.85	85.00	(6)	350.00	
566	15¢ Statue of Liberty, 1922	30.00	.10	325.00	(6)	350.00	
567	20¢ Golden Gate, 1923	32.50	.13	325.00	(6)	400.00	
568	25¢ Niagara Falls, 1922	35.00	.60	325.00	(6)	600.00	
569	30¢ Buffalo, 1923	53.50	.35	500.00	(6)	700.00	

537

547

548

549

550

551

552

553

554

555

556

557

558

559

560

561

562

563

564

565

566

567

568

569

570

571

572

573

610

611

	1922-25 continued	Un	U	PB	#	FDC	Q
570	50¢ Arlington Amphitheater, 1922	95.00	.15	1,450.00	(6)	900.00	
571	$1 Lincoln Memorial, 1923	90.00	.45	600.00	(6)	4,250.00	
572	$2 U.S. Capitol, 1923	200.00	11.75	2,000.00	(6)	8,500.00	
573	$5 Head of Freedom,						
	Capitol Dome, 1923	450.00	17.50	6,500.00	(8)	11,000.00	
	Issues of 1923-25, Imperf.						
575	1¢ green Franklin (552), 1923	15.00	4.00	145.00	(6)		
576	1½¢ yel. brown Harding (553),-25	2.50	1.95	45.00	(6)	50.00	
577	2¢ carmine Washington (554)	3.35	2.25	40.00	(6)		

For listings of other perforated stamps of issues 551-573 see:

Nos. 578 and 579	Perf. 11x10
Nos. 581 to 591	Perf. 10
Nos. 594 and 595	Perf. 11
Nos. 622 and 623	Perf. 11
Nos. 632 to 642, 653, 692 to 696	Perf. 11x10½
Nos. 697 to 701	Perf. 10½x11

	Perf. 11x10						
578	1¢ green Franklin (552)	85.00	75.00	850.00			
579	2 ¢ carmine Washington (554)	60.00	55.00	450.00			

	Issues of 1923-26, Perf. 10	Un	U	PB	#	FDC	Q
581	1¢ green Franklin (552), 1923	7.50	.75	120.00		*2,000.00*	
582	1½¢ brown Harding (553), 1925	5.00	.75	45.00		52.50	
583	2¢ carmine Washington (554), 1924	3.00	.09	30.00			
583a	Booklet pane of 6	87.50	*25.00*				
584	3¢ violet Lincoln (555), 1925	35.00	1.95	325.00		62.50	
585	4¢ yellow brown						
	M. Washington (556)	20.00	.35	200.00			
586	5¢ blue T. Roosevelt (557), 1925	20.00	.25	200.00		62.50	
587	6¢ red orange Garfield (558), 1925	10.00	.50	65.00		77.50	
588	7¢ black McKinley (559), 1926	12.50	6.50	120.00		75.00	
589	8¢ olive green Grant (560), 1926	36.50	3.25	325.00		80.00	
590	9¢ rose Jefferson (561), 1926	7.50	2.75	45.00		85.00	
591	10¢ orange Monroe (562), 1925	80.00	.10	750.00		110.00	
	Perf. 11						
594	1¢ green Franklin,						
	19¾x22¼mm (552)	*7,000.00*	*1,850.00*				
595	2¢ carmine Washington,						
	19¾x22¼mm (554)	225.00	165.00	1,750.00			
596	1¢ green Franklin,						
	19¼x22¾mm (552)	—	*13,500.00*				
	Coil Stamps 1923-29, Perf. 10 Vertically						
597	1¢ green Franklin (552), 1923	.40	.10			450.00	
598	1½¢ brown Harding (553), 1925	.90	.13			60.00	
599	2¢ carmine Washington,						
	type I (554), 1929	.40	.09			750.00	
599A	2¢ carmine Washington,						
	type II (554), 1929	200.00	11.00				
600	3¢ violet Lincoln (555)	7.50	.11			80.00	
601	4¢ yellow brown						
	M. Washington (556), 1923	3.75	.45				
602	5¢ dark blue						
	Theodore Roosevelt (557), 1924	1.50	.18			85.00	
603	10¢ orange Monroe (562), 1924	3.75	.15			105.00	
	Coil Stamps 1923-25 Perf. 10 Horizontally						
604	1¢ yel. grn. Franklin (552), 1924	.25	.13			95.00	
605	1½¢ yel. brn. Harding (553), 1925	.30	.18			60.00	
606	2¢ carmine Washington (554), 1923	.30	.15			90.00	
	Harding Memorial Issue, 1923, Flat Plate Printing (19¼x22¼mm)						
610	2¢ Harding, Perf. 11, Sept. 1	1.00	.13	40.00	(6)	22.50	1,459,487,085
611	2¢ Harding Imperf., Nov. 15	18.50	6.25	185.00	(6)	100.00	770,000
	Rotary Press Printing (19¼x22¾mm)						
612	2¢ black, Perf. 10 (610), Sept. 12	25.00	2.25	425.00		110.00	99,950,300
613	2¢ black Perf. 11 (610)	—	*13,500.00*				

	Un	U	PB	#	FDC	
Huguenot-Walloon 300th Anniv. Issue, 1924, May 1						
614	1¢ Ship *New Netherland*	7.50	4.75	65.00	(6)	40.00	51,378,023
615	2¢ Landing at Fort Orange	11.00	3.00	115.00	(6)	55.00	77,753,423
616	5¢ Huguenot Monument, Florida	55.00	24.50	575.00	(6)	100.00	5,659,023
Lexington-Concord Issue, 1925, Apr. 4						
617	1¢ Washington at Cambridge	6.50	6.50	60.00	(6)	40.00	15,615,000
618	2¢ Birth of Liberty	11.00	7.00	125.00	(6)	50.00	26,596,600
619	5¢ Statue of Minute Man	57.50	23.75	450.00	(6)	90.00	5,348,800
Norse-American Issue, 1925, May 18						
620	2¢ Sloop *Restaurationen*	9.75	5.75	325.00	(8)	32.50	9,104,983
621	5¢ Viking Ship	35.00	25.00	1,000.00	(8)	55.00	1,900,983
Issues of 1925-26						
622	13¢ Benjamin Harrison, 1926	22.50	.65	250.00	(6)	35.00	
623	17¢ Woodrow Wilson, 1925	27.50	.30	275.00	(6)	35.00	
Issues of 1926						
627	2¢ Independence,						
	150th Anniv., May 10	5.00	.60	70.00	(6)	17.50	307,731,900
628	5¢ Ericsson Memorial, May 29	13.50	5.65	120.00	(6)	30.00	20,280,500
629	2¢ Battle of White Plains, Oct. 18	3.00	2.50	70.00	(6)	7.00	40,639,485

U.S. Pictorials Fade in Slowly

For the first 22 years of our philatelic history, U.S. stamps depicted only Presidents and Benjamin Franklin, a rather unimaginative start for such a unique nation. But in 1869, the Post Office issued the first U.S. pictorials. A 2¢ stamp showed a post rider on horseback (#113); a 3¢ issue depicted a steam locomotive (#114); and the 12¢ stamp carried a rendering of a steamship, the SS "Adriatic" (#117). Another first in this series was the use of works of art by well-known painters. The 15¢ stamp showed Vanderlyn's "Landing of Columbus" (#118) and on the 24¢ stamp was John Trumbull's "Signing the Declaration of Independence" (#120).

113

But collectors of this time only wanted their leaders, and it wasn't until the Columbian Exposition Series (#230-245) — another 23 years later—that Americans saw anything besides heroic portraits on their postage. This 16-stamp series marked the 400th anniversary of the arrival of Columbus in America with historical paintings of his life. The series also was the first commemorative-sized U.S. stamp and had the first depiction of Indians, the first depiction of foreign rulers and the first woman, Queen Isabella. This time the public approved.

118

120

615

616

618

619

621

622

623

629

631

633

643

644

645

646

647

648

649

650

654

	Un	U	PB	#	FDC	Q
International Philatelic Exhibition Issue, Oct. 18, Souvenir Sheet						
630	2¢ car. rose, sheet of 25 with					
	selvage inscription (629)	575.00	*425.00*			1,500.00	107,398*
Imperf.						
631	1½¢ Harding Aug. 27, 18½	4.25	2.00	80.00		40.00	
Issues of 1926-27, Perf. 11x10½						
632	1¢ green Franklin (552), 1927	.20	.08	3.00		60.00	
632a	Booklet pane of 6, 1927	5.00	.25				
633	1½¢ Harding, 1927	3.75	.12	110.00		60.00	
634	2¢ carmine Washington, type I						
	(554) 1956	.15	.08	1.20		62.50	
634d	Booklet pane of 6, 1927	2.50	*.15*				
634A	2¢ carmine Washington, type II						
	(554) 1926	475.00	16.50	2,500:00			
635	3¢ violet Lincoln (555), 1934	.70	.08	8.00		52.50	
636	4¢ yellow brown						
	M. Washington (556), 1927	4.75	.11	140.00		60.00	
637	5¢ dark blue T. Roosevelt (557),-27	4.75	.08	25.00		60.00	
638	6¢ red orange Garfield (558), 1927	4.75	.08	25.00		72.50	
639	7¢ black McKinley (559), 1927	4.75	.11	25.00		75.00	
640	8¢ olive green, Grant (560), 1927	4.75	.08	25.00		77.50	
641	9¢ orange red Jefferson						
	(561), 1927	4.75	.08	25.00		95.00	
642	10¢ orange Monroe (562), 1927	6.75	.08	42.50		100.00	
Issues of 1927, Perf. 11						
643	2¢ Vermont 150th Anniversary,						
	Aug. 3	1.75	1.75	60.00	(6)	5.00	39,974,900
644	2¢ Burgoyne Campaign, Aug. 3	6.50	4.75	75.00	(6)	20.00	25,628,450
Issues of 1928						
645	2¢ Valley Forge, May 26	1.35	.65	60.00	(6)	5.00	101,330,328
Perf. 11x10½						
646	2¢ Battle of Monmouth, Oct. 20	2.00	2.00	70.00		22.50	9,779,896
647	2¢ carmine , Aug. 13	8.50	6.50	200.00		22.50	5,519,897
648	5¢ Hawaii 150th Anniv., Aug. 13	27.50	25.00	400.00		40.00	1,459,897
Aeronautics Conference Issue, Dec. 12, Perf.11						
649	2¢ Wright Airplane	2.25	1.50	22.50	(6)	12.00	51,342,273
650	5¢ Globe and Airplane	11.50	5.00	110.00	(6)	18.00	10,319,700
Issues of 1929						
651	2¢ George Rogers Clark, Feb. 25	1.05	1.00	20.00	(6)	7.00	16,684,674
Perf. 11x10½						
653	½¢ olive brown Nathan Hale (551)	.11	.08	1.00		30.00	
Electric Light Jubilee Issue, Perf. 11						
654	2¢ Edison's First Lamp, June 5	1.10	1.10	50.00	(6)	11.00	31,679,200
Perf. 11x10½						
655	2¢ carmine rose (654), June 11	1.10	.30	75.00		77.50	210,119,474

*Sheets of 25

	1929 continued	Un	U	PB	#	FDC	
	Coil Stamp, Perf. 10 Vertically						
656	2¢ carmine rose (654), June 11	22.50	1.80			100.00	133,530,000
	Perf. 11						
657	2¢ Sullivan Expedition, June 17	1.00	.95	45.00	(6)	4.50	51,451,880
	Regular Issue of 1929						
	Perf. 11x10½, 658-668 Overprinted Kans.						
658	1¢ green Franklin	2.75	1.90	35.00		27.50	13,390,000
659	1½¢ brown Harding (553)	4.00	3.35	55.00		27.50	8,240,000
660	2¢ carmine Washington (554)	4.15	.75	55.00		27.50	87,410,000
661	3¢ violet Lincoln (555)	22.50	14.50	200.00		30.00	2,540,000
662	4¢ yellow brown						
	M. Washington (556)	22.50	8.50	185.00		32.50	2,290,000
663	5¢ deep blue T. Roosevelt (557)	18.75	11.50	200.00		35.00	2,700,000
664	6¢ red orange Garfield (558)	35.00	18.50	550.00		42.50	1,450,000
665	7¢ black McKinley (559)	40.00	27.50	450.00		42.50	1,320,000
666	8¢ olive green Grant (560)	100.00	85.00	850.00		80.00	1,530,000
667	9¢ light rose Jefferson (561)	16.75	12.50	225.00		72.50	1,130,000
668	10¢ orange yellow Monroe (562)	26.50	12.50	425.00		85.00	2,860,000
	669-679 Overprinted Nebr.						
669	1¢ green Franklin	2.75	2.75	35.00		27.50	8,220,000
670	1½¢ brown Harding (553)	3.75	2.85	50.00		25.00	8,990,000
671	2¢ carmine Washington (554)	2.75	2.90	35.00		25.00	73,220,000
672	3¢ violet Lincoln (555)	16.75	11.50	200.00		32.50	2,110,000
673	4¢ yellow brown						
	M. Washington (556)	25.00	15.00	225.00		37.50	1,600,000
674	5¢ deep blue T. Roosevelt (557)	22.50	15.00	275.00		37.50	1,860,000
675	6¢ red orange Garfield (558)	45.00	26.50	600.00		55.00	980,000
676	7¢ black McKinley (559)	27.50	18.75	275.00		57.50	850,000
677	8¢ olive green Grant (560)	37.50	28.50	375.00		60.00	1,480,000
678	9¢ light rose Jefferson (561)	45.00	27.50	425.00		62.50	530,000
679	10¢ orange yellow Monroe (562)	125.00	21.50	1,000.00		70.00	1,890,000
	Warning: Excellent forgeries of the Kansas and Nebraska overprints exist.						
	Perf. 11						
680	2¢ Battle of Fallen Timbers,						
	Sept. 14	1.25	1.20	50.00	(6)	4.75	29,338,274
681	2¢ Ohio River Canal, Oct. 19	.90	.90	32.50	(6)	4.00	32,680,900
	Issues of 1930						
682	2¢ Mass. Bay Colony, Apr. 8	.80	.70	55.00	(6)	3.75	74,000,774
683	2¢ Carolina-Charleston, Apr. 10	1.75	1.70	85.00	(6)	4.00	25,215,574
	Perf. 11x10½						
684	1½¢ Warren G. Harding	.50	.08	1.25		4.75	
685	4¢ William H. Taft	1.00	.09	8.50		10.00	

6 (Coil Pair) 657 658 669 680

682 683 684 685

688

689

690

702

703

704

705

706

707

708

709

10

711

712

	1930 continued	Un	U	PB	#	FDC	Q
	Coil Stamps, Perf. 10 Vertically						
686	1½¢ brown Harding (684)	2.25	.09			7.50	
687	4¢ brown Taft (685)	3.50	.45			30.00	
	Perf. 11						
688	2¢ Braddock's Field, July 9	1.40	1.40	60.00	(6)	5.25	25,609,470
689	2¢ Von Steuben, Sept. 17	.80	.70	35.00	(6)	5.00	66,487,000
	Issues of 1931						
690	2¢ Pulaski, Jan. 16	.30	.22	25.00	(6)	4.00	96,559,400
	Perf. 11x10½						
692	11¢ light blue Hayes (563)	4.50	.12	19.00		80.00	
693	12¢ brown violet Cleveland (564)	7.50	.08	35.00		80.00	
694	13¢ yellow green Harrison (622)	3.50	.18	17.50		85.00	
695	14¢ dark blue Indian (565)	5.25	.45	25.00		85.00	
696	15¢ gray Statue of Liberty (566)	15.00	.08	60.00		95.00	
	Perf. 10½x11						
697	17¢ black Wilson (623)	7.50	.25	30.00		325.00	
698	20¢ car. rose Golden Gate (567)	20.00	.08	70.00		160.00	
699	25¢ blue green Niagara						
	Falls (568)	17.50	.11	60.00		350.00	
700	30¢ brown Buffalo (569)	25.00	.11	110.00		275.00	
701	50¢ lilac Amphitheater (570)	90.00	.11	325.00		400.00	
	Perf. 11						
702	2¢ Red Cross, May 21	.18	.18	2.50		4.00	99,074,600
	The American Red Cross was founded by Clara Barton in 1881.						
703	2¢ Yorktown, Oct. 12	.45	.45	4.00		5.00	25,006,400
	Issues of 1932. Perf. 11x10½, Washington Bicentennial Issue , Jan. 1						
704	½¢ Portrait by Charles W. Peale	.10	.10	4.50		5.00	87,969,700
705	1¢ Bust by Jean Antoine Houdon	.16	.08	5.50		5.50	1,265,555,100
706	1½¢ Portrait by Charles W. Peale	.55	.13	25.00		5.50	304,926,800
707	2¢ Portrait by Gilbert Stuart	.13	.08	1.75		5.50	4,222,198,300
708	3¢ Portrait by Charles W. Peale	.80	.10	18.00		5.75	456,198,500
709	4¢ Portrait by Charles P. Polk	.45	.10	7.00		5.75	151,201,300
710	5¢ Portrait by Charles W. Peale	3.50	.13	24.00		6.00	170,565,100
711	6¢ Portrait by John Trumbull	7.00	.11	85.00		6.75	111,739,400
712	7¢ Portrait by John Trumbull	.55	.24	7.50		6.75	83,257,400
713	8¢ Portrait by Charles B.J.F.						
	Saint Memin	7.00	1.10	100.00		6.75	96,506,100
714	9¢ Portrait by W. Williams	6.00	.25	65.00		7.75	75,709,200
715	10¢ Portrait by Gilbert Stuart	26.50	.13	160.00		10.00	147,216,000
	Perf. 11						
716	2¢ Olympic Games, Jan. 25	.50	.28	17.50	(6)	5.00	51,102,800
	Perf. 11x10½						
717	2¢ Arbor Day, Apr. 22	.20	.12	12.50		3.25	100,869,300

	1932 continued	Un	U	PB	#	FDC	
	10th Olympic Games Issue, June 15						
718	3¢ Runner at Starting Mark	2.00	.09	25.00		5.75	168,885,300
719	5¢ Myron's Discobolus	2.75	.30	40.00		7.50	52,376,100
720	3¢ Washington, June 16	.25	.08	1.50		10.00	
720b	Booklet pane of 6	45.00	5.00				
	Coil Stamps, Perf. 10 Vertically						
721	3¢ deep violet (720), June 24	3.75	.09			20.00	
	Perf. 10 Horizontally						
722	3¢ deep violet (720), Oct. 12	2.00	.60			20.00	
	Perf. 10 Vertically						
723	6¢ red orange Garfield						
	(558), Aug. 18	22.50	.22			20.00	
	Perf. 11						
724	3¢ William Penn, Oct. 24	.45	.25	20.00	(6)	3.00	49,949,000
725	3¢ Daniel Webster, Oct. 24	.65	.38	32.50	(6)	3.00	49,538,500
	Issues of 1933						
726	3¢ Georgia 200th Anniv. Feb. 12	.45	.27	22.50	(6)	3.00	61,719,200
	Perf. 10½x11						
727	3¢ Peace of 1783, Apr. 19	.20	.15	7.00		3.50	73,382,400
	Century of Progress Issue, May 25						
728	1¢ Restoration of Ft. Dearborn	.15	.09	3.00		2.75	348,266,800
729	3¢ Fed. Building at Chicago 1933	.22	.08	4.00		2.75	480,239,300
	American Philatelic Society Issue, Souvenir Sheets, Aug. 25, Without Gum, Imperf.						
730	1¢ deep yellow green						
	sheet of 25 (728)	60.00	50.00			150.00	456,704
730a	Single stamp	1.10	.50			2.75	11,417,600

St. Louis "Bears"

In 1895, a janitor cleaning the basement of the Louisville, KY, Courthouse wisely refrained from destroying a sheaf of papers he had been ordered to burn when he saw some strange looking stamps affixed to a number of them. What the janitor had discovered was a set of some of the rarest stamps ever printed in America: the St. Louis "Bears" Postmaster's Provisionals. These were stamps printed in November 1845 by a regional postmaster before the United States Postal Service began printing its own standardized stamps. Until the Louisville find, very little was known about the provisionals and few copies had surfaced.

The stamps were originally issued in 5¢ and 10¢ denominations in black on greenish-gray wove paper and acquired the nickname "Bears" from the design which featured two bears supporting the St. Louis coat of arms. Later, a 20¢ denomination was also issued.

Unfortunately, as such stories sometimes go, the janitor turned his find over to the caretakers of the courthouse, who astutely realized some $20,000 on sale of the stamps.

718

719

720

723

724

725

726

727

728

729

UNDER AUTHORITY OF JAMES A. FARLEY, POSTMASTER GENERAL AT A CENTURY OF PROGRESS

PRINTED BY THE TREASURY DEPARTMENT, BUREAU OF ENGRAVING AND PRINTING

IN COMPLIMENT TO THE AMERICAN PHILATELIC SOCIETY FOR ITS CONVENTION AND EXHIBITION

CHICAGO, ILLINOIS, AUGUST 1933. PLATE NO. 21159

730

731

732

733

734

736

737

739

740

741

	1933 continued	Un	U	PB	#	FDC	Q
731	3¢ deep violet, sheet of 25 (729)	50.00	40.00			150.00	441,172
731a	Single stamp	1.10	.50			2.75	11,029,300
	Perf. 10½x11						
732	3¢ NRA, Aug. 15	.16	.08	2.00		3.00	1,978,707,300
	Perf. 11						
733	3¢ Byrd's Antarctic Expedition,						
	Oct. 9	1.00	1.00	30.00	(6)	7.00	5,735,944
734	5¢ Tadeusz Kosciuszko, Oct. 13	.80	.40	65.00	(6)	6.25	45,137,700
	Issues of 1934, National Stamp Exhibition Issue, Souvenir Sheet,						
	Feb. 10, Without Gum, Imperf.						
735	3¢ dk. blue sheet of 6 (733)	35.00	32.50			67.50	811,404
735a	Single stamp	4.50	2.65			6.75	4,868,424
	Perf. 11						
736	3¢ Maryland 300th Anniversary,						
	Mar. 23	.20	.20	15.00	(6)	2.00	46,258,300
	Mothers of America Issue, May 2, Perf. 11x10½						
737	3¢ Whistler's Mother	.16	.09	1.75		2.00	193,239,100
	Perf. 11						
738	3¢ deep violet (737)	.25	.25	7.25	(6)	2.00	15,432,200
739	3¢ Wisconsin 300th Anniversary,						
	July 7	.23	.15	7.00	(6)	2.00	64,525,400
	National Parks Issue						
740	1¢ El Capitan, Yosemite, Calif.	.12	.12	1.50	(6)	2.25	84,896,350
741	2¢ Grand Canyon, Arizona	.16	.12	2.00	(6)	2.25	74,400,200

Penny Black Precedent Renewed

The "penny black" was the world's first postage stamp. It was issued in 1840 by Great Britain and had the picture of a woman on it: Queen Victoria. This did not, however, set much of a precedent for the future gender of stamp subjects, because the next time a woman appeared on a British stamp was 96 years later.

306

In fact, women have had a very tough time getting themselves depicted on stamps. Until recently, the only way a woman could do so was to be of royal blood or be married to a President. Queen Isabella became the first woman on U.S. postage (#234) because Columbus asked her for money and ships to sail west. Martha Washington was the first American woman on a U.S. stamp (#306) and the 1930 Red Cross stamp (#702) had the picture of a nurse who might be Clara Barton, founder of the Red Cross, but Barton's name wasn't on the stamp.

702

But with the issuance of a 3¢ stamp bearing the picture and name of Susan B. Anthony in 1936 (#784), women have become stamp subjects more regularly and are no longer excluded from our philatelic expression.

784

	1934 continued	Un	U	PB	#	FDC	
742	3¢ Mt. Rainier and Mirror Lake, Washington	.25	.12	3.50	(6)	2.50	95,089,000
743	4¢ Mesa Verde, Colorado	.60	.60	12.00	(6)	3.25	19,178,650
744	5¢ Old Faithful, Yellowstone, Wyoming	1.50	.90	14.50	(6)	3.25	30,980,100
745	6¢ Crater Lake, Oregon	2.25	1.50	30.00	(6)	4.00	16,923,350
746	7¢ Great Head, Acadia Park, Maine	1.35	1.30	20.00	(6)	4.00	15,988,250
747	8¢ Great White Throne, Zion Park, Utah	3.35	2.65	35.00	(6)	4.25	15,288,700
748	9¢ Mt Rockwell and Two Medicine Lake, Glacier National Park, Montana	3.50	.85	32.50	(6)	4.50	17,472,600
749	10¢ Great Smoky Mountains, North Carolina	6.00	1.40	57.50	(6)	7.50	18,874,300
	American Philatelic Society Issue, Souvenir Sheet, Imperf.						
750	3¢ deep violet sheet of six (742), Aug. 28	50.00	45.00			65.00	511,391
750a	Single stamp	6.00	4.00			7.00	3,068,346
	Trans-Mississippi Philatelic Issue						
751	1¢ green sheet of six (740), Oct. 10	20.00	18.50			45.00	793,551
751a	Single stamp	3.00	1.50			4.50	4,761,306
	Special Printing (Nos. 752 to 771 inclusive), Issued March 15, 1935, Without Gum						
	Issues of 1935, Perf. 10½x11						
752	3¢ violet Peace of 1783 (727) Issued in sheets of 400, Mar. 15	.17	.17	16.00		13.00	3,274,556
	Perf. 11						
753	3¢ blue Byrd's Antarctic Expedition (733)	.60	.60	25.00	(6)	15.00	2,040,760
	Imperf.						
754	3¢ dp. vio. Whistler's Mother (737)	1.00	.90	40.00	(6)	15.00	2,389,288
755	3¢ deep violet Wisconsin 300th Anniversary (739)	1.00	.90	40.00	(6)	15.00	2,294,948
756	1¢ green Yosemite (740)	.25	.25	6.50	(6)	15.00	3,217,636
757	2¢ red Grand Canyon (741)	.35	.35	7.50	(6)	15.00	2,746,640
758	3¢ dp. vio. Mt. Rainier (742)	.85	.85	22.50	(6)	16.00	2,168,088
759	4¢ brown Mesa Verde (743)	1.95	1.85	27.50	(6)	16.00	1,822,684
760	5¢ blue Yellowstone (744)	3.00	2.75	37.50	(6)	16.00	1,724,576
761	6¢ dk. blue Crater Lake (745)	3.95	2.65	47.50	(6)	16.50	1,647,696
762	7¢ black Acadia (746)	3.00	2.65	45.00	(6)	16.50	1,682,948
763	8¢ sage green Zion (747)	3.15	2.65	60.00	(6)	17.00	1,638,644
764	9¢ red orange Glacier Nat'l Park (748)	3.75	2.65	60.00	(6)	18.00	1,625,224
765	10¢ gray black Smoky Mts. (749)	7.25	5.50	80.00	(6)	20.50	1,644,900

742

743

744

745

46

748

72

773

774

	1935 continued	Un	U	PB	#	FDC	Q
766	1¢ yellow green (728)	60.00	50.00				98,712
	Pane of 25						
766a	Single stamp	1.10	.50			11.00	2,467,800
767	3¢ violet (729)	55.00	45.00				85,914
	Pane of 25						
767a	Single stamp	1.10	.50			11.00	2,147,850
768	3¢ dark blue (733)	32.50	25.00			267,200	
	Pane of 6						
768a	Single stamp	4.50	2.65			13.00	1,,603,200
769	1¢ green (740)	15.00	12.00				279,960
	Pane of 6						
769a	Single stamp	1.60	1.50			8.00	1,679,760
770	3¢ deep violet (742)	37.50	25.00				215,920
	Pane of 6						
770a	Single stamp	4.50	4.00			10.00	1,295,520
771	16¢ dark blue Seal of U.S. (CE2),						
	issued in sheets of 200	4.75	4.00	100.00	(6)	25.00	1,370,560
	Perf. 11x10½						
772	3¢ Connecticut 300th Anniv.,						
	Apr. 26	.20	.09	2.00		9.50	70,726,800
773	3¢ California-Pacific Exposition,						
	May 29	.14	.09	2.00		9.50	100,839,600
	Perf. 11						
774	3¢ Boulder Dam, Sep. 30	.14	.09	2.75	(6)	13.00	73,610,650
	Perf. 11x10½						
775	3¢ Michigan 100th Anniv., Nov. 1	.14	.09	2.00		9.00	75,823,900
	Issues of 1936						
776	3¢ Texas 100th Anniv., Mar. 2	.15	.09	2.00		9.00	124,324,500
	Perf.10½x11						
777	3¢ Rhode Island 300th Anniv.,						
	May 4	.20	.09	2.00		9.00	67,127,650
	Third International Philatelic Exhibition Issue, Souvenir Sheet, Imperf.						
778	Violet, sheet of 4 different stamps						
	(772, 773, 775 and 776), May 9	4.00	4.00			17.50	2,809,039
	Perf. 11x10½						
782	3¢ Arkansas 100th Anniv., June 15	.14	.09	2.00		9.00	72,992,650
783	3¢ Oregon Territory, July 14	.14	.09	2.00		9.00	74,407,450
784	3¢ Susan B. Anthony, Aug. 26	.14	.08	.75		17.50	269,522,200

	Issues of 1936-37	Un	U	PB	#	FDC	Q
	Army Issue						
785	1¢ George Washington						
	and Nathanael Greene, 1936	.10	.09	1.00		6.00	105,196,150
786	2¢ Andrew Jackson and						
	Winfield Scott, 1937	.13	.09	1.10		6.00	93,848,500
787	3¢ Generals Sherman,						
	Grant and Sheridan, 1937	.25	.10	1.50		6.00	87,741,150
788	4¢ Generals Robert E. Lee						
	and "Stonewall" Jackson, 1937	.70	.30	13.00		6.75	35,794,150
789	5¢ U.S. Military Academy,						
	West Point, 1937	1.10	.30	15.00		8.00	36,839,250
	Navy Issue						
790	1¢ John Paul Jones						
	and John Barry, 1936	.10	.09	1.00		6.00	104,773,450
791	2¢ Stephen Decatur						
	and Thomas MacDonough, 1937	.13	.09	1.10		6.00	92,054,550
792	3¢ Admirals David G. Farragut						
	and David D. Porter, 1937	.25	.10	1.50		6.00	93,291,650
793	4¢ Admirals William T. Sampson,						
	George Dewey and Winfield						
	S. Schley, 1937	.70	.30	13.00		6.75	34,552,950
794	5¢ Seal of U.S. Naval Academy						
	and Naval Cadets, 1937	1.10	.30	15.00		8.00	36,819,050
	Issues of 1937						
795	3¢ Northwest Ordinance						
	150th Anniversary, July 13	.14	.09	2.00		8.50	84,825,250
	Perf. 11						
796	5¢ Virginia Dare, Aug. 18	.35	.28	11.50		9.50	25,040,400
	Society of Philatelic Americans, Souvenir Sheet, Imperf.						
797	10¢ blue green (749), Aug. 26	1.30	.95			8.00	5,277,445
	Perf. 11x10½						
798	3¢ Constitution 150th Anniv.,						
	Sept. 17	.17	.09	1.65		8.50	99,882,300
	Territorial Issues, Perf. 10½x11						
799	3¢ Hawaii, Oct. 18	.18	.10	2.00		9.50	78,454,450
	Perf. 11x10½						
800	3¢ Alaska, Nov. 12	.18	.10	2.00		9.50	77,004,200
801	3¢ Puerto Rico, Nov. 25	.16	.10	1.75		9.50	81,292,450
802	3¢ Virgin Islands, Dec. 15	.16	.10	2.00		9.50	76,474,550

		Un	U	PB	#	FDC	Q
	Presidential Issue, 1938						
803	½¢ Benjamin Franklin	.08	.08	.40		1.25	
804	1¢ George Washington	.08	.08	.25		1.35	
804b	Booklet pane of 6	2.50	.20				
805	1½¢ Martha Washington	.08	.08	.30		1.35	
806	2¢ John Adams	.09	.08	.35		1.65	
806b	Booklet pane of 6	5.50	.50				
807	3¢ Thomas Jefferson	.10	.08	.50		1.65	
807a	Booklet pane of 6	11.00	.50				
808	4¢ James Madison	.45	.08	1.80		1.65	
809	4½¢ White House	.20	.10	1.60		2.25	
810	5¢ James Monroe	.40	.08	1.80		2.25	
811	6¢ John Q. Adams	.42	.08	2.00		2.25	
812	7¢ Andrew Jackson	.45	.08	2.00		2.50	
813	8¢ Martin Van Buren	.55	.08	2.25		2.50	
814	9¢ William H. Harrison	.60	.08	2.75		2.65	
815	10¢ John Tyler	.45	.08	2.00		2.75	
816	11¢ James K. Polk	1.00	.10	4.50		2.75	
817	12¢ Zachary Taylor	1.75	.09	6.00		3.00	
818	13¢ Millard Fillmore	1.50	.13	5.50		3.00	
819	14¢ Franklin Pierce	1.40	.13	5.50		3.25	
820	15¢ James Buchanan	.80	.08	3.60		3.25	
821	16¢ Abraham Lincoln	1.75	.60	7.00		3.50	
822	17¢ Andrew Johnson	1.60	.13	7.00		3.75	
823	18¢ Ulysses S. Grant	2.95	.12	3.00		4.25	
824	19¢ Rutherford B. Hayes	1.75	.70	8.00		4.25	
825	20¢ James A. Garfield	1.00	.08	5.50		4.50	
826	21¢ Chester A. Arthur	1.85	.14	8.25		5.00	
827	22¢ Grover Cleveland	1.75	.65	8.25		5.25	
828	24¢ Benjamin Harrison	6.75	.23	26.50		5.25	
829	25¢ William McKinley	1.30	.08	7.25		6.50	
830	30¢ Theodore Roosevelt	10.00	.08	38.50		10.00	
831	50¢ William Howard Taft	15.00	.08	52.50		20.00	
	Perf. 11						
832	$1 Woodrow Wilson	19.50	.12	60.00		55.00	
832b	Wmkd. USIR	325.00	85.00				
833	$2 Warren G. Harding	50.00	6.50	200.00		100.00	
834	$5 Calvin Coolidge	185.00	6.00	675.00		175.00	

This series was in use for approximately 16 years when the Liberty Series began replacing it. Various shades of these stamps are in existence due to the numerous reprintings.

		Un	U	PB	#	FDC	
	Issues of 1938, Perf. 11x10½						
835	3¢ Constitution Ratification,						
	June 21	.25	.10	6.00		8.50	73,043,650
	Perf. 11						
836	3¢ Swedish-Finnish 300th Anniv.,						
	June 27	.23	.12	6.00	(6)	8.50	58,564,368
	Perf. 11x10½						
837	3¢ Northwest Territory, July 15	.23	.10	16.50		8.50	65,939,500
838	3¢ Iowa Territory 100th Anniv.,						
	Aug. 24	.25	.13	9.50		8.50	47,064,300
	Issues of 1939, Coil Stamps, Perf. 10 Vertically						
839	1¢ green Washington (804)	.40	.08			10.00	
840	1½¢ bistre brown						
	M. Washington (805)	.40	.10			10.00	
841	2¢ rose car. Adams (806)	.40	.08			11.00	
842	3¢ deep violet Jefferson (807)	.65	.08			12.00	
843	4¢ red violet Madison (808)	9.65	.40			12.50	
844	4½¢ dk. gray White House (809)	.70	.60			12.50	
845	5¢ bright blue Monroe (810)	7.00	.35			14.00	
846	6¢ red orange J.Q. Adams (811)	1.35	.15			15.00	
847	10¢ brown red Tyler (815)	16.00	.50			37.50	
	Perf. 10 Horizontally						
848	1¢ green Washington (804)	.85	.12			9.00	
849	1½¢ bistre brown						
	M. Washington (805)	1.60	.50			9.00	
850	2¢ rose car. Adams (806)	2.85	.50			10.00	
851	3¢ deep violet Jefferson (807)	2.50	.50			10.00	
	Perf. 10½x11						
852	3¢ Golden Gate Exposition,						
	Feb. 18	.14	.09	1.65		7.50	114,439,600
853	3¢ New York World's Fair, Apr. 1	.15	.09	2.00		8.50	101,699,550
	Perf. 11						
854	3¢ Washington's Inauguration,						
	Apr. 30	.35	.11	4.75	(6)	7.50	72,764,550
	Perf. 11x10½						
855	3¢ Baseball Anniversary						
	100th, June 12	.35	.10	3.50		17.50	81,269,600
	Perf. 11						
856	3¢ Panama Canal, Aug. 15	.30	.10	6.00	(6)	7.50	67,813,350
	Perf. 10½x11						
857	3¢ 300th Anniv. of Printing,						
	Sept. 25	.14	.10	1.65		7.50	71,394,750
	Perf. 11x10½						
858	3¢ 50th Anniv. of Statehood,						
	Nov. 2	.14	.10	1.65		7.00	66,835,000

836

837

838

853

854

856

857

859

860

861

862

863

864

865

866

867

868

869

870

871

872

873

874

875

876

877

878

		Un	U	PB	#	FDC	Q
Famous Americans Issue, 1940, Perf. 10½x11							
	Authors						
859	1¢ Washington Irving	.09	.09	1.10		2.00	56,348,320
860	2¢ James Fenimore Cooper	.10	.10	1.25		2.00	53,177,110
861	3¢ Ralph Waldo Emerson	.12	.09	2.00		2.00	53,260,270
862	5¢ Louisa May Alcott	.35	.30	12.00		5.00	22,104,950
863	10¢ Samuel L. Clemens						
	(Mark Twain)	2.00	2.00	55.00		8.25	13,201,270
	Poets						
864	1¢ Henry W. Longfellow	.12	.12	1.50		2.00	51,603,580
865	2¢ John Greenleaf Whittier	.12	.10	1.50		2.00	52,100,510
866	3¢ James Russell Lowell	.15	.09	3.50		2.00	51,666,580
867	5¢ Walt Whitman	.40	.33	12.00		4.50	22,207,780
868	10¢ James Whitcomb Riley	3.00	2.25	55.00		8.25	11,835,530
	Educators						
869	1¢ Horace Mann	.10	.10	1.50		2.00	52,471,160
870	2¢ Mark Hopkins	.12	.10	1.40		2.00	52,366,440
871	3¢ Charles W. Eliot	.28	.09	3.25		2.00	51,636,270
872	5¢ Frances E. Willard	.60	.30	13.00		4.75	20,729,030
873	10¢ Booker T. Washington	2.00	2.00	35.00		8.25	14,125,580
	Scientists						
874	1¢ John James Audubon	.09	.09	1.10		2.00	59,409,000
875	2¢ Dr. Crawford W. Long	.10	.09	1.20		2.00	57,888,600
876	3¢ Luther Burbank	.12	.09	1.25		2.00	58,273,180
877	5¢ Dr. Walter Reed	.28	.22	10.50		4.50	23,779,000
878	10¢ Jane Addams	1.75	1.65	35.00		8.25	15,112,580
	Composers						
879	1¢ Stephen Collins Foster	.08	.08	1.25		2.00	57,322,790
880	2¢ John Philip Sousa	.17	.09	1.25		2.00	58,281,580
881	3¢ Victor Herbert	.16	.09	1.75		2.00	56,398,790
882	5¢ Edward MacDowell	.60	.30	13.00		4.50	21,147,000
883	10¢ Ethelbert Nevin	5.75	2.00	50.00		7.75	13,328,000

	1940 continued	Un	U	PB	#	FDC	
	Artists						
884	1¢ Gilbert Charles Stuart	.08	.08	1.10		2.00	54,389,510
885	2¢ James A. McNeill Whistler	.10	.09	1.10		2.00	53,636,580
886	3¢ Augustus Saint-Gaudens	.12	.09	1.25		2.00	55,313,230
887	5¢ Daniel Chester French	.45	.25	12.50		4.00	21,720,580
888	10¢ Frederic Remington	2.85	2.25	45.00		7.75	13,600,580
	Inventors						
889	1¢ Eli Whitney	.12	.10	2.50		2.00	47,599,580
890	2¢ Samuel F. B. Morse	.14	.10	1.50		2.00	53,766,510
891	3¢ Cyrus Hall McCormick	.25	.09	2.50		2.00	54,193,580
892	5¢ Elias Howe	1.45	.50	22.50		5.00	20,264,580
893	10¢ Alexander Graham Bell	17.50	3.00	135.00		13.50	13,726,580
	Issues of 1940, Perf. 11x10½						
894	3¢ Pony Express, Apr. 3	.45	.16	7.50		6.75	46,497,400
	Perf. 10½x11						
895	3¢ Pan American Union, Apr. 14	.45	.12	7.00		5.25	47,700,000
	Perf. 11x10½						
896	3¢ Idaho Statehood,						
	50th Anniversary, July 3	.23	.10	3.75		5.25	50,618,150
	Perf. 10½x11						
897	3¢ Wyoming Statehood,						
	50th Anniversary, July 10	.23	.10	3.25		5.25	50,034,400
	Perf. 11x10½						
898	3¢ Coronado Expedition, Sept. 7	.23	.10	3.25		5.25	60,943,700
	National Defense Issue, Oct. 16						
899	1¢ Statue of Liberty	.08	.08	.60		5.00	
900	2¢ Anti-aircraft Gun	.09	.08	.70		5.00	
901	3¢ Torch of Enlightenment	.13	.08	1.40		5.00	
	Perf. 10½x11						
902	3¢ Thirteenth Amendment,						
	Oct. 20	.28	.15	8.25		6.00	44,389,550
	Issue of 1941, Perf. 11x10½						
903	3¢ Vermont Statehood, Mar. 4	.20	.11	2.75		5.50	54,574,550
	Issues of 1942						
904	3¢ Kentucky Statehood, June 1	.18	.11	2.25		5.00	63,558,400
905	3¢ Win the War, July 4	.11	.05	.60		4.75	

884

885

886

887

888

889

890

891

892

893

894

895

896

897

898

899

900

901

902

903

904

905

906   907   908

909   910   911

912   913   914

915   916   917

918   919   920

921   922   923

	1942 continued	Un	U	PB	#	FDC	Q
906	5¢ Chinese Resistance, July 7	.35	.25	25.00		7.00	21,272,800
	Issues of 1943						
907	2¢ Allied Nations, Jan. 14	.07	.05	.50		4.25	1,671,564,200
908	1¢ Four Freedoms, Feb. 12	.06	.05	1.00		4.25	1,227,334,200
	Overrun Countries Issue, 1943-44, Perf. 12						
909	5¢ Poland, June 22	.28	.25	15.00		5.75	19,999,646
910	5¢ Czechoslovakia, July 12	.32	.18	6.00		5.50	19,999,646
911	5¢ Norway, July 27	.18	.17	3.50		5.00	19,999,646
912	5¢ Luxembourg, Aug. 10	.18	.17	3.50		5.00	19,999,646
913	5¢ Netherlands, Aug. 24	.18	.17	3.50		5.00	19,999,646
914	5¢ Belgium, Sept. 14	.18	.17	3.50		5.00	19,999,646
915	5¢ France, Sept. 28	.18	.17	3.50		5.00	19,999,646
916	5¢ Greece, Oct. 12	.85	.65	25.00		5.00	14,999,646
917	5¢ Yugoslavia, Oct. 26	.50	.40	14.00		5.00	14,999,646
918	5¢ Albania, Nov. 9	.50	.40	8.50		5.00	14,999,646
919	5¢ Austria, Nov. 23	.35	.35	8.50		5.00	14,999,646
920	5¢ Denmark, Dec. 7	.50	.40	10.00		5.00	14,999,646
921	5¢ Korea, Nov. 2, 1944	.25	.25	12.50		6.50	14,999,646
	Issues of 1944, Perf. 11x10½						
922	3¢ Transcontinental Railroad,						
	May 10	.25	.11	2.50		6.75	61,303,000
923	3¢ Steamship, May 22	.13	.11	2.50		4.50	61,001,450

Pony Express Rides Again

From April 1860 to November 1861, Wells Fargo & Co. acted as agent for one of the more daring and colorful attempts to link California with the East—the Pony Express. Until the telegraph, Pony Express was the fastest method of sending messages across a wild and unpredictable continent.

Of course, even today California weather can itself be wild and unpredictable. On April 9, 1983, a 40-mile stretch of Route 50 between Sacramento and Lake Tahoe was closed to all forms of transportation by a mudslide. The California Dept. of Transportation promised to have the road reopened by April 23. But what about the time in between?

Since the mail must always go through members of the Pony Express Association were authorized to carry first class mail for the USPS for the first time since November 1861. The revival began on April 15, 1983, and lasted for about a week, starting at Pollack Pines with stops at Pacific House, Kyburz, Twin Bridges and Little Norway. Though short-lived, it was declared a success.

1944 continued	Un	U	PB #	FDC	
924	3¢ Telegraph, May 24	.12	.11	1.60	4.00	60,605,000
925	3¢ Philippines, Sept. 27	.12	.11	3.00	4.00	50,129,350
926	3¢ 50th Anniversary of					
	Motion Picture, Oct. 31	.12	.11	2.00	4.00	53,479,400
Issues of 1945						
927	3¢ Florida Statehood, Mar. 3	.10	.10	1.00	4.00	61,617,350
928	5¢ United Nations Conference,					
	Apr. 25	.15	.07	.70	4.00	75,500,000
Perf. 10½x11						
929	3¢ Iwo Jima (Marines), July 11	.10	.06	.60	5.00	137,321,000
Issues of 1945-46, Perf. 11x10½						
Franklin D. Roosevelt Issue						
930	1¢ F.D.R. and home at Hyde Park	.05	.05	.30	3.00	128,140,000
931	2¢ Roosevelt and "Little					
	White House," Ga.	.07	.07	.50	3.00	67,255,000
932	3¢ Roosevelt and White House	.10	.07	.55	3.00	133,870,000
933	5¢ F.D.R., Globe and					
	Four Freedoms, 1946	.14	.07	.75	3.00	76,455,400
934	3¢ U.S. Army in Paris, Sept. 28	.10	.07	.50	3.00	128,357,750
935	3¢ U.S. Navy, Oct. 27	.10	.07	.50	3.00	135,863,000
936	3¢ U.S. Coast Guard, Nov. 10	.10	.07	.50	3.00	111,616,700
937	3¢ Alfred E. Smith, Nov. 26	.10	.05	.50	3.00	308,587,700
938	3¢ Texas Statehood, Dec. 29	.10	.05	.50	3.00	170,640,000
Issues of 1946						
939	3¢ Merchant Marine, Feb. 26	.10	.05	.50	3.00	135,927,000

Bicycle Mail

By the 1890s, railroads dominated transportation in this country so much so that a small town with a railroad station grew bigger and one that didn't often shrank or vanished. In 1894, however, the American Railway Union went on strike, isolating many of these small communities without freight, passenger and even mail service.

In Fresno, CA, Arthur Banter, also in the transportation business, decided emergency measures were needed. He owned the Victor Cyclery and decided to start his own mail service between Fresno and San Francisco via bicycle. The 210-mile route was covered in 18 hours by bicycle riders in relays, much like the Pony Express.

The service lasted only 12 days, but 380 letters were carried, franked by Banter's own 25¢ stamp which showed a cyclist speeding along a mountain landscape. An oval band all around the scene was inscribed "Fresno and San Francisco Bicycle Mail Route 1894."

924

925

926

927

928

929

930

931

932

933

934

935

936

937

938

939

940

941

942

943

944

945

946

947

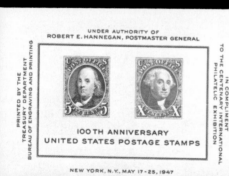

948

949

950

951

952

	1946 continued	Un	U	PB	#	FDC	Q
940	3¢ Veterans of World War II, May 9	.10	.05	.55		3.00	260,339,100
941	3¢ Tennessee Statehood, June 1	.10	.05	.50		3.00	132,274,500
942	3¢ Iowa Statehood, Aug.3	.10	.05	.50		3.00	132,430,000
943	3¢ Smithsonian Institution, Aug. 10	.10	.05	.50		3.00	139,209,500
944	3¢ Kearny Expedition, Oct. 16	.10	.05	.50		3.00	114,684,450
	Issues of 1947, Perf. 10½x11						
945	3¢ Thomas A. Edison, Feb. 11	.10	.05	.50		3.00	156,540,510
	Perf. 11x10½						
946	3¢ Joseph Pulitzer, Apr. 10	.10	.05	.50		3.00	120,452,600
947	3¢ 100th Anniv. of the						
	Postage Stamp, May 17	.10	.05	.50		3.00	127,104,300
	Imperf.						
948	Souvenir sheet of two, May 19	1.50	1.25			3.00	10,299,600
948a	5¢ blue, single stamp (1)	.55	.40				
948b	10¢ brn. org., single stamp (2)	.75	.40				
	Issued in sheets of two with marginal inscription commemorating the 100th anniversary of U.S. postage stamps and the Centenary International Philatelic Exhibition, held in New York in 1947.						
	Perf. 11x10½						
949	3¢ Doctors, June 9	.10	.05	.50		2.00	132,902,000
950	3¢ Utah, July 24	.10	.05	.50		2.00	131,968,000
951	3¢ U.S. Frigate Constitution,						
	Oct. 21	.11	.05	.50		2.00	131,488,000
	Perf. 10½x11						
952	3¢ Everglades Nat'l Park, Dec. 5	.10	.05	.50		2.00	122,362,000

Philately in Fiction

Stamps have been the subject of novels and movies for some time. It's surprising, however, that philately hasn't been used more often as a foil in fiction. A stamp's small size (easy to conceal), detailed history and sometimes significant value seem to make it a perfect plot device to bring out the desires and fateful choices of a wide range of characters.

The first instance of philately in fiction that comes to mind is Edgar Allan Poe's "The Purloined Letter," which was about a letter everyone was looking for in every conceivable place except the most logical. The movie, "Charade", also used this theme, but the characters were specifically searching for a stamp. Robert Graves wrote the mystery, "The Antigua Stamp", in 1940 for the 100th anniversary of the postage stamp, and more recently, John D. MacDonald wrote "The Scarlet Ruse", another mystery for which he did extensive philatelic research in conjunction with a prominent Miami, FL, dealer.

The movie "The Barefoot Mailman" was based on a real mail carrier whose route was along the beach from Miami to Jupiter, FL, in the 1880s. He disappeared one day while crossing a stream, presumably attacked by alligators. Rain, sleet and snow can be overcome…hungry reptiles are another story.

	Issues of 1948	Un	U	PB	#	FDC	
953	3¢ Dr. George Washington Carver,						
	Jan. 5	.10	.05	.50		2.00	121,548,000
	Perf. 11x10½						
954	3¢ Calif. Gold 100th Anniversary,						
	Jan. 24	.10	.05	.50		2.00	131,109,500
955	3¢ Mississippi Territory, Apr. 7	.10	.05	.50		2.00	122,650,500
956	3¢ Four Chaplains, May 28	.10	.05	.50		2.00	121,953,500
957	3¢ Wisconsin Statehood, May 29	.10	.05	.50		2.00	115,250,000
958	5¢ Swedish Pioneer, June 4	.14	.10	1.00		2.00	64,198,500
959	3¢ Progress of Women, July 19	.10	.05	.50		2.00	117,642,500
	Perf. 10½x11						
960	3¢ William Allen White, July 31	.10	.06	.60		2.00	77,649,600
	Perf. 11x10½						
961	3¢ U.S.-Canada Friendship,						
	Aug. 2	.10	.06	.50		2.00	113,474,500
962	3¢ Francis Scott Key, Aug. 9	.11	.06	.50		2.00	120,868,500
963	3¢ Salute to Youth, Aug. 11	.10	.06	.50		2.00	77,800,500
964	3¢ Oregon Territory, Aug. 14	.10	.09	.90		2.00	52,214,000
	Perf. 10½x11						
965	3¢ Harlan Fiske Stone, Aug. 25	.11	.09	1.70		2.00	53,958,100
966	3¢ Palomar Mt. Obs., Aug. 30	.12	.09	2.50		2.00	61,120,010
	Perf. 11x10½						
967	3¢ Clara Barton, Sept. 7	.10	.09	.60		1.50	57,823,000
968	3¢ Poultry Industry, Sept. 9	.10	.09	.80		1.50	52,975,000
	Perf. 10½x11						
969	3¢ Gold Star Mothers, Sept. 21	.11	.07	.65		1.50	77,149,000
970	3¢ Fort Kearny, Sept. 22	.10	.09	.65		1.50	58,332,000
971	3¢ Volunteer Firemen, Oct. 4	.10	.09	.75		1.50	56,228,000

Pan-American Exhibition Invert

On May 4, 1901, Brooklynite F.W. Davis eagerly awaited the delivery by his postman of a pane of 50 2¢ stamps commemorating that month's Pan-American Exhibition in Buffalo. This stamp was to feature the famous "Empire State Express," making it doubly interesting to New Yorkers. Collector Davis quickly realized the find he had. On every stamp on the sheet, the train had been printed upside down (#295a). Davis was so elated by his fortune that he immediately gave one of the stamps to his postman.

Then, however, worried that the government might have printed the whole issue as inverts, Davis tried to sell his stamps quickly, before more were discovered. The buyers to whom he sold them had the same worry, and Davis only received from $2 to $75 per stamp. The sad truth later surfaced that only one sheet of 200 2¢ inverts had been printed, and Davis had sold a fortune for a pittance.

953

954

955

956

957

958

959

960

961

962

963

964

965

966

967

968

970

971

972

973

974

975

976

977

978

979

980

981

982

983

984

985

986

987

988

989

990

	1948 continued	Un	U	PB	#	FDC	Q
972	3¢ Five Indian Tribes, Oct. 15	.10	.08	.75		1.50	57,832,000
973	3¢ Rough Riders, Oct. 27	.10	.10	1.20		1.50	53,875,000
974	3¢ Juliette Low, Oct. 29	.10	.09	.65		1.50	63,834,000
	Perf. 10½x11						
975	3¢ Will Rogers, Nov. 4	.10	.08	1.00		1.50	67,162,200
976	3¢ Fort Bliss 100th Anniv., Nov. 5	.13	.09	2.00		1.50	64,561,000
	Perf. 11x10½						
977	3¢ Moina Michael, Nov. 9	.10	.07	.65		1.50	64,079,500
978	3¢ Gettysburg Address, Nov. 19	.10	.09	.70		1.50	63,388,000
	Perf. 10½x11						
979	3¢ American Turners, Nov. 20	.10	.09	.65		1.50	62,285,000
980	3¢ Joel Chandler Harris, Dec. 9	.10	.09	.75		1.50	57,492,610
	Issues of 1949, Perf. 11x10½						
981	3¢ Minnesota Territory, Mar. 3	.10	.05	.50		1.50	99,190,000
982	3¢ Washington & Lee University,						
	Apr. 12	.10	.05	.50		1.50	104,790,000
983	3¢ Puerto Rico Election, Apr. 27	.10	.05	.50		1.50	108,805,000
984	3¢ Annapolis 300th Anniv.,						
	May 23	.10	.05	.50		1.50	107,340,000
985	3¢ Grand Army of the Republic,						
	Aug. 29	.10	.05	.50		1.50	117,020,000
	Perf. 10½x11						
986	3¢ Edgar Allan Poe, Oct. 7	.10	.05	.60		1.50	122,633,000
	Issues of 1950, Perf. 11x10½						
987	3¢ American Bankers Association,						
	Jan. 3	.10	.05	.50		1.50	130,960,000
	Perf. 10½x11						
988	3¢ Samuel Gompers, Jan. 27	.10	.05	.55		1.50	128,478,000
	National Capital 150th Anniv. Issue, Perf. 10½x11, 11x10½						
989	3¢ Statue of Freedom	.10	.05	.50		1.50	132,090,000
990	3¢ Executive Mansion	.11	.05	.50		1.50	130,050,000

And the Edge of the Stamp

It wasn't until ten years after it had issued its first stamp that the United States Postal Service began ordering its stamps with perforations. On February 24, 1857 the USPS took delivery of perforated stamps printed by Toppan, Carpenter and Co. of Philadelphia, Pennsylvania. The designs of these stamps were the same as the 1851-1855 imperforates with the addition of the following: a 24¢ portrait of Washington; a 30¢ profile bust of Franklin; a 90¢ portrait of Washington.

The first actual coils, stamps printed in rolls with perforations on only two sides, were printed by the Bureau of Engraving in 1908. A version of the coil concept had been tried earlier in 1902 when sheets of 400 stamps had been cut into strips of 20 and then spliced together to form rolls.

	1950 continued	Un	U	PB	#	FDC	
991	3¢ Supreme Court Building	.10	.05	.50		1.50	131,350,000
992	3¢ U.S. Capitol Building	.10	.05	.50		1.50	129,980,000
	Perf. 11x10½						
993	3¢ Railroad Engineers, Apr. 29	.11	.05	.50		1.50	122,315,000
994	3¢ Kansas City, Mo., June 3	.10	.05	.50		1.50	122,170,000
995	3¢ Boy Scouts, June 30	.11	.05	.55		1.50	131,635,000
996	3¢ Indian Territory, July 4	.10	.05	.50		1.50	121,860,000
997	3¢ California Statehood, Sept. 9	.10	.05	.50		1.50	121,120,000
	Issues of 1951						
998	3¢ Confederate Veterans, May 30	.11	.05	.50		1.50	119,120,000
999	3¢ Nevada 100th Anniv., July 14	.10	.05	.50		1.50	112,125,000
1000	3¢ Landing of Cadillac, July 24	.10	.05	.50		1.50	114,140,000
1001	3¢ Colorado Statehood, Aug. 1	.11	.05	.50		1.50	114,490,000
1002	3¢ American Chem. Society,						
	Sept. 4	.10	.05				117,200,000
1003	3¢ Battle of Brooklyn, Dec. 10	.12	.05	.50		1.50	116,130,000
	Issues of 1952						
1004	3¢ Betsy Ross, Jan. 2	.13	.05	.50		1.50	116,175,000
1005	3¢ 4-H Club, Jan. 15	.10	.05	.50		1.50	115,945,000
1006	3¢ B&O Railroad, Feb. 28	.14	.05	.60		2.00	112,540,000
1007	3¢ American Auto. Assn., Mar. 4	.10	.05	.60		.85	117,415,000
1008	3¢ NATO, Apr. 4	.10	.05	.55		.85	2,899,580,000
1009	3¢ Grand Coulee Dam, May 15	.10	.05	.60		.85	114,540,000

Honoring Lafayette

In 1945, George B. Sloane, noted philatelist and author of "Sloane's Column," pointed out that one of the most prominent foreigners who came to the colonies to lend support to the fight against English rule had never been commemorated on a U.S. stamp.

1716

The Marquis de Lafayette sailed from France in 1777 in his privately owned ship to volunteer his services to General George Washington. He was 19 at the time. Lafayette remained in the U.S. after the war, developing a deep affection for the young nation. In 1824 when Lafayette returned to France, he bid a tearful adieu to President John Quincy Adams and the hugh crowd that had gathered to say farewell.

Apparently when Sloane spoke, the philatelic community listened. On June 13, 1952, the 175th anniversary of Lafayette's arrival in 1777 was honored with a 3¢ stamp (#1010). Two other stamps have also been issued picturing Lafayette: a 3¢ stamp for this 200th birthday, September 6, 1957, (#1097), and a Bicentennial 13¢ commemorative issue (#1716).

991

992

993

994

995

996

997

998

999

1000

1001

1002

1003

1004

1005

1006

1007

1008   1009

1010

1011

1012

1013

1014

1015

1016

1017

1018

1019

1020

1021

1022

1023

1024

1025

1026

1027

	1952 continued	Un	U	PB	#	FDC	Q
1010	3¢ General Lafayette, June 13	.11	.05	.60		.85	113,135,000
	Perf. 10½x11						
1011	3¢ Mt. Rushmore Mem., Aug. 11	.10	.05	.60		.85	116,255,000
	Perf. 11x10½						
1012	3¢ Engineering, Sept. 6	.10	.05	.60		.85	113,860,000
1013	3¢ Service Women, Sept. 11	.12	.05	.60		.85	124,260,000
1014	3¢ Gutenberg Bible, Sept. 30	.10	.05	.60		.85	115,735,000
1015	3¢ Newspaper Boys, Oct. 4	.10	.05	.60		.85	115,430,000
1016	3¢ Red Cross, Nov. 21	.10	.05	.60		.85	136,220,000
	Issues of 1953						
1017	3¢ National Guard, Feb. 23	.10	.05	.50		.85	114,894,600
1018	3¢ Ohio Statehood, Mar. 2	.10	.05	1.00		.85	118,706,000
1019	3¢ Washington Territory, Mar. 2	.10	.05	.50		.85	114,190,000
1020	3¢ Louisiana Purchase, Apr. 30	.10	.05	.50		.85	113,990,000
1021	5¢ Opening of Japan 100th Anniv.,						
	July 14	.16	.07	2.00		.85	89,289,600
1022	3¢ American Bar Assn., Aug. 24	.10	.05	.50		.85	114,865,000
1023	3¢ Sagamore Hill, Sep. 14	.10	.05	.50		1.00	115,780,000
1024	3¢ Future Farmers, Oct. 13	.10	.05	.50		.85	115,244,600
1025	3¢ Trucking Industry, Oct. 27	.10	.05	.50		.85	123,709,600
1026	3¢ General Patton, Nov. 11	.17	.05	.50		.85	114,798,600
1027	3¢ New York City						
	300th Anniversary, Nov. 20	.11	.05	.50		.85	115,759,600

Maps On Stamps

Maps have been used on U.S. stamps to show newly acquired territory or to commemorate statehood, geographical exploration and historical events. Recently, older stamps have been used on newer stamps to not only represent the area where an historical event occurred, but to also add a flavor of that era to the event's graphic depiction.

1690

A 13¢ commemorative of Ben Franklin (#1690) was issued for the U.S. Bicentennial (it was also a joint issue with Canada). In the background is a map of the northeastern U.S. and Canada dating from the Revolutionary War. It adds an effective and interesting sense of time passed, while also giving us a glimpse of the important cities and geographical features of that time.

Another interesting map effect is on a pair of se-tenant stamps that commemorate the Battle of Yorktown and Virginia Capes (#1937 & 1938). One stamp shows the land battle and the other depicts U.S. and British ships in battle formations, both against the background of a Revolutionary War map of Yorktown.

	1953 continued	Un	U	PB	#	FDC	
1028	3¢ Gadsden Purchase, Dec. 30	.10	.05	.50		.85	116,134,600
	Issues of 1954						
1029	3¢ Columbia University 200th						
	Anniv., Jan. 4	.10	.05	.50		.85	118,540,000
	Liberty Issue, 1954-68, Perf. 11x10½, 10½x11						
1030	½¢ Benjamin Franklin, 1955	.05	.05	.30		.85	Unlimited
1031	1¢ George Washington, 1954	.05	.05	.25		.85	Unlimited
1031A	1¼¢ Palace of the Governors,						
	Santa Fe, 1960	.05	.05	1.75		.85	Unlimited
1032	1½¢ Mount Vernon, 1956	.06	.06	7.50		.60	Unlimited
1033	2¢ Thomas Jefferson, 1954	.06	.05	.25		.60	Unlimited
1034	2½¢ Bunker Hill Monument						
	and Massachusetts flag, 1959	.09	.06	2.00		.60	Unlimited
1035	3¢ Statue of Liberty, 1954	.09	.05	.40		.60	Unlimited
1035a	Booklet pane of 6	4.00	.50				
1036	4¢ Abraham Lincoln, 1954	.11	.05	.50		.60	Unlimited
1036a	Booklet pane of 6	3.50	.50				
1037	4½¢ The Hermitage, 1959	.13	.06	1.75		.60	Unlimited
1038	5¢ James Monroe, 1954	.15	.05	.75		.60	Unlimited
1039	6¢ Theodore Roosevelt, 1955	.55	.05	2.00		.65	Unlimited
1040	7¢ Woodrow Wilson, 1956	.26	.05	1.50		.70	Unlimited
	Perf. 11						
1041	8¢ Statue of Liberty, 1954	.22	.06	5.00		.80	Unlimited
1042	8¢ Statue of Liberty, redrawn, 1958	.30	.05	1.75		.60	Unlimited
	Perf. 11x10½, 10½x11						
1042A	8¢ John J. Pershing, 1961	.30	.05	1.50		.60	Unlimited
1043	9¢ The Alamo, 1956	.30	.05	1.50		.90	Unlimited
1044	10¢ Independence Hall, 1956	.30	.05	1.65		.90	Unlimited
	Perf. 11						
1044A	11¢ Statue of Liberty, 1961	.30	.08	1.50		.90	Unlimited
	Perf. 11x10½, 10½x11						
1045	12¢ Benjamin Harrison, 1959	.50	.05	2.75		.90	Unlimited
1046	15¢ John Jay, 1958	.75	.05	3.35		1.00	Unlimited
1047	20¢ Monticello, 1956	.75	.05	4.50		1.20	Unlimited
1048	25¢ Paul Revere, 1958	2.75	.05	14.00		1.30	Unlimited
1049	30¢ Robert E. Lee, 1955	1.60	.05	10.00		1.50	Unlimited
1050	40¢ John Marshall, 1955	3.75	.06	18.00		1.75	Unlimited
1051	50¢ Susan B. Anthony, 1955	3.25	.05	18.00		6.00	Unlimited
1052	$1 Patrick Henry, 1955	13.50	.07	65.00		11.00	Unlimited
	Perf. 11						
1053	$5 Alexander Hamilton, 1956	125.00	6.75	475.00		65.00	Unlimited
	Coil Stamps, Perf. 10 Vertically						
1054	1¢ dark green Washington						
	(1031), 1954	.30	.05			.75	Unlimited

1029

1030

1031

1032

1033

1034

1035

1037

1038

1039

1040

042

1042A

1043

1044

1044A

1046

1047

1048

1049

060

1061

1062

063

1064

1065

066

1067

1068

069

1070

1071

072

1074

	1954-68 continued	Un	U	PB #	FDC	Q
	Perf. 10 Horizontally					
1054A	1¼¢ turquoise, Palace of the					
	Governors, Santa Fe (1031A), 1960	.30	.20		.90	Unlimited
	Perf. 10 Vertically					
1055	2¢ rose carmine					
	Jefferson (1033), -54	.06	.05		.75	Unlimited
1056	2½¢ gray blue, Bunker Hill Monument					
	and Massachusetts flag (1034), -59	.35	.30		1.20	Unlimited
1057	3¢ deep violet Statue of Liberty					
	(1035), 1954	.12	.05		.75	Unlimited
1058	4¢ red violet Lincoln (1036), 1958	.15	.05		.75	Unlimited
	Perf. 10 Horizontally					
1059	4½¢ blue grn. Hermitage (1037), -59	2.25	1.50		1.20	Unlimited
	Perf. 10 Vertically					
1059A	25¢ green P. Revere (1048)	.65	.20		1.20	Unlimited
	Issues of 1954, Perf. 11x10½					
1060	3¢ Nebraska Territory, May 7	.10	.05	.50	.75	115,810,000
1061	3¢ Kansas Territory, May 31	.10	.05	.50	.75	113,603,700
	Perf. 10½x11					
1062	3¢ George Eastman, July 12	.10	.05	.60	.75	128,002,000
	Perf. 11x10½					
1063	3¢ Lewis and Clark Expedition,					
	July 28	.10	.05	.50	.75	116,078,150
	Issues of 1955, Perf. 10½x11					
1064	3¢ Pennsylvania Academy of					
	Fine Arts, Jan. 15	.10	.05	.50	.75	116,139,800
	Perf. 11x10½					
1065	3¢ Land Grant Colleges, Feb. 12	.10	.05	.50	.75	120,484,800
1066	8¢ Rotary International, Feb. 23	.25	.08	1.75	.90	53,854,750
1067	3¢ Armed Forces Reserve, May 21	.11	.05	.50	.75	176,075,000
	Perf. 10½x11					
1068	3¢ New Hampshire, June 21	.12	.05	.50	.75	125,944,400
	Perf. 11x10½					
1069	3¢ Soo Locks, June 28	.10	.05	.50	.75	122,284,600
1070	3¢ Atoms for Peace, July 28	.10	.05	.80	.75	133,638,850
1071	3¢ Fort Ticonderoga, Sept. 18	.11	.05	.50	.75	118,664,600
	Perf. 10½x11					
1072	3¢ Andrew W. Mellon, Dec. 20	.10	.05	.60	.75	112,434,000
	Issues of 1956					
1073	3¢ Benjamin Franklin, Jan. 17	.10	.05	.50	.75	129,384,550
	Perf. 11x10½					
1074	3¢ Booker T. Washington, Apr. 5	.10	.05	.50	.75	121,184,600
	Fifth International Philatelic Exhibition, Souvenir Sheet, Imperf.					
1075	Sheet of 2, Apr. 28	4.25	4.25			2,900,731
1075a	3¢ deep violet (1035)	1.75	1.75			

	1956 continued	Un	U	PB	#	FDC	
1075b	8¢ dk. vio. bl. & car. (1041)	2.00	2.00				
	Perf. 11x10½						
1076	3¢ New York Coliseum and						
	Columbus Monument, Apr. 30	.10	.05	.50		.75	119,784,200
	Wildlife Conservation Issue						
1077	3¢ Wild Turkey, May 5	.12	.05	.65		1.00	123,159,400
1078	3¢ Pronghorn Antelope, June 22	.12	.05	.65		1.00	123,138,800
1079	3¢ King Salmon, Nov. 9	.12	.05	.65		1.00	109,275,000
	Perf. 10½x11						
1080	3¢ Pure Food and Drug Laws,						
	June 27	.10	.05	.50		.80	112,932,200
	Perf. 11x10½						
1081	3¢ Wheatland, Aug. 5	.10	.05	.50		.80	125,475,000
	Perf. 10½x11						
1082	3¢ Labor Day, Sept. 3	.10	.05	.50		.80	117,855,000
	Perf. 11x10½						
1083	3¢ Nassau Hall, Sept. 22	.10	.05	.50		.80	122,100,000
	Perf. 10½x11						
1084	3¢ Devils Tower, Sept. 24	.10	.05	.50		.80	118,180,000
	Perf. 11x10½						
1085	3¢ Children's Issue, Dec. 15	.10	.05	.50		.80	100,975,000
	Issues of 1957						
1086	3¢ Alexander Hamilton, Jan. 11	.10	.05	.50		.80	115,299,450
	Perf. 10½x11						
1087	3¢ Polio, Jan. 15	.10	.05	.50		.80	186,949,627
	Perf. 11x10½						
1088	3¢ Coast and Geodetic Survey,						
	Feb. 11	.10	.05	.50		.80	115,235,000
1089	3¢ Architects, Feb. 23	.10	.05	.50		.80	106,647,500
	Perf. 10½x11						
1090	3¢ Steel Industry, May 22	.10	.05	.50		.80	112,010,000
	Perf. 11x10½						
1091	3¢ Int'l. Naval Review, June 10	.10	.05	.50		.80	118,470,000
1092	3¢ Oklahoma Statehood, June 14	.10	.05	.60		.80	102,230,000
1093	3¢ School Teachers, July 1	.10	.05	.50		.80	102,410,000

WILDLIFE CONSERVATION
WILD TURKEY
UNITED STATES POSTAGE

1077

WILDLIFE CONSERVATION
PRONGHORN ANTELOPE
UNITED STATES POSTAGE

1078

CONSERVATION
STATES POSTAGE

UNITED STATES POSTAGE
HARVEY WILEY
50TH ANNIVERSARY
PURE FOOD AND DRUG LAWS

1080

UNITED STATES POSTAGE 3¢
WHEATLAND
THE HOME OF JAMES BUCHANAN

1081

LABOR DAY
LABOR PROSPERS
U.S.POSTAGE

1082

SARY OF NASSAU HALL
1756 1956
STATES POSTAGE 3¢

U.S. POSTAGE
50th ANNIVERSARY
DEVILS TOWER
NATIONAL MONUMENT

1084

FRIENDSHIP - THE KEY TO WORLD PEACE
CHILDREN'S STAMP
1956
UNITED STATES POSTAGE

1085

UNITED STATES POS
1757 1957
ALEXANDER HAMILTON

1086

COAST AND GEODETIC SURVEY
1807 1957
U.S. POSTAGE 3 CENTS

1088

CENTENNIAL
AMERICAN
INSTITUTE
OF
ARCHITECTS
1957
UNITED STATES POSTAGE

1089

AMERICA AND STEEL
GROWING TOGETHER
U.S. POSTAGE

1090

NAL NAVAL REVIEW
U.S. POSTAGE 3¢

1907 ARROWS TO ATOMS 1957
50TH ANNIVERSARY OF
OKLAHOMA STATEHOOD
UNITED STATES POSTAGE

HONORING THE
TEACHERS OF AMERICA
NATIONAL EDUCATION ASSOCIATION
1857 1957
UNITED STATES POSTAGE

094

1095

1096

1097

098

1099

1100

1104

105

1106

1107

108

1109

1110

1111

	1957 continued	Un	U	PB	#	FDC	Q
	Perf. 11						
1094	4¢ Flag Issue, July 4	.12	.05	.60		.80	84,054,400
	Perf. 10½x11						
1095	3¢ Shipbuilding, Aug. 15	.10	.05	.70		.80	126,266,000
	Perf. 11						
1096	8¢ Champion of Liberty, Aug. 31,						
	Ramon Magsaysay	.24	.12	1.90		.80	39,489,600
	Perf. 10½x11						
1097	3¢ Lafayette, Sept. 6	.10	.05	.50		.80	122,990,000
	Perf. 11						
1098	3¢ Wildlife Conservation, Nov. 22	.10	.05	.65		1.00	174,372,800
	Perf. 10½x11						
1099	3¢ Religious Freedom, Dec. 27	.10	.05	.50		.80	114,365,000
	Issues of 1958						
1100	3¢ Gardening-Horticulture, Mar. 15	.10	.05	.50		.80	122,765,200
	Perf. 11x10½						
1104	3¢ Brussels Fair, Apr. 17	.10	.05	.50		.80	113,660,200
1105	3¢ James Monroe, Apr. 28	.10	.05	.60		.80	120,196,580
1106	3¢ Minnesota Statehood, May 11	.10	.05	.50		.80	120,805,200
	Perf. 11						
1107	3¢ Geophysical Year, May 31	.10	.05	.75		.80	125,815,200
	Perf. 11x10½						
1108	3¢ Gunston Hall, June 12	.10	.05	.50		.80	108,415,200
	Perf. 10½x11						
1109	3¢ Mackinac Bridge, June 25	.10	.05	.50		.80	107,195,200
1110	4¢ Champion of Liberty, July 24,						
	Simon Bolivar	.12	.05	.60		.80	115,745,280
	Perf. 11						
1111	8¢ Champion of Liberty, July 24,						
	Simon Bolivar	.24	.15	6.00		.80	39,743,640
	Perf. 11x10½						
1112	4¢ Atlantic Cable 100th Anniversary,						
	Aug. 15	.12	.05	.50		.80	114,570,200

	1958 continued	Un	U	PB	#	FDC	
	Lincoln 150th Anniv. Issue, 1958-59, Perf. 10½x11, 11x10½						
1113	1¢ Portrait by George Healy,						
	Feb. 12, '59	.05	.05	.40		.80	120,400,200
1114	3¢ Sculptured Head						
	by Gutzon Borglum, Feb. 27, '59	.10	.07	.60		.80	91,160,200
1115	4¢ Lincoln and Stephen Douglas						
	Debating, Aug. 27, 1958	.12	.05	.55		.80	114,860,200
1116	4¢ Statue in Lincoln Memorial						
	by Daniel Chester French,						
	May 30, '59	.12	.05	.65		.80	126,500,000
	Issues of 1958, Perf. 10½x11						
1117	4¢ Champion of Liberty, Sept. 19,						
	Lajos Kossuth	.12	.05	.60		.80	120,561,280
	Perf. 11						
1118	8¢ Champion of Liberty, Sept. 19,						
	Lajos Kossuth	.24	.14	4.25		.80	44,064,576
	Perf. 10½x11						
1119	4¢ Freedom of Press, Sept. 22	.12	.05	.50		.80	118,390,200
	Perf. 11x10½						
1120	4¢ Overland Mail, Oct. 10	.12	.05	.50		.80	125,770,200
	Perf. 10½x11						
1121	4¢ Noah Webster, Oct. 16	.12	.05	.50		.80	114,114,280
	Perf. 11						
1122	4¢ Forest Conservation, Oct. 27	.12	.05	.60		.80	156,600,200
	Perf. 11x10½						
1123	4¢ Fort Duquesne, Nov. 25	.12	.05	.50		.80	124,200,200
	Issues of 1959						
1124	4¢ Oregon Statehood, Feb. 14	.12	.05	.50		.80	120,740,200
	Perf. 10½x11						
1125	4¢ Champion of Liberty, Feb. 25,						
	José de San Martin	.12	.05	.55		.80	133,623,280
	Perf. 11						
1126	8¢ Champion of Liberty, Feb. 25,						
	José de San Martin	.24	.14	2.25		.80	45,569,088
	Perf. 10½x11						
1127	4¢ NATO, Apr. 1	.12	.05	.50		.80	122,493,280
	Perf. 11x10½						
1128	4¢ Arctic Explorations, Apr. 6	.12	.05	.85		.80	131,260,200
1129	8¢ World Peace through World						
	Trade, Apr. 20	.24	.10	1.50		.80	47,125,200
1130	4¢ Nevada Silver, June 8	.12	.05	.50		.80	123,105,000
	Perf. 11						
1131	4¢ St. Lawrence Seaway, June 26	.12	.05	.50		.80	126,105,050

1113

1114

1115

1116

1117

1118

1119

1120

1121

1122

1123

1124

1125

1126

1127

1128

1129

1130

1131

1132

1133

1134

1135

1136

1137

1138

1139

1140

1141

1142

1143

1144

1145

1146

1147

1148

	1959 continued	Un	U	PB	#	FDC	Q
1132	4¢ 49-Star Flag, July 4	.12	.05	.50		.80	209,170,000
1133	4¢ Soil Conservation, Aug. 26	.12	.05	.65		.80	120,835,000
	Perf. 10½x11						
1134	4¢ Petroleum Industry, Aug. 27	.12	.05	.50		.80	115,715,000
	Perf. 11x10½						
1135	4¢ Dental Health, Sept. 14	.12	.05	.50		.80	118,445,000
	Perf. 10½x11						
1136	4¢ Champion of Liberty, Sept. 29,						
	Ernst Reuter	.12	.05	.60		.80	111,685,000
	Perf. 11						
1137	8¢ Champion of Liberty, Sept. 29,						
	Ernst Reuter	.24	.14	2.25		.80	43,099,200
	Perf. 10½x11						
1138	4¢ Dr. Ephraim McDowell, Dec. 3	.12	.05	.50		.80	115,444,000
	Issues of 1960-61, Perf. 11, American Credo						
1139	4¢ Quotation from Washington's						
	Farewell Address	.12	.05	1.00		.80	126,470,000
1140	4¢ B. Franklin Quotation	.12	.05	1.00		.80	124,560,000
1141	4¢ T. Jefferson Quotation	.14	.05	1.00		.80	115,455,000
1142	4¢ Francis Scott Key Quotation	.14	.05	1.00		.80	122,060,000
1143	4¢ Lincoln Quotation	.20	.05	1.00		.80	120,540,000
1144	4¢ Patrick Henry Quotation, 1961	.18	.05	1.00		.80	113,075,000
1145	4¢ Boy Scout Jubilee, Feb. 8	.12	.05	.50		.80	139,325,000
	Perf. 10½x11						
1146	4¢ Olympic Winter Games, Feb. 18	.12	.05	.50		.80	124,445,000
1147	4¢ Champion of Liberty, Mar. 7,						
	Masaryk	.12	.05	.60		.80	113,792,000
	Perf. 11						
1148	8¢ Champion of Liberty, Masaryk	.24	.14	2.50		.80	44,215,200

	1960-61 continued	Un	U	PB	#	FDC	
	Perf. 11x10½						
1149	4¢ World Refugee Year, Apr. 7	.12	.05	.50		.80	113,195,000
	Perf. 11						
1150	4¢ Water Conservation, Apr. 18	.12	.05	.65		.80	121,805,000
	Perf. 10½x11						
1151	4¢ SEATO, May 31	.12	.05	.50		.80	115,353,000
	Perf. 11x10½						
1152	4¢ American Woman, June 2	.12	.05	.50		.80	111,080,000
	Perf. 11						
1153	4¢ 50-Star Flag, July 4	.12	.05	.50		.80	153,025,000
	Perf. 11x10½						
1154	4¢ Pony Express 100th Anniv., July 19	.12	.05	.50		.80	119,665,000
	Perf. 10½x11						
1155	4¢ Employ the Handicapped, Aug. 28	.12	.05	.50		.80	117,855,000
1156	4¢ World Forestry Congress, Aug. 29	.12	.05	.50		.80	118,185,000
	Perf. 11						
1157	4¢ Mexican Independence, Sept. 16	.12	.05	.50		.80	112,260,000
1158	4¢ U.S.-Japan Treaty, Sept. 28	.12	.05	.50		.80	125,010,000
	Perf. 10½x11						
1159	4¢ Champion of Liberty, Oct. 8, I.J. Paderewski	.12	.05	.55		.80	119,798,000
	Perf. 11						
1160	8¢ Champion of Liberty, I.J. Paderewski	.24	.14	2.00		.80	42,696,000
	Perf. 10½x11						
1161	4¢ Sen. Taft Memorial, Oct. 10	.12	.05	.50		.80	106,610,000
	Perf. 11x10½						
1162	4¢ Wheels of Freedom, Oct. 15	.12	.05	.50		.80	109,695,000
	Perf. 11						
1163	4¢ Boy's Clubs of America, Oct. 18	.12	.05	.50		.80	123,690,000
1164	4¢ Automated P.O., Oct. 20	.12	.05	.50		.80	123,970,000
	Perf. 10½ x 11						
1165	4¢ Champion of Liberty, Oct. 26, Baron Gustaf Mannerheim	.12	.05	.55		.80	124,796,000
	Perf. 11						
1166	8¢ Champion of Liberty, Baron Gustaf Mannerheim	.24	.14	2.25		.80	42,076,800

1149

1150

SEATO

1151

1152

1153

1154

1155

1156

1157

1158

1159

1160

1161

1162

1163

1164

1165

1166

1167

1168

1169

1170

1171

1172

1173

1174

1175

1176

1177

1178

1179

1180

1181

1182

1183

1184

	1960-61 continued	Un	U	PB #	FDC	Q
1167	4¢ Camp Fire Girls, Nov. 4	.12	.05	.50	.80	116,210,000
	Perf. 10½x11					
1168	4¢ Champion of Liberty, Nov. 2,					
	Giuseppe Garibaldi	.12	.05	.55	.80	126,252,000
	Perf. 11					
1169	8¢ Champion of Liberty,					
	Giuseppe Garibaldi	.24	.14	2.25	.80	42,746,400
	Perf. 10½x11					
1170	4¢ Sen. George Memorial, Nov. 5	.12	.05	.50	.80	124,117,000
1171	4¢ Andrew Carnegie, Nov. 25	.12	.05	.50	.80	119,840,000
1172	4¢ John Foster Dulles Memorial,					
	Dec. 6	.12	.05	.55	.80	117,187,000
	Perf. 11x10½					
1173	4¢ Echo I—Communications for					
	Peace, Dec. 15	.30	.06	2.25	1.40	124,390,000
	Issues of 1961, Perf. 10½x11					
1174	4¢ Champion of Liberty, Jan. 26,					
	Mahatma Gandhi	.12	.05	.55	.80	112,966,000
	Perf. 11					
1175	8¢ Champion of Liberty,					
	Mahatma Gandhi	.24	.14	2.25	.80	41,644,200
1176	4¢ Range Conservation, Feb. 2	.12	.05	.65	.75	110,850,000
	Perf. 10½x11					
1177	4¢ Horace Greeley, Feb. 3	.12	.05	.55	.75	98,616,000
	Civil War 100th Anniv. Issue, 1961-1965, Perf. 11x10½					
1178	4¢ Fort Sumter Centenary, 1961	.16	.05	1.10	1.25	101,125,000
1179	4¢ Shiloh Centenary, 1962	.13	.05	1.00	1.25	124,865,000
	Perf. 11					
1180	5¢ Gettysburg Centenary, 1963	.16	.05	1.00	1.25	79,905,000
1181	5¢ Wilderness Centenary, 1964	.16	.05	1.00	1.25	125,410,000
1182	5¢ Appomattox Centenary, 1965	.16	.05	1.10	1.25	112,845,000
	Issue dates: #1178, Apr. 12, 1961; #1179, Apr. 7, 1962; #1180, July 1, 1963; #1181, May 5, 1964; #1182, Apr. 9, 1965.					
	Issues of 1961					
1183	4¢ Kansas Statehood, May 10	.12	.05	.55	.75	106,210,000
	Perf. 11x10½					
1184	4¢ Sen. George W. Norris, July 11	.12	.05	.55	.75	110,810,000

	1961 continued	Un	U	PB	#	FDC	
1185	4¢ Naval Aviation, Aug. 20	.12	.05	.55		.90	116,995,000
	Perf. 10½x11						
1186	4¢ Workmen's Comp., Sept. 4	.12	.05	.55		.75	121,015,000
	Perf. 11						
1187	4¢ Frederic Remington, Oct. 4	.14	.05	1.00		.75	111,600,000
	Perf. 10½x11						
1188	4¢ Republic of China, Oct. 10	.12	.05	.55		.75	110,620,000
1189	4¢ Naismith-Basketball, Nov. 6	.15	.05	.55		.90	109,110,000
	Perf. 11						
1190	4¢ Nursing, Dec. 28	.12	.05	.70		.75	145,350,000
	Issues of 1962						
1191	4¢ New Mexico Statehood, Jan. 6	.12	.05	.55		.75	112,870,000
1192	4¢ Arizona Statehood, Feb. 14	.12	.05	.75		.75	121,820,000
1193	4¢ Project Mercury, Feb. 20	.12	.05	.75		1.50	289,240,000
1194	4¢ Malaria Eradication, Mar. 30	.12	.05	.55		.75	120,155,000
	Perf. 10½x11						
1195	4¢ Charles Evans Hughes, Apr. 11	.12	.05	.55		.75	124,595,000
	Perf. 11						
1196	4¢ Seattle World's Fair, Apr. 25	.12	.05	.70		.75	147,310,000
1197	4¢ Louisiana Statehood, Apr. 30	.12	.05	.55		.75	118,690,000
	Perf. 11x10½						
1198	4¢ Homestead Act, May 20	.12	.05	.55		.75	122,730,000
1199	4¢ Girl Scout Jubilee, July 24	.12	.05	.55		.75	126,515,000
1200	4¢ Sen. Brien McMahon, July 28	.12	.05	.75		.75	130,960,000
1201	4¢ Apprenticeship, Aug. 31	.12	.05	.55		.75	120,055,000

Cars Need Stamps, Too

One would expect to see one of this country's most important industries displayed on a good number of stamps, but the American automobile industry has been ignored for the most part as a philatelic subject. In spite of the fact that a good deal of our mail is delivered by truck, automotive vehicles have been depicted on U.S. postage rather infrequently.

1007

The first time was on the 4¢ stamp of the Pan-American series of 1901 (#296), and the auto has been used as a backdrop on six other stamps, most notably on the American Automobile Association 3¢ stamp (#1007), for Henry Ford's 12¢ stamp (#1286A) and, most recently, on the Electric Auto stamp (#1905) in the Transportation Series.

1185

1186

1187

1188

1189

1190

1191

1192

1193

1194

1195

1196

1197

1198

1199

1200

1201

1202

1203

1204

1205

1206

1207

1208

1209

1213

1230

1231

1232

1233

1234

1235

1236

1237

The Pony Express and The Overland Mail

A close look at the 1940 3¢ stamp commemorating the Pony Express (#894) reveals an interesting bit of historical misinformation. Horse and rider are leaving a relay depot that displays a sign reading, "Station, Overland Mail." In fact, the words, "overland mail," imply the name of the Butterfield Southern Overland Mail, a stage-line running the San Francisco-St. Louis route. The Pony Express was their direct competitor, having been devised to better the 25-day stage delivery by completing the route in less than half the time. The Pony Express also ran a more northerly course to avoid the growing hostilities of the Civil War. Thus, the stamp seemingly depicts the pony rider as leaving a rival's station many miles south of his own route.

	1963 continued	Un	U	PB	#	FDC	
1238	5¢ City Mail Delivery, Oct. 26	.14	.05	.60		.75	128,450,000
1239	5¢ Red Cross 100th Anniv., Oct. 29	.14	.05	.60		.75	118,665,000
1240	5¢ Christmas Issue, Nov. 1	.14	.05	.60.		75	1,291,250,000
1241	5¢ John James Audubon, Dec. 7	.14	.05	1.25		.75	175,175,000
	Issues of 1964, Perf. 10½x11						
1242	5¢ Sam Houston, Jan. 10	.14	.05	.60		.75	125,995,000
	Perf. 11						
1243	5¢ Charles M. Russell, Mar. 9	.18	.05	1.20		.75	128,925,000
	Perf. 11x10½						
1244	5¢ New York World's Fair, Apr. 22	.14	.05	1.00		.75	145,700,000
	Perf. 11						
1245	5¢ John Muir, Apr. 29	.14	.05	.60		.75	120,310,000
	Perf. 11x10½						
1246	5¢ Kennedy Memorial, May 29	.14	.05	.60		.75	511,750,000
	Perf. 10½x11						
1247	5¢ New Jersey 300th Anniv., June 15	.15	.05	.60		.75	123,845,000
	Perf. 11						
1248	5¢ Nevada Statehood, July 22	.14	.05	.60		.75	122,825,000
1249	5¢ Register and Vote, Aug. 1	.14	.05	.60		.75	453,090,000
	Perf. 10½x11						
1250	5¢ Shakespeare, Aug. 14	.14	.05	.60		.75	123,245,000
1251	5¢ Doctors Mayo, Sept. 11	.14	.05	.60		.75	123,355,000
1252	5¢ American Music, Oct. 15,						
	Perf. 11	.14	.05	.60		.75	126,970,000
1253	5¢ Homemakers, Oct. 26, Perf. 11	.14	.05	.60		.75	121,250,000

Roosevelt's Famous Americans

The Famous American Series of 1940 (#859-893) was a commemorative issue to which President Roosevelt was devoted. Himself a noted stamp enthusiast, he labored for three months over the lists of "recommended" and "alternate" selections for the proposed 35-stamp issue.

859

The series was comprised of seven groups of five stamps each (over the years additional stamps have been added). The group categories were Authors, Poets, Educators, Scientists, Composers, Artists and Inventors. With all the possible choices, FDR knew he would need an authority to fall back on to handle the inevitable criticism for leaving out someone's favorite Famous American. Then, New York University published a "Hall of Fame," and FDR made sure all his choices were listed there.

But this didn't make his task any easier. For example, Robert Fulton was an "alternate" in the Inventor category, but FDR chose him, then replaced him with Cyrus McCormick. In June 1940, the final list included Fulton again. But when the issue came out, it was McCormick "in" and Fulton "out." Fulton was later honored in 1965 (#1270) on the 200th anniversary of his birth.

1238

1239

1240

1241

1242

1243

1244

1245

1246

1247

1248

1249

1252

1253

1254 1255
1256 1257

1258

1259

1260

1261

1262

1263

1264

1265

1266

1267

1268

1269

1270

1271

1272

	1964 continued	Un	U	PB #	FDC	Q
	Christmas Issue, Nov. 9					
1254	5¢ Holly, Perf. 11	.65	.05		.75	351,940,000
1255	5¢ Mistletoe, Perf. 11	.65	.05		.75	351,940,000
1256	5¢ Poinsettia, Perf. 11	.65	.05		.75	351,940,000
1257	5¢ Sprig of Conifer, Perf. 11	.65	.05		.75	351,940,000
	Block of four, #1254-1257	4.50	1.25	5.50		
	Perf. 10½x11					
1258	5¢ Verrazano-Narrows Bridge,					
	Nov. 21	.14	.05	.60	.75	120,005,000
	Perf. 11					
1259	5¢ Fine Arts, Dec. 2	.14	.05	.75	.75	125,800,000
	Perf. 10½x11					
1260	5¢ Amateur Radio, Dec. 15	.14	.05	.75	.75	122,230,000
	Issues of 1965, Perf. 11					
1261	5¢ Battle of New Orleans, Jan. 8	.14	.05	.75	.75	115,695,000
1262	5¢ Physical Fitness-Sokol, Feb. 15	.14	.05	.75	.75	115,095,000
1263	5¢ Crusade Against Cancer, Apr. 1	.14	.05	.75	.75	119,560,000
	Perf. 10½x11					
1264	5¢ Churchill Memorial, May 13	.14	.05	.75	.75	125,180,000
	Perf. 11					
1265	5¢ Magna Carta, June 15	.14	.05	.75	.75	120,135,000
1266	5¢ Intl. Cooperation Year, June 26	.14	.05	.75	.75	115,405,000
1267	5¢ Salvation Army, July 2	.14	.05	.75	.75	115,855,000
	Perf. 10½x11					
1268	5¢ Dante Alighieri, July 17	.14	.05	.75	.75	115,340,000
1269	5¢ Herbert Hoover, Aug. 10	.14	.05	.75	.75	114,840,000
	Perf. 11					
1270	5¢ Robert Fulton, Aug. 19	.14	.05	.75	.75	116,140,000
1271	5¢ Settlement of Florida, Aug. 28	.14	.05	1.00	.75	116,900,000
1272	5¢ Traffic Safety, Sept. 3	.14	.05	1.00	.75	114,085,000

Christmas Stamps

The U.S. Postal Service only began printing special Christmas stamps in 1962. For the first four years the issues depicted only secular aspects of the holiday, "Wreath and Candles," "National Christmas Tree and White House," for example. In 1966 Hans Memling's masterpiece from the National Gallery of Art, "Madonna and Child," appeared (#1321) and was repeated in 1967 on a larger Christmas stamp (#1336).

The present format was adopted in 1970. Now the USPS offers two special Christmas issues each year: an "art masterpiece" and a "contemporary or popular scene."

Christmas stamps go on sale in the middle of October. The combined printing of the two issues usually approaches the 2 billion mark.

	1965 continued	Un	U	PB	#	FDC	
1273	5¢ John Singleton Copley, Sept. 17	.15	.05	1.25		.75	114,880,000
1274	11¢ International Telecommunication Union,						
	Oct. 6	.45	.25	15.00		.75	26,995,000
1275	5¢ Adlai E. Stevenson, Oct. 23	.14	.05	.75		.75	128,495,000
1276	5¢ Christmas Issue, Nov. 2	.14	.05	.60		.75	1,139,930,000

Issues of 1965-78, Prominent Americans, Perf. 11x10½, 10½x11

		Un	U	PB	#	FDC	
1278	1¢ Thomas Jefferson, 1968	.05	.05	.20		.35	
1278a	Booklet pane of 8, 1968	1.00	.25				
1278b	Booklet pane of 4, 1971	.80	.20				
1279	1¼¢ Albert Gallatin, 1967	.09	.09	22.50		.35	
1280	2¢ Frank Lloyd Wright, 1966	.06	.05	.30		.35	
1280a	Booklet pane of 5 + label, 1968	1.25	.40				
1280c	Booklet pane of 6, 1971	1.00	.35				
1281	3¢ Francis Parkman, 1967	.09	.05	.70		.35	
1282	4¢ Abraham Lincoln, 1965	.13	.05	.40		.35	
1283	5¢ George Washington, 1966	.16	.05	.50		.45	
1283B	5¢ Washington redrawn, 1967	.12	.05	1.00		.45	
1284	6¢ Franklin D. Roosevelt, 1966	.20	.05	.65		.45	
1284b	Booklet pane of 8, 1967	1.75	.50				
1284c	Booklet pane of 5 + label, 1968	1.50	.50				
1285	8¢ Albert Einstein, 1966	.25	.05	1.25		.50	
1286	10¢ Andrew Jackson, 1967	.26	.05	1.30		.60	
1286A	12¢ Henry Ford, 1968	.30	.05	1.75		.50	
1287	13¢ John F. Kennedy, 1967	.35	.05	1.65		.65	
1288	15¢ Oliver Wendell Holmes, 1968	.45	.05	1.50		.60	
1288B	15¢ dk. rose claret Holmes (1288),						
	Perf. 10, 1978	.40	.05			.75	
1288c	Booklet pane of 8, 1978	2.85	1.25				
1289	20¢ George C. Marshall, 1967	.35	.05	2.00		.80	
1290	25¢ Frederick Douglass, 1967	.42	.05	2.50		1.00	
1291	30¢ John Dewey, 1968	.75	.05	3.00		1.20	
1292	40¢ Thomas Paine, 1968	.70	.06	4.00		1.60	
1293	50¢ Lucy Stone, 1968	1.25	.05	5.00		3.25	
1294	$1 Eugene O'Neill, 1967	2.75	.10	10.00		7.50	
1295	$5 John Bassett Moore, 1966	11.00	3.25	50.00		60.00	
	No. 1288B issued only in booklets.						

Coil Stamps, Issues of 1966-78, Perf. 10 Horizontally

		Un	U	PB	#	FDC	
1297	3¢ violet Parkman (1281), 1975	.07	.05			.75	
1298	6¢ gray brown F.D.R. (1284), 1967	.16	.05			.75	
	Perf. 10 Vertically						
1299	1¢ green Jefferson (1278), 1968	.05	.05			.75	
1303	4¢ black Lincoln (1282), 1966	.11	.11			.75	
1304	5¢ blue Washington (1283), 1966	.14	.05			.75	
1305	6¢ Franklin D. Roosevelt, 1968	.22	.05			.75	

1273

1274

1275

5c U.S. POSTAGE
CHRISTMAS
1276

1278

1279

1280

1281

1282

1283

1283B

1284

1285

1286

1286A

1287

1288

1289

1290

1291

1292

1293

1294

1295

1305

147

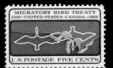

1306

1307

1308

1309

1310

1312

1313

1314

1311

1315

1316

1317

1318

1319

	Un	U	PB	#	FDC	Q
Coil Stamps, Issues of 1966-78, continued						
1305E 15¢ rose claret Holmes (1288), 1978	.40	.05			.75	
1305C $1 dull purple Eugene O'Neill						
(1294), 1973	2.00	.95			3.00	
Issues of 1966, Perf. 11						
1306 5¢ Migratory Bird Treaty, Mar. 16	.14	.05	1.00		.75	116,835,000
1307 5¢ Humane Treatment of Animals,						
Apr. 9	.14	.05	.90		.75	117,470,000
1308 5¢ Indiana Statehood, Apr. 16	.14	.05	.75		.75	123,770,000
1309 5¢ American Circus, May 2	.14	.05	.90		.75	131,270,000
Sixth International Philatelic Exhibition Issues						
1310 5¢ Stamped Cover, May 21	.14	.05	.90		.75	122,285,000
Imperf.						
1311 5¢ Souvenir Sheet, May 23	.22	.22			.75	14,680,000
Issued in sheets of one stamp with marginal inscription commemorating the Sixth International Philatelic Exhibition (SIPEX), held in Washington, D.C. from May 21-30.						
Perf. 11						
1312 5¢ Bill of Rights, July 1	.14	.05	.75		.75	114,160,000
Perf. 10½x11						
1313 5¢ Polish Millennium, July 30	.14	.05	.90		.75	128,475,000
Perf. 11						
1314 5¢ National Park Service, Aug. 25	.14	.05	.75		.75	119,535,000
1315 5¢ Marine Corps Reserve, Aug. 29	.14	.05	1.00		.75	125,110,000
1316 5¢ General Federation of Women's						
Clubs, Sept. 12	.14	.05	1.00		.75	114,853,200
1317 5¢ Johnny Appleseed, Sept. 24	.14	.05	1.00		.75	124,290,000
1318 5¢ Beautification of America, Oct. 5	.14	.05	1.75		.75	128,460,000
1319 5¢ Great River Road, Oct. 21	.14	.05	1.00		.75	127,585,000

Early U.S. Stamps

The first American postage stamp was not issued by the United States Postal Service, but by a private delivery service. During the 1840s the U.S. Mail was only delivered to post offices; individuals picked up and brought their mail to these offices. This led to the creation of private postal services which set up their own boxes in certain areas and, for a fee, shuttled the mail between their own facilities and the government post offices.

Alexander Grieg, founder of one of the earliest of these services, the City Despatch Post of New York City, commissioned a New York bank note firm to print engraved 3¢ stamps in sets of 42. The stamp was a small, nonperforated rectangle which carried the legend "City Despatch Post" and a bust of George Washington. In August 1842, the United States Postal Service bought out Grieg's service and continued to use his stamps. Stamps of this era bear the cancellation of the New York Post Office, a small "U.S." within an octagon. Later issues were reingraved to read "United States City Despatch Post."

	1966 continued	Un	U	PB	#	FDC	Q
1320	5¢ Savings Bond—Servicemen,						
	Oct. 26	.14	.05	1.00		.75	115,875,000
1321	5¢ Christmas Issue, Nov. 1	.14	.05	.75		.75	1,173,547,420
1322	5¢ Mary Cassatt, Nov. 17	.17	.05	2.75		.75	114,015,000
	Issues of 1967						
1323	5¢ National Grange, Apr. 17	.14	.05	.90		.75	121,105,000
1324	5¢ Canada 100th Anniv., May 25	.14	.05	.90		.25	132,045,000
1325	5¢ Erie Canal, July 4	.14	.05	.90		.75	118,780,000
1326	5¢ "Peace"—Lions, July 5	.14	.05	.90		.75	121,985,000
1327	5¢ Henry David Thoreau, July 12	.14	.05	.90		.75	111,850,000
1328	5¢ Nebraska Statehood, July 29	.14	.05	.90		.75	117,225,000
1329	5¢ Voice of America, Aug. 1	.14	.05	1.00		.75	111,515,000
1330	5¢ Davy Crockett, Aug. 17	.14	.05	1.00		.75	114,270,000
	Space Accomplishments Issue, Sept. 29						
1331	5¢ Space-Walking Astronaut	.80	.20				60,432,500
1332	5¢ Gemini 4 Capsule and Earth	.80	.20				60,432,500
	Pair, #1331-1332	3.25	1.50	11.00		10.00	
1333	5¢ Urban Planning, Oct. 2	.16	.05	2.00		.75	110,675,000
1334	5¢ Finnish Independence, Oct. 6	.16	.05	2.00		.75	110,670,000
	Perf. 12						
1335	5¢ Thomas Eakins, Nov. 2	.16	.05	2.50		.75	113,825,000
	Perf. 11						
1336	5¢ Christmas Issue, Nov. 6	.14	.05	.60		.75	1,208,700,000
1337	5¢ Mississippi Statehood, Dec. 11	.16	.05	2.00		.75	113,330,000
	Issues of 1968-71						
1338	6¢ Flag and White House	.17	.05	.60		.75	

Citizens' Stamp Advisory Committee

In the 1940s the pressures brought to bear on the Postal Service to issue stamps grew to unmanageable proportions. Between the interest taken by a stamp collecting President Roosevelt in honoring various causes and occasions and the commemoratives that Congress authorized to satisfy constituents, the Postal Service was induced to print an unwieldy variety of special stamps.

Congress finally agreed to relinquish its power to authorize special stamps, and in 1957 the first Citizens' Stamp Advisory Committee was formed. It was made up of three philatelists, three artists and a representative of the United States Information Agency. Over the years the committee has grown and its members now reflect a diversity of educational, geographical and occupational backgrounds. Appointed by the Postmaster General, they consider thousands of suggestions for commemorative stamps each year.

WE APPRECIATE OUR SERVICEMEN

UNITED STATES SAVINGS BONDS 25TH ANNIVERSARY 5¢

1320

1321

Mary Cassatt American Artist 5¢ U.S. POSTAGE

1322

1867-1967 NATIONAL GRANGE U.S. 5 CENTS

1323

CANADA 1867-1967 U.S. POSTAGE 5¢

1324

U.S. POSTAGE ERIE CANAL 1817 1967 5¢

1325

Search for Peace Lions International 5¢ United States

1326

THOREAU U.S. 5 cents

1327

NEBRASKA STATEHOOD 1867-1967 U.S. POSTAGE 5¢

1328

VOICE OF AMERICA 5¢ U.S. POSTAGE

1329

United States 5¢ U.S. POSTAGE Davy Crockett

1330

plan for better cities UNITED STATES POSTAGE 5¢

1333

Finland Independence 1917-67 United States 5¢

1334

US 5¢ US 5¢

1331   1332

UNITED STATES 6¢

1338

U.S. CHRISTMAS 5¢ U.S.

1336

5¢ UNITED STATES POSTAGE

1335

MISSISSIPPI 1817 1967 5¢ U.S. POSTAGE 5¢

1337

339

1340

1341

1342

343

1344

1345

1346

347

1348

1349

350

1351

1352

	1968-71 continued	Un	U	PB #	FDC	Q
	Perf. 11x10½					
1338D	6¢ dark blue, red & green					
	(1338), 1970	.18	.05	3.25 (20)	.75	
1338F	8¢ multicolored (1338), 1971	.20	.05	3.50 (20)	.75	
	Coil Stamps of 1969-71, Perf. 10 Vertically					
1338A	6¢ dark blue, red & green					
	(1338), 1969	.18	.05			
1338G	8¢ multicolored (1338), 1971	.25	.05			
	Issues of 1968, Perf. 11					
1339	6¢ Illinois Statehood, Feb. 12	.18	.05	1.00	.75	141,350,000
1340	6¢ HemisFair '68, Mar. 30	.18	.05	1.00	.75	144,345,000
1341	$1 Airlift, Apr. 4	6.25	2.95	32.50	6.50	
1342	6¢ "Youth"—Elks, May 1	.18	.05	1.00	.75	147,120,000
1343	6¢ Law and Order, May 17	.18	.05	1.00	.75	130,125,000
1344	6¢ Register and Vote, June 27	.18	.05	1.00	.75	158,700,000
	Historic Flag Series, July 4					
1345	6¢ Ft. Moultrie Flag (1776)	1.35	.50		4.00	23,153,000
1346	6¢ Ft. McHenry Flag (1795-1818)	1.35	.50		4.00	23,153,000
1347	6¢ Washington's Cruisers Flag					
	(1775)	.45	.45		4.00	23,153,000
1348	6¢ Bennington Flag (1777)	.45	.40		4.00	23,153,000
1349	6¢ Rhode Island Flag (1775)	.45	.40		4.00	23,153,000
1350	6¢ First Stars and Stripes Flag					
	(1777)	.45	.40		4.00	23,153,000
1351	6¢ Bunker Hill Flag (1775)	.45	.40		4.00	23,153,000
1352	6¢ Grand Union Flag (1776)	.45	.40		4.00	23,153,000
1353	6¢ Phila. Light Horse Flag (1775)	.75	.40		4.00	23,153,000
1354	6¢ First Navy Jack (1775)	.75	.40		4.00	23,153,000
	Strip of 10, (1345-1354)	8.25	7.50			
	Plate Block of 20			22.50		
	Perf. 12					
1355	6¢ Walt Disney, Sept. 11	.22	.05	1.75	1.00	153,015,000

The Motto

Do you know the origin of the quotation, "Neither snow, nor rain, nor heat, nor gloom of night stays these couriers from the swift completion of their appointed rounds"? It became famous because it was inscribed on the New York City Main Post Office. Architect William Mitchell Kendall composed the actual words, but the motto was a modification of a fourth century B.C. quote. The Greek historian Herodotus wrote of Persian messengers that they "travel with a velocity which nothing human can equal....Neither snow, nor rain, nor heat, nor darkness, are permitted to obstruct their speed."

	1968 continued	Un	U	PB #	FDC	
	Perf. 11					
1356	6¢ Father Marquette, Sept. 20	.17	.05	1.10	.75	132,560,000
1357	6¢ Daniel Boone, Sept. 26	.17	.05	1.10	.75	130,385,000
1358	6¢ Arkansas River, Oct. 1	.17	.05	1.10	.75	132,265,000
1359	6¢ Leif Erikson, Oct. 9	.17	.05	1.20	.75	128,710,000
	Perf. 11x10½					
1360	6¢ Cherokee Strip, Oct. 15	.20	.05	1.65	.75	124,775,000
	Perf. 11					
1361	6¢ John Trumbull, Oct. 18	.28	.05	2.25	.75	128,295,000
1362	6¢ Waterfowl Conservation, Oct. 24	.27	.05	3.00	.75	142,245,000
1363	6¢ Christmas Issue, Nov. 1	.17	.05	2.75 (10)	.75	1,410,580,000
1364	6¢ American Indian, Nov. 4	.32	.05	3.00	.75	125,100,000
	Issues of 1969, Beautification of America, Jan. 16					
1365	6¢ Capitol, Azaleas and Tulips	.90	.09	10.00	2.00	48,142,500
1366	6¢ Washington Monument,					
	Potomac River and Daffodils	.90	.09	10.00	2.00	48,142,500
1367	6¢ Poppies and Lupines					
	along Highway	.90	.09	10.00	2.00	48,142,500
1368	6¢ Blooming Crabapples					
	along Street	.90	.09	10.00	2.00	48,142,500
	Block of four	6.50	3.50	10.00	2.00	
1369	6¢ American Legion, Mar. 15	.17	.05	1.10	.75	148,770,000
1370	6¢ Grandma Moses, May 1	.17	.05	1.35	.75	139,475,000
1371	6¢ Apollo 8, May 5	.25	.05	3.00	2.00	187,165,000
1372	6¢ W. C. Handy, May 17	.17	.05	1.00	.75	125,555,000

The Stamp of Approval

It is a matter of more than passing interest that all five of the artists selected for the Artists set of the Famous American Series of 1940 contributed works which previously had been used as subjects for U.S. stamps.

Gilbert Stuart's (#884) portrait of Washington was used on definitive issue stamps; Whistler's (#885) portrait of his mother was used for the Mothers of America issue in 1934; Augustus Saint-Gaudens (#886) is known for his Lincoln head on the 2¢ Lincoln Memorial of 1909; Daniel Chester French (#887) is also well known for his statue of the Minute Man used on the 5¢ stamp of the Lexington-Concord issue of 1925; and two of Remington's (#888) paintings appeared on the Trans-Mississippi Series of 1898.

885

888

1356

1357

1358

1359

1360

1361

1362

1363

1364

1365   1366
1367   1368

1369

1370

1371

1372

1373

1374

1375

1376
1378

1377
1379

1380

1381

1382

1383

1384

1384a

1385

1386

1969 continued		Un	U	PB #	FDC	Q
1373	6¢ California Settlement, July 16	.17	.05	1.00	.75	144,425,000
1374	6¢ John Wesley Powell, Aug. 1	.17	.05	1.00	.75	135,875,000
1375	6¢ Alabama Statehood, Aug. 2	.17	.05	1.00	.75	151,110,000
	Botanical Congress Issue					
1376	6¢ Douglas Fir (Northwest)	1.35	.11		2.00	39,798,750
1377	6¢ Lady's Slipper (Northeast)	1.35	.11		2.00	39,798,750
1378	6¢ Ocotillo (Southwest)	1.35	.11		2.00	39,798,750
1379	6¢ Franklinia (Southeast)	1.35	.11		2.00	39,798,750
	Block of four, #1376-1379			12.00	5.00	
	Perf. 10½x11					
1380	6¢ Dartmouth College Case,					
	Sept. 22	.17	.05	1.35	.75	129,540,000
	Perf. 11					
1381	6¢ Professional Baseball, Sept. 24	.25	.05	1.75	.75	130,925,000
1382	6¢ Intercollegiate Football,					
	Sept. 26	.22	.05	1.85	.75	139,055,000
1383	6¢ Dwight D. Eisenhower, Oct. 14	.17	.05	1.00	.75	150,611,200
	Perf. 11x10½					
1384	6¢ Christmas Issue, Nov. 3	.17	.05	2.25 (10)	.75	1,709,795,000
1384a	Precanceled	.75	.06			
1385	6¢ Hope for Crippled, Nov. 20	.17	.05	1.00	.75	127,545,000
1386	6¢ William M. Harnett, Dec. 3	.17	.05	1.20	.75	145,788,800

FDR the Stamp Maker

President Franklin D. Roosevelt was a noted philatelist and is known to have taken a hand in designing quite a few stamp issues.

It's been reported that FDR suggested the basic design for the 25¢ (#C20) and 20¢ (#C21) Trans-Pacific Air Mail stamps that featured Pan Am's new China Clipper "flying boat." He also requested that the stamps show one of the old American Clipper ships formerly involved with the China trade, along with an early steamship, a Chinese junk and a modern merchant vessel, all sailing across the Pacific to Chinese seaports.

C20

C21

The Bureau of Engraving and Printing developed two design models of this stamp and sent them to the Post Office Department for approval. An interesting fact comes to light here…the date of approval for model #2, October 29, 1935, was also the same day on which the die was cast for model #2. The Bureau had been working on model #2 before approval was given. How did they know? Obviously, FDR and the Bureau had a close working relationship.

		Un	U	PB #	FDC	
	Issues of 1970, Natural History, May 6					
1387	6¢ American Bald Eagle	.18	.09		2.00	50,448,550
1388	6¢ African Elephant Herd	.18	.09		2.00	50,448,550
1389	6¢ Tlingit Chief in					
	Haida Ceremonial Canoe	.18	.09		2.00	50,448,50
1390	6¢ Brontosaurus, Stegosaurus					
	and Allosaurus from Jurassic					
	Period	.18	.09		2.00	50,448,550
	Block of four, #1387-1390	1.10	.80	2.75	3.00	
1391	6¢ Maine Statehood, July 9	.17	.05	1.10	.75	171,850,000
	Perf. 10½x11					
1392	6¢ Wildlife Conservation, July 20	.17	.05	1.10	.75	142,205,000
	Issues of 1970-74, Perf. 11x10½, 10½x11, 11					
1393	6¢ Dwight D. Eisenhower, 1970	.12	.05	.60	.75	
	Booklet pane of 8	1.50	.50			
	Booklet pane of 5 + label	1.25	.35			
1393D	7¢ Benjamin Franklin, 1972	.18	.05	1.35	.75	
1394	8¢ Eisenhower, 1971	.20	.05	1.00	.75	
1395	8¢ Eisenhower (1393), 1971	.30	.05		.75	
	Booklet pane of 8, 1971	2.00	1.25			
	Booklet pane of 6, 1971	1.60	.75			
	Booklet pane of 4 + 2 labels, -72	1.35	.50			
	Booklet pane of 7 + label, 1972	2.00	1.00			
1396	8¢ U.S. Postal Service, 1971	.20	.05	7.50 (12)	.75	
1397	14¢ Fiorello H. LaGuardia, 1972	.25	.09	2.35	.85	
1398	16¢ Ernie Pyle, 1971	.40	.05	2.35	.75	
1399	18¢ Dr. Elizabeth Blackwell, 1974	.42	.06	1.80	1.25	
1400	21¢ Amadeo P. Giannini, 1973	.45	.20	2.10	1.00	
	Coil Stamps, Perf. 10 Vertically					
1401	6¢ dark blue gray Eisenhower					
	(1393), 1970	.12	.05		.75	
1402	8¢ deep claret Eisenhower					
	(1395), -71	.20	.05		.75	
	Issues of 1970, Perf. 11					
1405	6¢ Edgar Lee Masters, Aug. 22	.17	.05	1.00	.75	137,660,000
1406	6¢ Woman Suffrage, Aug. 26	.17	.05	1.00	.75	135,125,000
1407	6¢ South Carolina, Sept. 12	.17	.05	1.00	.75	135,895,000
1408	6¢ Stone Mountain Mem., Sept. 19	.17	.05	1.00	.75	132,675,000
1409	6¢ Fort Snelling, Oct. 17	.17	.05	1.00	.75	134,795,000

AMERICAN BALD EAGLE AFRICAN ELEPHANT HERD

U.S. 6c U.S. 6c

HAIDA CEREMONIAL CANOE THE AGE OF REPTILES

U.S. 6c U.S. 6c

387
389

1388
1390

MAINE STATEHOOD
1820-1970
U.S. POSTAGE SIX CENTS

1391

WILDLIFE CONSERVATION
UNITED STATES 6c

1392

EISENHOWER·USA
6c

393

U.S. 7c
Spirit of the Declaration of Constitution

1393D

EISENHOWER USA
8c

1394

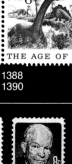

UNITED STATES POSTAL SERVICE
U.S. MAIL
8 cents

1396

LaGuardia 14c
US

1397

Ernie Pyle
Journalist
16c

898

ELIZABETH BLACKWELL FIRST WOMAN PHYSICIAN
US POSTAGE 18c

1399

GIANNINI
AMADEO P.
USA 21c
BANKER

1400

EDGAR LEE MASTERS
AMERICAN POET

UNITED STATES 6c

1405

WOMAN SUFFRAGE
1920-1970
VOTES FOR WOMEN
50TH ANNIVERSARY

1406

SOUTH CAROLINA
1670-1970
6c

Stone Mountain Memorial
UNITED STATES 6 CENTS

GREAT NORTHWEST
1820 FORT SNELLING 1970
US 6c

SAVE OUR SOIL · SAVE OUR CITIES

SAVE OUR WATER · SAVE OUR AIR

1411
1413

Christmas 6us.

1414

Christmas 6us.

1414a

Christmas 6us.
Christmas 6us.
Christmas 6us.
Christmas 6us.

1416
1418

UNITED STATES POSTAGE 6 CENTS
UN
United Nations 25ᵗʰ Anniversary

1419

U.S. POSTAGE 6 CENTS

1420

50 of service · HONORING U.S. SERVICEMEN
PRISONERS OF WAR
MISSING AND KILLED IN ACTION
6¢ STATES · UNITED 6 STATES

1422

UNITED STATES
6
AMERICA'S WOOL

1423

DOUGLAS MacARTHUR
6¢ US

1424

giving BLOOD saves lives
United States Postage
6

1425

ouri 1821-1971 United States

UNITED STATES
TROUT
8¢

UNITED STATES
ALLIGATOR
8¢

		Un	U	PB	#	FDC	Q
	Perf. 11x10½, Anti-Pollution Issue, Oct. 28						
1410	6¢ Save Our Soil	.30	.13			2.00	40,400,000
1411	6¢ Save Our Cities	.30	.13			2.00	40,400,000
1412	6¢ Save Our Water	.30	.13			2.00	40,400,000
1413	6¢ Save Our Air	.30	.13			2.00	40,400,000
	Block of four, #1410-1413	3.00	1.95	7.00		3.00	
	(1410/1412)			7.00 (10)			
	(1411/1413)			7.00 (10)			
	Christmas Issue, Nov. 5, Perf. 10½x11						
1414	6¢ Nativity, by Lorenzo Lotto	.17	.05	3.00		1.40	638,730,000
1414a	Precanceled	.20	.06				358,245,000
	Perf. 11x10½						
1415	6¢ Tin and Cast-Iron Locomotive	.60	.08			1.40	122,313,750
1415a	Precanceled	1.50	.10				109,912,500
1416	6¢ Toy Horse on Wheels	.60	.08			1.40	122,313,750
1416a	Precanceled	1.50	.10				109,912,500
1417	6¢ Mechanical Tricycle	.60	.08			1.40	122,313,750
1417a	Precanceled	1.50	.10				109,912,500
1418	6¢ Doll Carriage	.60	.08			1.40	122,313,750
1418a	Precanceled	1.50	.10			3.00	109,912,500
	Plate Block (1415/1417)			10.00		3.00	
	(1416/1418)			10.00		3.00	
	Perf. 11						
1419	6¢ United Nations, Nov. 20	.17	.05	1.25		.75	127,610,000
1420	6¢ Landing of the Pilgrims, Nov. 21	.17	.05	1.25		.75	129,785,000
	Disabled Veterans and Servicemen Issue, Nov. 24						
1421	6¢ Disabled American Veterans						
	Emblem	.17	.07			.75	67,190,000
1422	6¢ U.S. Servicemen	.17	.07			.75	67,190,000
	Pair (1421/1422)	.75	.35	4.00		1.20	
	Issues of 1971						
1423	6¢ American Wool Industry, Jan. 19	.17	.05	1.00		.75	135,305,000
1424	6¢ Gen. Douglas MacArthur,						
	Jan. 26	.17	.05	1.00		.75	134,840,000
1425	6¢ Blood Donor, Mar. 12	.17	.05	1.00		.75	130,975,000
	Perf. 11x10½						
1426	8¢ Missouri 150th Anniv., May 8	.20	.05	3.50 (12)		.75	161,235,000
	Perf. 11, Wildlife Conservation Issue, June 12						
1427	8¢ Trout	.20	.09			1.75	43,920,000
1428	8¢ Alligator	.20	.09			1.75	43,920,000
1429	8¢ Polar Bear and Cubs	.20	.09			1.75	43,920,000
1430	8¢ California Condor	.20	.09			1.75	43,920,000
	Block of four #1427-1430	.90	.90	2.25		3.00	

	1971 continued	Un	U	PB #	FDC	
1431	8¢ Antarctic Treaty, June 23	.20	.05	1.65	.75	138,700,000
1432	8¢ American Revolution					
	200th Anniversary, July 4	.30	.05	4.00	.75	138,165,000
1433	8¢ John Sloan, Aug. 2	.20	.05	1.65	.75	152,125,000
	Decade of Space Achievements Issue, Aug. 2					
1434	8¢ Earth, Sun, Landing Craft					
	on Moon	.20	.08		.75	88,147,500
1435	8¢ Lunar Rover and Astronauts	.20	.08		.75	88,147,500
	Pair (1434/1435)	.40	.90	1.75	1.75	
1436	8¢ Emily Dickinson, Aug. 28	.20	.05	1.25	.75	142,845,000
1437	8¢ San Juan, Sept 12	.20	.05	1.25	.75	148,755,000
	Perf. 10½x11					
1438	8¢ Prevent Drug Abuse, Oct. 5	.20	.05	1.85 (6)	.75	139,080,000
1439	8¢ CARE, Oct. 27	.20	.05	2.10 (8)	.75	130,755,000
	Perf. 11, Historic Preservation Issue, Oct. 29					
1440	8¢ Decatur House,					
	Washington, D.C.	.22	.09		1.20	42,552,000
1441	8¢ Whaling Ship					
	Charles W. Morgan	.22	.09		1.20	42,552,000
1442	8¢ Cable Car, San Francisco, Calif.	.22	.09		1.20	42,552,000
1443	8¢ San Xavier del Bac Mission, Ariz.	.22	.09		1.20	42,552,000
	Block of four, #1440-1443	.90	1.15	1.85	3.00	
	Perf. 10½x11, Christmas Issue, Nov. 10					
1444	8¢ Adoration of the Shepherds,					
	by Giorgione	.20	.05	2.50 (12)	.75	1,074,350,000
1445	8¢ Partridge in a Pear Tree,					
	by Jamie Wyeth	.20	.05	2.50 (12)	.75	979,540,000
	Issues of 1972, Perf. 11					
1446	8¢ Sidney Lanier, Feb. 3	.20	.05	1.00	.75	137,355,000
	Perf. 10½x11					
1447	8¢ Peace Corps. Feb. 11	.20	.05	1.50	.75	150,400,000

The Matter of Peculiar Mail

Americans have been known to send just about anything through the mails, including pet snakes and papier-mache clocks. Back in 1889, "McCleans Stamp Collector's Guide" discussed how the U.S. government simply could not properly educate the populace as to the proper use of their mail service. Some of the curious parcels passing through the post at that time included unboxed glassware, hewn lumber, fireproof safes, poodles and even packages of nitro-glycerin, which, according to the "Guide," "can make great confusion when they are stamped."

1971-1972

1431

AMERICAN
REVOLUTION
BICENTENNIAL
1776-1976

1432

1433

1434   1435

1436   1437

1438   1439

1440   1441
1442   1443

1444

1445

1446

1447

1452

1448 1449
1450 1451

1453

1454

1455

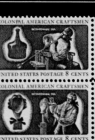

1456 1457
1458 1459

1460

1461

1462

1463

1464 1465
1466 1467

	1972 continued	Un	U	PB #	FDC	Q
	National Parks 100th Anniversary Issue, Perf. 11					
1448	2¢ Hulk of Ship, Apr. 5	.05	.05		1.25	172,730,000
1449	2¢ Cape Hatteras Lighthouse,					
	Apr. 5	.05	.05		1.25	172,730,000
1450	2¢ Laughing Gulls on Driftwood,					
	Apr. 5	.05	.05		1.25	172,730,000
1451	2¢ Laughing Gulls and Dune,					
	Apr. 5	.05	.05		1.25	172,730,000
	Block of four, (1448-1451)	.20	.30	1.60	1.25	
1452	6¢ Wolf Trap Farm, June 26	.17	.09	1.25	.75	104,090,000
1453	8¢ Yellowstone, Mar. 1	.20	.05	1.00	.75	164,096,000
1454	15¢ Mt. McKinley, July 28	.35	.30	2.50	.75	53,920,000

Note: Beginning with this issue, the U.S.P.S. began to offer stamp collectors first day cancellations affixed to 8x10½ inch souvenir pages. The pages are similar to the stamp announcements that have appeared on post office bulletin boards since Scott No. 1132.

		Un	U	PB #	FDC	Q
1455	8¢ Family Planning, Mar. 18	.20	.05	1.00	.75	153,025,000
	Perf. 11x10½, American Revolution Bicentennial Issue, Jul. 4,					
	Craftsmen in Colonial America					
1456	8¢ Glassmaker	.22	.08		1.00	50,472,500
1457	8¢ Silversmith	.22	.08		1.00	50,472,500
1458	8¢ Wigmaker	.22	.08		1.00	50,472,500
1459	8¢ Hatter	.22	.08		1.00	50,472,500
	Block of four, #1456-1459	1.00	1.10	2.25	2.50	
	Olympic Games Issue, Aug. 17					
1460	6¢ Bicycling and Olympic Rings	.17	.16	2.00 (10)	.75	67,335,000
1461	8¢ Bobsledding	.20	.05	2.25 (10)	.85	179,675,000
1462	15¢ Running	.40	.40	4.00 (10)	1.00	46,340,000
1463	8¢ P.T.A. 75th Anniv., Sept. 15	.20	.05	1.00	.75	180,155,000
	Perf. 11, Wildlife Conservation Issue, Sep. 20					
1464	8¢ Fur Seals	.20	.07		2.00	49,591,200
1465	8¢ Cardinal	.20	.07		2.00	49,591,200
1466	8¢ Brown Pelican	.20	.07		2.00	49,591,200
1467	8¢ Bighorn Sheep	.20	.07		2.00	49,591,200
	Block of 4, #1464-1467	.90	1.00	1.40	3.00	

Note: With this issue the U.S.P.S. introduced the "American Commemorative Series" Stamp Panels. Each panel contains a block of four mint stamps, mounted with text, and background illustrations.

	1972 continued	Un	U	PB #	FDC	
	Perf. 11x10½					
1468	8¢ Mail Order 100th Anniv.,					
	Sept. 27	.20	.05	2.75 (12)	.75	185,490,000
	Perf. 10½x11					
1469	8¢ Osteopathic Medicine, Oct. 9	.20	.05	1.35 (6)	.75	162,335,000
	Perf. 11					
1470	8¢ American Folklore Issue,					
	Oct. 13	.20	.05	1.00	.75	162,789,950
	Perf. 10½x11, Christmas Issue, Nov. 9					
1471	8¢ Angel form "Mary,					
	Queen of Heaven"	.20	.05	2.75 (12)	.75	1,003,475,000
1472	8¢ Santa Claus	.20	.05	2.75 (12)	.75	1,017,025,000
	Perf. 11					
1473	8¢ Pharmacy, Nov. 11	.20	.05	1.00	.75	165,895,000
1474	8¢ Stamp Collecting, Nov. 17	.20	.05	1.00	.75	166,508,000
	Issues of 1973, Perf. 11x10½					
1475	8¢ Love, Jan. 26	.20	.05	1.35 (6)	.75	330,055,000
	This "special stamp for someone special" depicts "Love" by contemporary artist Robert Indiana.					
	Perf. 11					
	American Revolution Bicentennial Issues, Communications in Colonial America					
1476	8¢ Printer and Patriots Examining					
	Pamphlet, Feb. 16	.20	.05	1.35	.75	166,005,000
1477	8¢ Posting a Broadside, Apr. 13	.20	.05	1.35	.75	163,050,000
1478	8¢ Postrider, June 22	.20	.05	1.35	.75	159,005,000
1479	8¢ Drummer, Sept. 28	.20	.05	1.35	.75	147,295,000
	Boston Tea Party, July 4					
1480	8¢ British Merchantman	.20	.09		1.75	49,068,750
1481	8¢ British Three-master	.20	.09		1.75	49,068,750
1482	8¢ Boats and Ship's Hull	.20	.09		1.75	49,068,750
1483	8¢ Boat and Dock	.20	.09		1.75	49,068,750
	Block of four, #1480-1483	.80	.90	1.35	3.75	
	American Arts Issue					
1484	8¢ George Gershwin, Feb. 28	.20	.05	2.75 (12)	.75	139,152,000

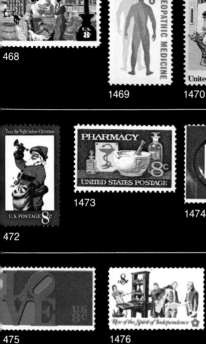

468

1469

1470

1471

472

1473

1474

475

1476

1477

478

1479

1484

1486

1487

8CUS

1488

U.S. POSTAL SERVICE 8¢ • U.S. POSTAL SERVICE 8¢ • U.S. POSTAL SERVICE 8¢ • U.S. POSTAL SERVICE 8¢

Mail is
picked up
from nearly
a third of a million
local collection
boxes, as well
as your mailbox.

More than
87 billion letters
and packages
are handled
yearly—almost
300 million every
delivery day.

The People
in your
Postal Service
handle and
deliver more
than 500 million
packages yearly.

Thousands of
machines, buildings,
and vehicles
must be operated
and maintained
to keep your
mail moving.

People Serving You

People Serving You

People Serving You

People Serving You

90

1491

1492

1493

U.S. POSTAL SERVICE 8¢ • U.S. POSTAL SERVICE 8¢ • U.S. POSTAL SERVICE 8¢ • U.S. POSTAL SERVICE 8¢

Employees
use modern, high-
speed equipment
to sort and process
huge volumes of
mail in central
locations.

Thirteen billion
pounds of mail are
handled yearly by
postal employees
as they speed
your letters and
packages.

Our customers
include
54 million urban
and 12 million
rural families,
plus 9 million
businesses.

Employees
cover
4 million miles
each delivery day
to bring mail to
your home or
business.

People Serving You

People Serving You

People Serving You

People Serving You

	1973 continued	Un	U	PB #	FDC	Q
1485	8¢ Robinson Jeffers, Aug. 13	.20	.05	2.75 (12)	.75	128,048,000
1486	8¢ Henry Ossawa Tanner, Sept. 10	.20	.05	2.75 (12)	.75	146,008,000
1487	8¢ Willa Cather, Sept. 20	.20	.05	2.75 (12)	.75	139,608,000
1488	8¢ Nicolaus Copernicus, Apr. 23	.20	.05	.80	.75	159,475,000
	Perf. 10½x11, Postal Service Employees Issue, Apr. 30					
1489	8¢ Stamp Counter	.20	.09		1.10	48,602,000
1490	8¢ Mail Collection	.20	.09		1.10	48,602,000
1491	8¢ Letter Facing Conveyor	.20	.09		1.10	48,602,000
1492	8¢ Parcel Post Sorting	.20	.09		1.10	48,602,000
1493	8¢ Mail Cancelling	.20	.09		1.10	48,602,000
1494	8¢ Manual Letter Routing	.20	.09		1.10	48,602,000
1495	8¢ Electronic Letter Routing	.20	.09		1.10	48,602,000
1496	8¢ Loading Mail on Truck	.20	.09		1.10	48,602,000
1497	8¢ Mailman	.20	.09		1.10	48,602,000
1498	8¢ Rural Mail Delivery	.20	.09		1.10	48,602,000
	Strip of ten, #1489-1498	2.00	2.00		6.00	
	Plate Block of 10			4.50		

"Hardships of Emigration"

The Trans-Mississippi, or "Omaha," Exposition Issue of June 17, 1898, (#285-293) is one of the most popular and interesting issues of U.S. stamps. It was a series of nine pictorial stamps displaying life west of the Mississippi. The fate of one of the paintings, "Hardships of Emigration" by A. G. Heaton (#290), has made the 10¢ stamp bearing the same name all the more distinguished.

290

Heaton painted "Hardships of Emigration" in Oklahoma around 1892. It shows travellers in a covered wagon on the plains, examining one of their two horses. The animal is lying on the ground, either dead or exhausted; and one can only wonder how the family could move any farther with just one horse pulling their possessions.

It appears that the painting itself fell on hard times. It was reported after Heaton's death that a number of his canvases that were stored in a garage were found to be badly damaged by water and vandals—"Hardships of Emigration" among them. The works had to be destroyed. Since there was never a photograph made of the painting, the 10¢ stamp is the only remaining reproduction of this powerful picture.

	1973 continued	Un	U	PB #	FDC	
	Perf. 11					
1499	8¢ Harry S. Truman, May 8	.20	.05	1.00	.75	157,052,800
	Electronics Progress Issue, July 10					
1500	6¢ Marconi's Spark Coil and Gap	.17	.14	1.25	.75	53,005,000
1501	8¢ Transistor and					
	Printed Circuit Board	.20	.05	1.00	.75	159,775,000
1502	15¢ Microphone, Speaker,					
	Vacuum Tube, TV Camera	.35	.35	2.25	.80	39,005,000
1503	8¢ Lyndon B. Johnson, Aug. 27	.20	.05	2.50 (12)	.75	152,624,000
	Issues of 1973-74, Rural America Issue					
1504	8¢ Angus and Longhorn Cattle,					
	by F.C. Murphy, Oct. 5, 1973	.20	.05	1.00	.75	145,840,000
1505	10¢ Chautauqua centenary,					
	Aug. 6, 1974	.23	.05	1.00	.75	151,335,000
1506	10¢ Kansas hard winter wheat					
	centenary, Aug. 16, 1974	.23	.05	1.00	.75	141,085,000
	Perf. 10½x11, Christmas Issue, Nov. 7, 1973					
1507	8¢ Madonna and Child by Raphael	.20	.05	2.10 (12)	.75	885,160,000
1508	8¢ Christmas Tree in Needlepoint	.20	.05	2.10 (12)	.75	939,835,000
	Issue of 1973-74, Perf. 11x10½					
1509	10¢ 50-Star and 13-Star Flags, 1973	.23	.05	4.50 (20)	.75	
1510	10¢ Jefferson Memorial					
	and Signature, 1973	.23	.05	1.00	.75	
1510b	Booklet pane of 5 + label, 1973	1.50	.30			
1510c	Booklet pane of 8, 1973	2.00	.30			
1510d	Booklet pane of 6, 1974	3.50	.30			
1511	10¢ Mail Transport; "ZIP", 1974	.23	.05	1.80 (8)	.75	
	Coil Stamps, Perf. 10 Vertically					
1518	6.3¢ Bells, Oct. 1, 1974	.15	.15		.75	
1519	10¢ red & blue Flags (1509), 1973	.28	.05		.75	
1520	10¢ blue Jefferson Memorial					
	(1510),-73	.25	.05		.75	

The National Philatelic Collection

In 1979 the philatelic holdings of the Smithsonian Institution were upgraded to the status of a national collection. It is now known as the National Philatelic Collection and includes, besides foreign holdings, the United States National Postage Collection. Well over 14 million objects are maintained in this collection, with a fine representative sample of stamps, covers and postal history objects on display in the Hall of Stamps housed on the third floor of the National Museum of History and Technology building.

One of the largest philatelic libraries in the world is part of the National Collection, including a photographic file of over 6,000 prints relating to philatelic and postal history subjects covering virtually every country in the world.

1499

1500

1501

1502

1503

1504

1505

1506

1507

1508

1509

1510

1511

1518

1519

1520

1974

1525

1526

1527

1528

1529

1530   1531   1532   1533
1534   1535   1536   1537

	Issues of 1974, Perf. 11	Un	U	PB	#	FDC	Q
1525	10¢ V.F.W. Emblem, Mar. 11	.22	.05	1.25		.75	143,930,000
	Perf. 10½x11						
1526	10¢ Robert Frost, Mar. 26	.22	.05	1.00		.75	145,235,000
	Perf. 11						
1527	10¢ Cosmic Jumper and Smiling						
	Sage, by Peter Max, Apr. 18	.22	.05	2.60		.75	135,052,000
	Perf. 11x10½						
1528	10¢ Horses Rounding Turn, May 4	.22	.05	2.60		.75	156,750,000
	Perf. 11						
1529	10¢ Skylab II, May 14	.22	.05	1.00		1.25	164,670,000
	Centenary of UPU Issue, June 6						
1530	10¢ Michelangelo, by Raphael	.22	.20			1.10	23,769,600
1531	10¢ "Five Feminine Virtues,"						
	by Hokusai	.22	.20			1.10	23,769,600
1532	10¢ Old Scraps,						
	by John Frederick Peto	.22	.20			1.10	23,769,600
1533	10¢ The Lovely Reader,						
	by Jean Liotard	.22	.20			1.10	23,769,600
1534	10¢ Lady Writing Letter, by Terborch	.22	.20			1.10	23,769,600
1535	10¢ Inkwell and Quill,						
	by Jean Chardin	.22	.20			1.10	23,769,600
1536	10¢ Mrs. John Douglas,						
	by Thomas Gainsborough	.22	.20			1.10	23,769,600
1537	10¢ Don Antonio Noriega, by Goya	.22	.20			1.10	23,769,600
	Block or strip of 8, #1530-37	1.65	1.50			4.25	
	Plate Block of 16			2.60			

Free Franking

Not everybody has to lick stamps in order to get a letter through the United States Postal Service. Some people have the privilege of merely signing their name and neither licking nor paying. The "free frank" is a privilege that began in England in 1652. In free franking, the signature of an official on a cover serves in lieu of postage. The tradition of free frank was carried across the Atlantic and legislative franks with written signatures are a common part of the congressional scene. Today's franks are almost all printed facsimile signatures reproduced by handstamps or mechanical devices, but earlier congressmen nearly all signed their names by hand. In fact, the signatures of all the members of Congress prior to 1873 are theoretically possible to obtain. This makes franked covers attractive to autograph and manuscript collectors, as well as to those interested in postal history and frank collecting.

Franks exist for some of the great names in American history: Clay, Webster, Calhoun, James Madison, William H. Seward, Jefferson Davis. Although the most readily available of these men's franks are from their congressional years, franks from other posts can be found as well.

	1974 continued	Un	U	PB #	FDC	
	Mineral Heritage Issue, June 13					
1538	10¢ Petrified Wood	.23	.09		1.50	41,803,200
1539	10¢ Tourmaline	.23	.09		1.50	41,803,200
1540	10¢ Amethyst	.23	.09		1.50	41,803,200
1541	10¢ Rhodochrosite	.23	.09		1.50	41,803,200
	Block of 4, #1538-1541	.90	.90	1.25	3.00	
1542	10¢ Fort Harrod, June 15	.22	.05	1.00	.75	156,265,000
	American Revolution Bicentennial, First Continental Congress, July 4					
1543	10¢ Carpenter's Hall	.23	.07		1.10	48,896,250
1544	10¢ "We ask but for Peace,					
	Liberty and Safety"	.23	.07		1.10	48,896,250
1545	10¢ "Deriving their Just Powers"	.23	.07		1.10	48,896,250
1546	10¢ Independence Hall	.23	.07	1.20	1.10	48,896,250
	Block of four, #1543-1546	.90	.90	1.20	3.00	
1547	10¢ Molecules and Drops of					
	Gasoline and Oil, Sept. 22	.22	.05	1.00	.75	148,850,000
1548	10¢ The Headless Horsemen,					
	Oct. 10	.22	.05	1.00	.75	157,270,000
1549	10¢ Little Girl, Oct. 12	.22	.05	1.00	.75	150,245,000
	Christmas Issues, 1974					
1550	10¢ Angel, Oct. 23	.22	.05	2.20 (10)	.75	835,180,000
1551	10¢ Sleigh Ride, by Currier and					
	Ives, Oct. 23	.22	.05	2.60 (12)	.75	882,520,000
1552	10¢ Weather Vane; precanceled,					
	Nov. 15, Imperf. Self-adhesive	.23	.06	5.50 (20)	.75	213,155,000

The Birth of the "Chicken" Stamp

Before the present Citizen's Stamp Advisory Committee was formed, the decision to issue a certain kind of stamp was left up to the Postmaster General. In certain circumstances, however, another route could be taken.

In 1939, the poultry industry clamored for a stamp to commemorate that year's Poultry Congress in Cleveland. Despite pleas from 75 senators and congressmen, the Postmaster General absolutely refused such an issue.

In 1947, the poultry lobby began the battle anew and appealed directly to Congress to honor the hundredth anniversary of the first American poultry show held in Boston in 1849. Resolutions were introduced and passed in both houses directing the Postmaster General to issue a series of stamps commemorating the poultry industry.

Although poultry enthusiasts were united in wanting a stamp, no agreement was reached on any aspect of the stamp. The choice of breed especially elicited complaint. The Light Brahma Cock depicted on the stamp was derided both as Asiatic rather than American and as a poor example of the breed. However, #968 became popular...and popularly known as the "Chicken Stamp."

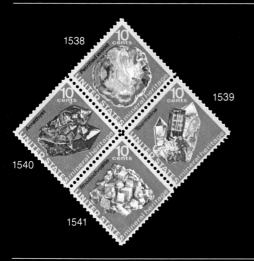

1538

1539

1540

1541

1542

1543
1545

1544
1546

1547

1548

1549

1550

1551

1552

Benjamin West

American artist
10 cents U.S. postage

1553

Paul Laurence **Dunbar**

American poet

10 cents U.S. postage

1554

MOVIEMAKER US 10 c
DW GRIFFITH

1555

PIONEER ★ JUPITER
US 10c

1556

MARINER 10 ★ VENUS/MERCURY
US 10c

1557

UNITED STATES
collective bargaining
out of conflict...accord
10c

1558

Contributors To The Cause U.S. 8c
Sybil Ludington ★ *Youthful Heroine*

1559

YOUTHFUL HEROINE
On the dark night of April 26, 1777,
16-year-old Sybil Ludington rode
her horse "Star" alone through the
Connecticut countryside rallying
her father's militia to repel a
raid by the British on Danbury.

1559

Contributors To The Cause U.S. 10c
Salem Poor ★ *Gallant Soldier*

GALLANT SOLDIER
The conspicuously courageous
actions of black foot soldier
Salem Poor at the Battle of
Bunker Hill on June 17, 1775,
earned him citations for his
bravery and leadership ability.

1560

Contributors To The Cause U.S. 10c
Haym Salomon ★ *Financial Hero*

FINANCIAL HERO
Businessman and broker Haym
Salomon was responsible for
raising most of the money
needed to finance the American
Revolution and later to save
the new nation from collapse.

1561

Contributors To The Cause U.S. 18c
Peter Francisco ★ *Fighter Extraordinary*

FIGHTER EXTRAORDINARY
Peter Francisco's strength
and bravery made him a
legend around campfires.
He fought with distinction
at Brandywine, Yorktown
and Guilford Court House.

1562

Lexington & Concord 1775 by Sandham
US Bicentennial 10cents

1563

Bunker Hill 1775 by Trumbull
US Bicentennial 10c

1564

	Un	U	PB #	FDC	Q
Issues of 1975					
American Art Issue, Perf. 10½x11, 11					
1553 10¢ Benjamin West, Self-portrait,					
Feb. 10	.22	.05	2.20 (10)	.75	156,995,000
1554 10¢ Paul Laurence Dunbar, May 1	.22	.05	2.20 (10)	.75	146,365,000
1555 10¢ D. W. Griffith, May 27	.22	.05	1.00	.75	148,805,000
Space Issue, Perf. 11					
1556 10¢ Pioneer 10, Feb. 28	.22	.05	1.00	1.10	173,685,000
1557 10¢ Mariner 10, Apr. 4	.22	.05	1.00	1.10	158,600,000
1558 10¢ "Labor and Management",					
Mar. 13	.22	.05	1.80 (8)	.75	153,355,000
American Bicentennial Issues, Contributors to the Cause, Mar. 25, Perf. 11x10½					
1559 8¢ Sybil Ludington	.20	.15	1.75 (10)	.75	63,205,000
1560 10¢ Salem Poor	.22	.05	2.20 (10)	.75	157,865,000
1561 10¢ Haym Salomon	.22	.05	2.20 (10)	.75	166,810,000
1562 18¢ Peter Francisco	.45	.45	4.00 (10)	.75	44,825,000
Perf. 11					
1563 10¢ "Birth of Liberty",					
by Henry Sandham, April 19	.22	.05	2.60 (12)	.75	144,028,000
Perf. 11x10½					
1564 10¢ Battle of Bunker Hill,					
by John Trumbull, June 17	.22	.05	2.60 (12)	.75	139,928,000

Cancelled-To-Order Stamps

Have you come across stamps that are fully gummed on back but still have a cancellation mark in the corner as if they were used? You may have what is known as a CTO (cancelled-to-order) stamp.

Some governments actually print simulated postmarks on sets of new issues to prevent their postal use. These cancelled sets are produced solely for sale at discount prices and are intended primarily as inexpensive and inoffensive stamps for beginners and collectors with limited budgets. Although CTOs are in what looks like "mint" condition, they are worth much less than actual mint stamps that were originally intended for postal use. Genuinely used copies of the same issue are also usually worth more than CTOs.

Despite the fact that CTOs may have no real philatelic or postal historical value, the collector should be aware that their condition is often excellent and some issues are easily obtainable only as CTOs.

	1975 continued	Un	U	PB	#	FDC	Q
	Military Uniforms, July 4, Perf. 11						
1565	10¢ Soldier with Flintlock Musket,						
	Uniform Button	.24	.07			.90	44,963,750
1566	10¢ Sailor with Grappling Hook,						
	First Navy Jack, 1775	.24	.07			.90	44,963,750
1567	10¢ Marine with Musket,						
	Full-rigged Ship	.24	.07			.90	44,963,750
1568	10¢ Militiaman with Musket,						
	Powder Horn	.24	.07			.90	44,963,750
	Block of 4, #1565-1568	.95	1.10			2.40	
	Plate Block of 12			2.60			
	Apollo-Soyuz Space Issue, July 15, Perf. 11x10½						
1569	10¢ Apollo and Soyuz after						
	Docking, and Earth	.23	.11			1.00	80,931,600
1570	10¢ Spacecraft before Docking,						
	Earth and Project Emblem	.23	.11			1.00	80,931,600
	Pair, #1569-1570	.45	.55				
	Plate Block of 12			2.60			
1571	10¢ Worldwide Equality for Women,						
	Aug. 26	.22	.05	1.40		.75	145,640,000
	Postal Service Bicentennial Issue, Sep. 3						
1572	10¢ Stagecoach and Trailer Truck	.24	.08			.75	42,163,750
1573	10¢ Old and New Locomotives	.24	.08			.75	42,163,750
1574	10¢ Early Mail Plane and Jet	.24	.08			.75	42,163,750
1575	10¢ Satellite for Transmission						
	of Mailgrams	.24	.08			.75	42,163,750
	Block of 4, #1572-1575	.95	1.10				
	Plate Block of 12			2.60			
	Perf. 11						
1576	10¢ World Peace, Sept. 29	.20	.05	1.00		.75	146,615,000
	Banking and Commerce Issue, Oct. 6						
1577	10¢ Engine Turning, Indian Head						
	Penny and Morgan Silver Dollar	.23	.06			.75	73,098,000
1578	10¢ Seated Liberty, Quarter,						
	$20 Gold (Double Eagle),						
	Engine Turning	.23	.06			.75	73,098,000
	Pair, #1577-1578	.45	.50	1.00		1.00	

1569
1570

1565   1566
1567   1568

1571

1572   1573
1574   1575

1576

1577   1578

1582b

1579

1580

1581
1584

1582
1585

1591
1593

1592
1594

1596
1598

1618
1599

1595d

1603
1605

1604
1606

1608
1611

1610
1612

	1975 continued	Un	U	PB #	FDC	Q
	Christmas Issue, Oct. 14, Perf. 11					
1579	(10¢) Madonna by					
	Domenico Ghirlandaio	.22	.05	2.60 (12)	.75	739,430,000
1580	(10¢) Christmas Card,					
	by Louis Prang, 1878	.22	.05	2.60 (12)	.75	878,690,000
	Issues of 1975-79, Americana, Perf. 11x10½					
1581	1¢ Inkwell & Quill, 1977	.05	.05	.15	.40	
1582	2¢ Speaker's Stand, 1977	.05	.05	.20	.40	
1584	3¢ Early Ballot Box, 1977	.06	.05	.30	.40	
1585	4¢ Books, Bookmark, Eyeglasses,	.07	.05	.40	.40	
	Size: 17½x20½mm., 1977					
1590	9¢ Capitol Dome (1591), 1977	.80	.30		1.00	
1590a	Perf. 10	25.00	10.00			
	Size: 18½x22½mm.					
1591	9¢ Capitol Dome, 1975	.16	.05	.90	.60	
1592	10¢ Contemplation of Justice, 1977	.17	.05	1.00	.60	
1593	11¢ Printing Press, 1975	.24	.05	1.10	.60	
1594	12¢ Torch	.20	.05	1.15	.60	
1595	13¢ Liberty Bell, 1975	.35	.05		.60	
1595a	Booklet pane of 6	2.25	.50			
1595b	Booklet pane of 7 + label	2.50	.50			
1595c	Booklet pane of 8	2.75	.50			
1595d	Booklet pane of 5 + label, 1976	2.15	.50			
1596	13¢ Eagle and Shield, 1975	.30	.05	3.50	.60	
	Perf. 11					
1597	15¢ Fort McHenry Flag, 1978	.33	.05	2.10	.65	
	Perf. 11x10½					
1598	15¢ Fort McHenry Flag (1597), 1978	.40	.06			
1598a	Booklet pane of 8	3.00	.60			
1599	16¢ Head of Liberty, 1978	.35	.10	1.60	.65	
1603	24¢ Old North Church, 1975	.55	.05	2.40	.75	
1604	28¢ Fort Nisqually, 1978	.65	.05	2.80	1.10	
1605	29¢ Sandy Hook Lighthouse, 1978	.65	.12	2.90	1.10	
1606	30¢ One-room Schoolhouse	.50	.07	3.00	1.10	
	No. 1590 is on white paper. No. 1591 on gray paper. Nos. 1590 and 1590a, 1595, 1598 issued only in booklets. Additional American Series, see No. 1813.					
1608	50¢ Whale Oil Lamp	.85	.06	5.00	1.25	
1610	$1 Candle and Rushlight Holder	1.65	.08	10.00	3.00	
1611	$2 Kerosene Table Lamp	3.35	.40	20.00	5.75	
1612	$5 Railroad Lantern	8.50	3.00	50.00	15.00	

	1975-1979 continued	Un	U	PB #	FDC	
	Coil Stamps, Perf. 10 Vertically					
1613	3.1¢ Guitar	.10	.08		.40	
1614	7.7¢ Saxhorns, 1976	.25	.10		.60	
1615	7.9¢ Drum, 1976	.18	.10		.60	
1615C	8.4¢ Piano, 1978	.20	.09		.60	
1616	9¢ Capitol Dome (1591), 1976	.22	.07		.60	
1617	10¢ Contemplation of Justice					
	(1592), 1977	.20	.06		.60	
1618	13¢ Liberty Bell (1595), 1975	.25	.05		.65	
1618C	15¢ Fort McHenry Flag (1597),					
	1978	.33	.05		.65	
1619	16¢ Head of Liberty (1599), 1978	.35	.12		.60	
	Perf. 11x10½					
1622	13¢ Flag over Independence					
	Hall, 1975	.25	.05	5.50 (20)	.65	
1623	13¢ Flag over Capitol, 1977	.35	.06		1.00	
1623a	Booklet pane of 8	2.75	.60			
1623b	Perf. 10	.80	.50			
1623c	Booklet pane of 8, Perf. 10	31.50	—			
	Nos. 1623, 1623b issued only in booklets					
	Coil Stamp. Perf. 10 Vertically					
1625	13¢ Flag over Independence Hall					
	(1622), 1975	.35	.05		.65	
	Issues of 1976					
1629	13¢ Drummer Boy	.30	.07		.65	
1630	13¢ Old Drummer	.30	.07		.65	
1631	13¢ Fifer	.30	.07		.65	
	Plate Block of 12			3.40 (12)		
	Strip of 3 (1629/1631)	.90	.90			218,585,000
1632	13¢ Interphil	.30	.05		.65	157,825,000
	American Bicentennial, State Flags Issue, Feb. 23, 1976					
1633	13¢ Delaware	.55	.45		1.75	8,720,100
1634	13¢ Pennsylvania	.55	.45		1.75	8,720,100
1635	13¢ New Jersey	.55	.45		1.75	8,720,100
1636	13¢ Georgia	.55	.45		1.75	8,720,100
1637	13¢ Connecticut	.55	.45		1.75	8,720,100
1638	13¢ Massachusetts	.55	.45		1.75	8,720,100

1613

1614

1615

1615c

1616

1622

1623a

1629   1630   1631

1632

1633

1634

1635

1636

1637

1638

1639

1640

1641

1642

1643

1644

1645

1646

1647

1648

1649

1650

1651

1652

1653

1654

1655

1656

	1976 continued	Un	U	PB	#	FDC	Q
1639	13¢ Maryland	.55	.45			1.75	8,720,100
1640	13¢ South Carolina	.55	.45			1.75	8,720,100
1641	13¢ New Hampshire	.55	.45			1.75	8,720,100
1642	13¢ Virginia	.55	.45			1.75	8,720,100
1643	13¢ New York	.55	.45			1.75	8,720,100
1644	13¢ North Carolina	.55	.45			1.75	8,720,100
1645	13¢ Rhode Island	.55	.45			1.75	8,720,100
1646	13¢ Vermont	.55	.45			1.75	8,720,100
1647	13¢ Kentucky	.55	.45			1.75	8,720,100
1648	13¢ Tennessee	.55	.45			1.75	8,720,100
1649	13¢ Ohio	.55	.45			1.75	8,720,100
1650	13¢ Louisiana	.55	.45			1.75	8,720,100
1651	13¢ Indiana	.55	.45			1.75	8,720,100
1652	13¢ Mississippi	.55	.45			1.75	8,720,100
1653	13¢ Illinois	.55	.45			1.75	8,720,100
1654	13¢ Alabama	.55	.45			1.75	8,720,100
1655	13¢ Maine	.55	.45			1.75	8,720,100
1656	13¢ Missouri	.55	.45			1.75	8,720,100

Multiple-Stamp Sheets

May 9, 1936, was opening day for the Third International Philatelic Exposition in New York City. At a temporary post office in Grand Central Palace, the first sheets of U.S. postage stamps to contain more than one variety of stamp were placed on sale. This multiple-stamp souvenir sheet consisted of four purple, ungummed, unperforated 3¢ stamps: one of the California-Pacific International Exposition (#773), one Texas Centennial Issue of 1936 (#776), one Connecticut Tercentenary issue of 1935 (#772) and one Michigan Centenary issue of 1935 (#775).

Subsequently, souvenir stamp sheets were issued in 1947 for the centennial of U.S. philately (#948) and in 1956 for the Sixth International Philatelic Exposition in Washington, D.C. (#1075).

However, issuance of multiple stamp sheets, whether a souvenir sheet, a commemorative or other special issue, didn't really take hold until November 9, 1964, when four different 5¢ Christmas stamps portraying holly, mistletoe, poinsettia and a sprig of conifer were issued in panes of 100, each containing 25 blocks of the four different se-tenant stamps (#1254-1257). This issue seems to have brought multiple issues into vogue. Some other notables include the Centenary of the UPU (#1530-1537), the Bicentennial Series of the 50 state flags in 1976 (#1633-1682), the 50 state Birds and Flowers Series in 1982 (#1953-2002) and the Space Achievement Series in 1981 (#1912-1919), which featured one scene broken into eight se-tenant stamps in two sizes.

	1976 continued	Un	U	PB	#	FDC	
1657	13¢ Arkansas	.55	.45			1.75	8,720,100
1658	13¢ Michigan	.55	.45			1.75	8,720,100
1659	13¢ Florida	.55	.45			1.75	8,720,100
1660	13¢ Texas	.55	.45			1.75	8,720,100
1661	13¢ Iowa	.55	.45			1.75	8,720,100
1662	13¢ Wisconsin	.55	.45			1.75	8,720,100
1663	13¢ California	.55	.45			1.75	8,720,100
1664	13¢ Minnesota	.55	.45			1.75	8,720,100
1665	13¢ Oregon	.55	.45			1.75	8,720,100
1666	13¢ Kansas	.55	.45			1.75	8,720,100
1667	13¢ West Virginia	.55	.45			1.75	8,720,100
1668	13¢ Nevada	.55	.45			1.75	8,720,100
1669	13¢ Nebraska	.55	.45			1.75	8,720,100
1670	13¢ Colorado	.55	.45			1.75	8,720,100
1671	13¢ North Dakota	.55	.45			1.75	8,720,100
1672	13¢ South Dakota	.55	.45			1.75	8,720,100
1673	13¢ Montana	.55	.45			1.75	8,720,100
1674	13¢ Washington	.55	.45			1.75	8,720,100

So You Want to Be a Living Legend…

According to the standards of stamp selection, it is not possible to honor a living person by issuing a stamp that carries his or her likeness until 10 years after death (except Presidents). But there is a circuitous route to living philatelic recognition if you're dead-set on it. You only need to do something like invent the light bulb, be the first to fly across the Atlantic alone or take the first step on the moon. These are the only instances in which the achievements of living people have been honored on U.S. stamps. But take heed, you'll never see your face on U.S. postage.

C10

The Lindbergh 10¢ air mail stamp of 1927 (#C10) shows an accurate reproduction of the "Spirit of St. Louis" in flight with Lindy's Atlantic route in the background. Also appearing on the stamp is Lindbergh's name, but not his face.

654

Edison's light bulb was honored on its 50th anniversary in 1929. This stamp (#654) carried a picture of Edison's electric lamp with Edison's name above it, but Edison's face was nowhere to be seen.

C76

Neil Armstrong of NASA came the closest of the three. The 1969 10¢ air mail stamp (#C76) carries a rendering of that famous first step, and the man in the space suit unquestionably is Armstrong. But is his face visible? Of course not. After all, the law is the law.

1657

1658

1659

1660

1661

1662

1663

1664

1665

1666

1667

1668

1669

1670

1671

1672

1673

1674

1675

1676

1677

1678

1679

1680

1681

1682

1683

1684

1685

The Surrender of Lord Cornwallis at Yorktown
From a Painting by John Trumbull

1686

	1976 continued	Un	U	PB #	FDC	Q
1675	13¢ Idaho	.55	.45		1.75	8,720,100
1676	13¢ Wyoming	.55	.45		1.75	8,720,100
1677	13¢ Utah	.55	.45		1.75	8,720,100
1678	13¢ Oklahoma	.55	.45		1.75	8,720,100
1679	13¢ New Mexico	.55	.45		1.75	8,720,100
1680	13¢ Arizona	.55	.45		1.75	8,720,100
1681	13¢ Alaska	.55	.45		1.75	8,720,100
1682	13¢ Hawaii	.55	.45		1.75	8,720,100
	Pane of 50, #1633-1682	—	21.75		32.50	
1683	13¢ Bell's Telephone Patent					
	Application, Mar. 10	.30	.05	1.30	.65	159,915,000
1684	13¢ Ford-Pullman Monoplane					
	and Laird Swallow Biplane, Mar. 19	.30	.05	2.90	.65	156,960,000
1685	13¢ Various Flasks, Separatory					
	Funnel, Computer Tape, Apr. 6	.30	.05	3.40	.65	158,470,00
American Bicentennial Issues, Souvenir Sheets, May 29						
	Sheets of 5 Stamps Each					
1686	13¢ Surrender of Cornwallis at					
	Yorktown, by John Trumbull	4.75	4.75		6.00	1,990,000

Blockbusters

U.S. philately took a design leap in 1967 when one design was spread over two stamps. The Space Achievement issue (#1331-1332) pictured a space walking astronaut attached by his "umbilical cord" to a Gemini space capsule in Earth orbit.

This technique was soon expanded to include blocks of four stamps on the Cape Hatteras landscape for the National Parks 100th anniversary issue of 1972 (#1448-51). In 1981, another Space Achievement issue (#1912-1919) came out which featured one design over a block of eight stamps. But the most inventive blockbuster style is found on the American Bicentennial Souvenir Sheets (#1686, 1687, 1688, 1689). These five-stamp sheets are composed of famous paintings of historic events. The design creates individual stamps by outlining the highlights and principles of the painting with perforation.

Two other Bicentennial issues employ this multiple stamp/one image technique: the Spirit of '76 (#1629-1631) and the Declaration of Independence commemoratives (#1691-1694). A recent issue with this technique is the Balloon issue of 1983 (#2032-2035).

1976 continued	Un	U	PB	#	FDC	Q
1687 18¢ Declaration of Independence, by John Trumbull	6.50	6.50			7.50	1,983,000
1688 24¢ Washington Crossing the Delaware, by Emanuel Leutze/ Eastman Johnson	8.75	8.75			8.50	1,953,000
1689 31¢ Washington Reviewing Army at Valley Forge, by William T. Trego	11.00	11.00			9.50	1,903,000

"Farming in the West"

One picture can generate thousands of words, as was the case with the 2¢ commemorative stamp, "Farming in the West" from the 1898 Trans-Mississippi Series (#285-293). This stamp (#286) featured a North Dakota farming scene taken from a photograph of one of the Amenia & Sharon Land Co. farms near Amenia, ND. When the stamp appeared, it met with a good deal of criticism.

286

Apparently, no one out east believed that any farm in the U.S. used such an aggregation of agricultural machinery as was pictured on the stamp. These critics were unaware of the bountiful Great Plains farming tradition that was growing in the West, aided by the development of more efficient farm machinery. In fact, the Amenia & Sharon Land Co. in 1888 farmed a total of 25,000 acres in the manner shown on the stamp.

The land company proudly had the photo lithographed onto their stationery (producing a cachet) and used only the 2¢ stamp for their correspondence. Thus, every letter mailed from their office depicted the photo twice; once on the stamp and again in the left hand corner of the envelope. Soon other business firms began asking the Amenia & Sharon Land Co. how they, too, could get their company on U.S. postage!

Most of the workers featured in the stamp's photo were flattered to be in the same company with Washington and Franklin, save one. As the camera clicked, a gust of wind rose, forcing Ed Nybakken to cover his face with his arm, obscuring his features. Poor Ed felt so cheated, he produced a veritable gale of lament and complaints over his misfortune until the day he died. And even then his newspaper obituary carried Ed's unlucky story at length—one more time.

The Declaration of Independence, 4 July 1776 at Philadelphia
From a Painting by John Trumbull

1687

Washington Crossing the Delaware
From a Painting by Emanuel Leutze / Eastman Johnson

1688

Washington Reviewing His Ragged Army at Valley Forge
From a Painting by William T. Trego

1689

191

1690

1691   1692   1693   1694

1699

1700

1695   1696
1697   1698

1701

1702

1703

1704

1705

	1976 continued	Un	U	PB #	FDC	Q
1690	13¢ Franklin and Map					
	of North America, 1776, June 1	.30	.05	1.30	.65	164,890,000
	American Bicentennial Issue, Declaration of Independence, by Trumbull, July 4					
1691	13¢	.33	.07		.65	51,008,750
1692	13¢	.33	.07		.65	51,008,750
1693	13¢	.33	.07		.65	51,008,750
1694	13¢	.33	.07		.65	51,008,750
	Strip of 4, #1691-1694	1.30	1.00		2.00	
	Plate Block of 20			5.50		
	Olympic Games Issue, July 16					
1695	13¢ Diving	.45	.07		.70	46,428,750
1696	13¢ Skiing	.45	.07		.70	46,428,750
1697	13¢ Running	.45	.07		.70	46,428,750
1698	13¢ Skating	.45	.07		.70	46,428,750
	Block of 4, #1695-1698	2.00	1.25		2.00	
	Plate block of 12			3.40		
1699	13¢ Clara Maass, Aug. 18	.30	.05	3.40 (12)	.65	130,592,000
1700	13¢ Adolph S. Ochs, Sept. 18	.30	.05	1.30	.65	158,332,800
	Christmas Issue, Oct. 27					
1701	13¢ Nativity,					
	by John Singleton Copley	.30	.05	3.40 (12)	.65	809,955,000
	Christmas Issue, Oct. 27, 1976 continued					
1702	13¢ "Winter Pastime",					
	by Nathaniel Currier	.30	.05	3.00 (10)	.65	481,685,000
1703	13¢ as 1702	.30	.05	5.70 (20)	.65	481,685,000

No. 1702 has overall tagging. Lettering at base is black and usually ½mm. below design. As a rule, no "snowflaking" in sky or pond. Pane of 50 has margins on 4 sides with slogans. No. 1703 has block tagging the size of the printed area. Lettering at base is gray black and usually ¾mm. below design. "Snowflaking" generally in sky and pond. Pane of 50 has margin only at right or left, and no slogans.

	Issues of 1977 American Bicentennial, Perf. 11					
1704	13¢ Washington,					
	by Charles Wilson Peale, Jan. 3	.30	.05	2.90 (10)	.65	150,328,000
1705	13¢ Tin Foil Phonograph, Mar. 23	.30	.05	1.30	.65	176,830,000

	1977 continued	Un	U	PB #	FDC	
	Pueblo Indian Art Issue, Apr. 13					
1706	13¢ Zia Pot	.32	.07		.65	48,994,000
1707	13¢ San Ildefonso Pot	.32	.07		.65	48,994,000
1708	13¢ Hopi Pot	.32	.07		.65	48,994,000
1709	13¢ Acoma Pot	.32	.07		.65	48,994,000
	Block of 4, #1706-1709	1.30	1.10		2.00	
	Plate Block of 10			3.00 (10)		
1710	13¢ Spirit of St. Louis, May 20	.30	.05	3.65 (12)	.65	208,820,000
1711	13¢ Columbine and Rocky					
	Mountains, May 21	.30	.05	3.65	.65	192,250,000
	Butterfly Issue, June 6					
1712	13¢ Swallowtail	.33	.07		.65	54,957,500
1713	13¢ Checkerspot	.33	.07		.65	54,957,500
1714	13¢ Dogface	.33	.07		.65	54,957,500
1715	13¢ Orange Tip	.33	.07		.65	54,957,500
	Block of 4, #1712-1715	1.35	1.10			
	Plate Block of 12 (1712/1714)			3.65 (12)		
	Plate Block of 12 (1713/1715)			3.65 (12)		
	American Bicentennial Issues					
1716	13¢ Marquis de Lafayette, June 13	.30	.05	1.30	.65	159,852,000
	Skilled Hands for Independence, July 4					
1717	13¢ Seamstress	.33	.07		.65	47,077,500
1718	13¢ Blacksmith	.33	.07		.65	47,077,500
1719	13¢ Wheelwright	.33	.07		.65	47,077,500
1720	13¢ Leatherworker	.33	.07		.65	47,077,500
	Block of 4, #1717-1720	1.35	1.10		2.00	
	Plate Block of 12			3.65 (12)		
	Perf. 11x10½					
1721	13¢ Peace Bridge and Dove,					
	Aug. 4	.30	.05	1.30	.65	163,625,000

Territorial Rates

If you're sending a package or letter to Guam or any other U.S. territory, be advised that you don't need to use international postal rates. All U.S. territories are occupied by U.S. citizens, are paying U.S. taxes and are considered domestic mailing addresses. Therefore, they are entitled to all the benefits and subject to all the regulations of a continental address.

Zia Museum of New Mexico
Pueblo Art USA 13c

San Ildefonso Denver Art Museum
Pueblo Art USA 13c

Hopi Heard Museum Phoenix
Pueblo Art USA 13c

Acoma School of American Research
Pueblo Art USA 13c

1706   1707
1708   1709

USA·13c
50th Anniversary Solo Transatlantic Flight

1710

COLORADO
13c USA
THE CENTENNIAL STATE

1711

Swallowtail
USA13c *Papilio oregonius*

Checkerspot
USA13c *Euphydryas phaeton*

Dogface
USA13c *Colias eurydice*

Orange-Tip
USA13c *Anthocaris midea*

1712   1713
1714   1715

Lafayette

US Bicentennial 13c

1716

the SEAMSTRESS
for INDEPENDENCE USA 13c

the BLACKSMITH
for INDEPENDENCE USA 13c

the WHEELWRIGHT
for INDEPENDENCE USA 13c

the LEATHERWORKER
for INDEPENDENCE USA 13c

1717   1718
1719   1720

United States & Canada
Peace Bridge 1927-77
USA13c

1721

195

Herkimer at Oriskany 1777 by Yohn
US Bicentennial 13 cents

1722

ENERGY
CONSERVATION
USA 13c

ENERGY
DEVELOPMENT
USA 13c

1723
1724

First Civil Settlement·Alta California·1777
USA 13c

1725

Drafting the Articles of Confederation
York Town, Pennsylvania 1777 13c USA

1726

13c
USA

1727

Surrender at Saratoga 1777 by Trumbull
US Bicentennial 13 cents

1728

VALLEY FORGE
Christmas
USA 13c

1729

Christmas 13c USA

1730

Carl Sandburg
USA 13c

1731

Alaska 1778 Capt" JAMES COOK 13c USA

Capt" JAMES COOK 13c USA
Hawaii 1778

1732
1733

USA 13c

1734

A
US Postage

1735

15c
USA

1737

USA 15c Virginia 1720
USA 15c Rhode Island 1790
USA 15c Massachusetts 1793
USA 15c Illinois 1860
USA 15c Texas 1890

USA 15c Virginia 1720
USA 15c Rhode Island 1790
USA 15c Massachusetts 1793
USA 15c Illinois 1860
USA 15c Texas 1890

1738   1739   1740   1741   1742

	1977 continued	Un	U	PB	#	FDC	Q
	American Bicentennial Issue, Perf. 11						
1722	13¢ Herkimer at Oriskany,						
	by Frederick Yohn, Aug. 6	.30	.05	3.10	(10)	.65	156,296,000
	Energy Issue, Oct. 20						
1723	13¢ Energy Conservation	.30	.06			.65	79,338,000
1724	13¢ Energy Development	.30	.06			.65	79,338,000
	Pair, #1723-1724	.60	.60	3.65	(12)		
	American Bicentennial Issues						
1725	13¢ Farm House, Sept. 9	.30	.05	1.30		.65	154,495,000
	First civil settlement in Alta, California, 200th anniversary.						
1726	13¢ Articles of Confederation,						
	Sept. 30	.30	.05	1.30		.65	168,050,000
	200th anniversary of the Drafting of the Articles of Confederation, York Town, Pa.						
1727	13¢ Movie Projector and						
	Phonograph, Oct. 6	.30	.05	1.30		.65	156,810,000
	American Bicentennial Issue						
1728	13¢ Surrender of Saratoga,						
	by John Trumbull, Oct. 7	.30	.05	3.10	(10)	.65	153,736,000
	Christmas Issue, Oct. 21						
1729	13¢ Washington at Valley Forge	.30	.05	5.70	(20)	.65	882,260,000
1730	13¢ Rural Mailbox	.30	.05	3.10	(10)	.65	921,530,000
	Issues of 1978, Perf. 11						
1731	13¢ Carl Sandburg, Jan. 6	.30	.05	1.30		.65	156,580,000
	Capt. Cook Issue, Jan. 20						
1732	13¢ Capt. Cook	.30	.06	1.30		.70	101,095,000
1733	13¢ "Resolution" and "Discovery"	.30	.06	1.30		.70	101,095,000
	Pair, #1732-1733	.60	.55			1.50	
1734	13¢ Indian Head Penny, 1877,						
	Jan. 11	.30	.08	1.30		.90	
1735	(15¢) Eagle (A), May 22	.33	.05	1.50		.65	
	Perf. 11x10½						
1736	(15¢) orange Eagle (1735), May 22	.35	.05			.65	
1736a	Booklet pane of 8	2.75	.60				
1737	15¢ Roses, July 11	.40	.05				
1737a	Booklet pane of 8	3.15	.60				
	Nos. 1736 and 1737 issued only in booklets.						
	1977 & 1980 Issues Windmills, Feb. 7, Perf. 11						
1738	15¢ Virginia, 1720	.45	.05			.65	
1739	15¢ Rhode Island, 1790	.45	.05			.65	
1740	15¢ Massachusetts, 1793	.45	.05			.65	
1741	15¢ Illinois, 1860	.45	.05			.65	
1742	15¢ Texas, 1890	.45	.05			.65	
	Booklet pane of 10	3.95				6.50	

1977-1980 continued	Un	U	PB	#	FDC	Q
Coil Stamp, Perf. 10 Vertically						
1743 (15¢) orange Eagle (1735), May 22	.35	.05			.65	
Perf. 11						
1744 13¢ Harriet Tubman, Feb. 1	.30	.05			.65	156,555,000
American Folk Art Issue, American Quilts, Mar. 8, 1978						
1745 13¢ Basket design, red & orange	.33	.07			.65	41,295,600
1746 13¢ Basket design, red	.33	.07			.65	41,295,600
1747 13¢ Basket design, orange	.33	.07			.65	41,295,600
1748 13¢ Basket design, black	.33	.07			.65	41,295,600
Block of 4, #1745-1748	1.35	1.00			2.00	
Plate Block of 12 (1745/1747)			3.65			
Plate Block of 12 (1746/1748)			3.65			
American Dance Issue, Apr. 26						
1749 13¢ Ballet	.33	.07			.65	39,399,600
1750 13¢ Theater	.33	.07			.65	39,399,600
1751 13¢ Folk Dance	.33	.07			.65	39,399,600
1752 13¢ Modern Dance	.33	.07			.65	39,399,600
Block of 4, #1749-1752	1.35	1.00			2.00	
Plate Block of 12 (1749/1751)			3.65			
Plate Block of 12 (1750/1752)			3.65			
1753 13¢ French Alliance, May 4	.30	.05	1.30		.65	102,920,000
Perf. 10½x11						
1754 13¢ Dr. Papanicolaou with						
Microscope, May 13	.30	.08	1.30		.65	152,355,000
Performing Arts Issue, Perf. 11						
1755 13¢ Jimmie Rodgers, May 24	.30	.08	3.65	(12)	.65	94,625,000
1756 15¢ George M. Cohan, July 3	.33	.05	4.20	(12)	.65	151,570,000

Private Stamps

Before 1861, when Congress declared the carrying of mail strictly a government operation, some 150 local postal services operated for varying lengths of time. Most of them followed the lead of Alexander Grieg (see page 149) in issuing private stamps. In the relatively short span of 1842 to 1861, some 280 different design types were in circulation. Most of them only bore the name of the issuing company without attempting any portrait or design, some even lacked any denomination.

Although the United States Postal Service itself did not begin issuing stamps until July 1, 1847, a few local postmasters produced their own issues. The first of these was the New York Postmaster's Provisional, issued July 14, 1845, a 5¢ stamp which carried a portrait of George Washington in black on bluish paper.

1744

1745 1746
1747 1748

1749

1750

1753

1752

1751

1754

1755

1756

1757a,b,c,d

1757e,f,g,h

1757

1758

1759

1760   1761
1762   1763

1768

1769

1764   1765
1766   1767

200

	1978 continued	Un	U	PB	#	FDC	Q
1757	13¢ Souvenir sheet of 8, June 10	2.25	2.25			3.50	15,170,400
1758	15¢ Photographic Equipment,						
	June 26	.33	.05	4.20	(12)	.65	163,200,00
1759	15¢ Viking I Landing on Mars,						
	July 20	.33	.05	1.50		.80	158,880,000
	American Owls, Aug. 26						
1760	15¢ Great Gray Owl	.40	.06			.65	46,637,500
1761	15¢ Saw-whet Owl	.40	.06			.65	46,637,500
1762	15¢ Barred Owl	.40	.06			.65	46,637,500
1763	15¢ Great Horned Owl	.40	.06			.65	46,637,500
	Block of 4, #1760-1763	1.50	1.20	1.50		2.00	
	American Trees, Oct. 9						
1764	15¢ Giant Sequoia	.40	.06			.65	42,034,000
1765	15¢ White Pine	.40	.06			.65	42,034,000
1766	15¢ White Oak	.40	.06			.65	42,034,000
1767	15¢ Gray Birch	.40	.06			.65	42,034,000
	Block of 4, #1764-1767	1.50	1.25			2.00	
	Plate Block of 12 (1764/1766)			4.20			
	Plate Block of 12 (1765/1767)			4.20			
	Christmas Issue, Oct. 18						
1768	15¢ Madonna and Child	.33	.05	4.20	(12)	.65	963,370,000
1769	15¢ Hobby Horse	.33	.05	4.20	(12)	.65	916,800,000

First American Stamps

An Act of Congress on March 3, 1847, authorized the United States Postal Service to issue its first stamps. The two Americans honored in that first issue were George Washington as "father" of his nation and Benjamin Franklin as "father" of the American postal service. The wisdom of those choices has been borne out by time; both have been depicted on more stamps than any other Americans. Washington has been on 75, while Franklin has appeared on 38 stamps. Abraham Lincoln comes next with 21 stamps.

This first issue went on sale July 1, 1847. Franklin appeared on a 5¢ red-brown stamp and Washington appeared on a 10¢ black stamp. They were printed by Rawdon, Wright, Hatch and Edson of New York City and are known as bank note issues because the portraits of these two patriots were taken from the stock dies of the Bank of Manchester (Michigan) bank notes.

For the next half-century, bank notes were the primary source for stamp artwork, until the Bureau of Engraving and Printing began the printing of stamps in 1894.

The original Washington and Franklin stamps remained in use until June 30, 1851, with 891,000 of the former eventually being printed and 3,712,200 of the latter.

1979

	Issues of 1979, Perf. 11	Un	U	PB	#	FDC	Q
1770	15¢ Robert F. Kennedy, Jan. 12	.33	.05	1.50		.65	159,297,600
1771	15¢ Martin Luther King, Jr., Jan. 13	.33	.05	4.20	(12)	.65	166,435,000
1772	15¢ Internt'l Year of the Child,						
	Feb. 15	.33	.05	1.50		.65	162,535,000
	Perf. 10½x11						
1773	15¢ John Steinbeck, Feb. 27	.33	.05	1.50		.65	155,000,000
1774	15¢ Albert Einstein, Mar. 4	.33	.05	1.50		.65	157,310,000
	American Folk Art Issue, Apr. 19, Pennsylvania Toleware						
1775	15¢ Coffeepot	.40	.06			.65	43,524,000
1776	15¢ Tea Caddy	.40	.06			.65	43,524,000
1777	15¢ Sugar Bowl	.40	.06			.65	43,524,000
1778	15¢ Coffeepot	.40	.06			.65	43,524,000
	Block of 4, #1775-1778	1.50	1.20			2.00	174,096,000
	Plate Block of 10			3.50			
	American Architecture Issue, June 4						
1779	15¢ Virginia Rotunda	.45	.06			.65	41,198,400
1780	15¢ Baltimore Cathedral	.45	.06			.65	41,198,400
1781	15¢ Boston State House	.45	.06			.65	41,198,400
1782	15¢ Philadelphia Exchange	.45	.06			.65	41,198,400
	Block of 4, #1779-1782	1.70	1.20	1.50		2.00	164,793,600
	Endangered Flora Issue, June 7						
1783	15¢ Persistent Trillium	.40	.06			.65	40,763,750
1784	15¢ Hawaiian Wild Broadbean	.40	.06			.65	40,763,750
1785	15¢ Contra Costa Wallflower	.40	.06			.65	40,763,750
1786	15¢ Antioch Evening Primrose	.40	.06			.65	40,763,750
	Block of 4, #1783-1786	1.50	1.20			2.00	163,055,000
	Plate Block of 12 (1783/1784)			4.20			
	Plate Block of 12 (1785/1786)			4.20			
1787	15¢ Seeing Eye Dogs, June 15	.33	.05	6.50		.65	161,860,000

1770

1771

International Year of the Child

1772

1773

1774

1775   1776
1777   1778

1779   1780
1781   1782

1787

1788   1789   1790

1791   1792
1793   1794

1799   1800

1795   1796
1797   1798

1801

1802

1803   1804

1979 continued		Un	U	PB	#	FDC	Q
1788	15¢ Special Olympics, Aug. 9	.33	.05	3.50	(10)	.65	165,775,000
1789	15¢ John Paul Jones,						
	by Charles Wilson Peale, Sept. 23	.40	.05	3.50	(10)	.65	160,000,000
	Olympic Games Issue, Sept.						
1790	10¢ Javelin	.27	.18	2.75	(12)	.60	67,195,000
1791	15¢ Running	.45	.07			.65	46,726,250
1792	15¢ Swimming	.45	.07			.65	46,726,250
1793	15¢ Canoeing	.45	.07			.65	46,726,250
1794	15¢ Equestrian	.45	.07			.65	46,726,250
	Block of 4, #1791-1794	1.75	1.60	4.25		2.00	187,650,000
	Issues of 1980						
	Winter Olympic Games Issue, Feb. 1						
1795	15¢ Speed Skating	.50	.06			.65	
1796	15¢ Downhill Skiing	.50	.06			.65	
1797	15¢ Ski Jump	.50	.06			.65	
1798	15¢ Hockey Goaltender	.50	.06			.65	
	Block of 4, #1795-1798	1.90	1.20	4.25		2.00	208,295,000
	Christmas Issue, Oct. 18, 1979						
1799	15¢ Virgin and Child,						
	by Gerard David	.33	.05	4.25	(12)	.65	873,710,000
1800	15¢ Santa Claus	.33	.05	4.25	(12)	.65	931,880,000
1801	15¢ Will Rogers, Nov. 4	.33	.05	4.25	(12)	.65	161,290,000
1802	15¢ Vietnam Veterans, Nov. 11	.33	.05	3.50	(10)	.65	172,740,000
	Perf. 11½x11½						
1803	15¢ W.C. Fields, Jan. 29	.33	.05	4.25	(12)	.65	168,995,000
	Perf. 11						
1804	15¢ Benjamin Banneker, Feb. 15	.33	.05	4.25	(12)	.65	160,000,000

The Headsville Post Office

If you take a close look at the 1972 8¢ commemorative honoring the 100th anniversary of the mail order business (#1468), you'll see a picture of an old-fashioned country store/post office, the kind that hasn't existed for some time now. The basis for this stamp was the post office of Headsville, WV, which operated from 1861 to 1914 and was later carefully taken apart, transported to the Smithsonian and reassembled on the first floor of the museum building.

1468

It has been renamed Smithsonian Station and visitors to the museum may purchase current postal issues there and have them postmarked with a special Smithsonian Station picture cancellation.

	1980 continued	Un	U	PB	#	FDC	Q
	Letter Writing Issue, Feb. 25						
1805	15¢ Letter Preserve Memories	.40	.09			.60	
1806	15¢ P.S. Write Soon	.40	.09			.60	
1807	15¢ Letters Lift Spirits	.40	.09			.60	
1808	15¢ P.S. Write Soon	.40	.09			.60	
1809	15¢ Letters Shape Opinions	.40	.09			.60	
1810	15¢ P.S. Write Soon	.40	.09			.60	
	Strip of 6, #1805-1810	2.25	1.75			3.00	233,598,000
	Plate Block of 36			11.00			
	Perf. 10						
1811	1¢ Americana Type Coil, March 6	.05	.05			.65	
1813	3.5¢ Coil, June 23	.10	.08			.65	
1816	12¢ Freedom of Conscience,						
	Apr. 8	.27	.07				
	Perf. 11x10½						
1818	(18¢) "B" Mar. 15	.45	.05	1.75		.75	
	Perf. 10						
1819	(18¢) "B" Booklet, Mar. 15	.50	.05				
	Perf. 10 Vert.						
1820	(18¢) "B" Coil, Mar. 15	.45	.05				
	Perf. 10½x11						
1821	15¢ Frances Perkins, April 10	.33	.05	1.50		.65	163,510,000
	Perf. 11						
1822	15¢ Dolley Madison, May 20	.33	.05	1.50		.65	256,620,000
1823	15¢ Emily Bissell, May 31	.33	.05	1.50		.65	95,695,000
1824	15¢ Helen Keller/Anne Sullivan,						
	June 27	.33	.05	1.50		.65	153,975,000
1825	15¢ Veterans Administration,						
	July 21	.33	.05	1.50		.65	160,000,000
1826	15¢ General Bernardo de Galvez,						
	July 23	.33	.05	1.50		.65	103,855,000
	Coral Reefs Issue, Aug. 26						
1827	15¢ Brain Coral	.40	.06			.65	
1828	15¢ Elkhorn Coral	.40	.06			.65	
1829	15¢ Chalice Coral	.40	.06			.65	
1830	15¢ Finger Coral	.40	.06			.65	
	Block of 4, #1827-1830	1.50	1.10			2.00	205,165,000
	Plate Block of 12 (1827/1828)			4.50			
	Plate Block of 12 (1829/1830)			4.50			

1811   1813

1805
1806   1807   1809
            1808   1810

1822

1816   1818

Frances Perkins
USA 15c

1821   1823

1824   1825   1826

1827   1828
1829   1830

Organized Labor
Proud and Free
USA 15c

1831

Edith Wharton
USA 15c

1832

Glow by Josef Albers USA 15c
Learning
never ends

1833

Heiltsuk, Bella Bella
Indian Art USA 15c

Chilkat Tlingit
Indian Art USA 15c

Tlingit
Indian Art USA 15c

Bella Coola
Indian Art USA 15c

1834   1835
1836   1837

Renwick 1818-1895 Smithsonian Washington
Architecture USA 15c

Richardson 1838-1886 Trinity Church Boston
Architecture USA 15c

Furness 1839-1912 Penn Academy Philadelphia
Architecture USA 15c

AJ Davis 1803-1892 Lyndhurst Tarrytown NY
Architecture USA 15c

1838   1839
1840   1841

Christmas USA 15c

1842

USA 15c
Season's Greetings

1843

208

1980-1981 continued		Un	U	PB #	FDC	Q
1831	15¢ Organized Labor, Sept. 1	.33	.05	4.50 (12)	.65	166,590,000
	Perf. 11x10½					
1832	15¢ Edith Wharton, Sept. 5	.33	.05	1.50	.65	163,275,000
	Perf. 11					
1833	15¢ American Education, Sept. 12	.33	.05	2.25	.65	160,000,000
	Indian Art—Masks Issue, Sept. 25					
1834	15¢ Bella Bella	.40	.06		.65	
1835	15¢ Chilkat	.40	.06		.65	
1836	15¢ Tlingit	.40	.06		.65	
1837	15¢ Bella Coola	.40	.06		.65	
	Block of 4, #1834-1837	1.50	1.10		2.00	152,404,000
	Plate Block of 10			3.50		
	American Architecture Issue, Oct. 9					
1838	15¢ Smithsonian	.42	.06		.65	
1839	15¢ Trinity Church	.42	.06		.65	
1840	15¢ Pennsylvania Academy of					
	Fine Arts	.42	.06		.65	
1841	15¢ Lyndhurst	.42	.06		.65	
	Block of 4, #1838-1841	1.60	1.10			155,024,000
	Plate Block of 4			1.50		
1842	15¢ Christmas Stained Glass					
	Windows, Oct. 16	.33	.05	4.25 (12)	.65	693,250,000
1843	15¢ Christmas Antique Toys,					
	Oct. 16	.33	.05	6.50 (20)	.65	718,715,000

Deja Vu Stamps

The Postal Service produced its first "deja vu stamp" in 1967. In a philatelic innovation, the design of the popular John James Audubon 5¢ stamp of 1963 (#1241) was enlarged and reproduced on the new 20¢ international air mail stamp (#C71). This issue went on sale April 26, 1967, in New York City and featured Audubon's aquatint of the "Columbian Jay."

The response to this new design was favorable enough for the Post Office to reproduce the "Madonna and Child With Angels" from the 1966 5¢ Christmas stamp (#1321) for the 1967 Christmas issue (#1336). More of the painting was visible in the 1967 issue. The painting is the work of the Flemish Renaissance artist Hans Memling. The image on the later issue was enlarged to display more of the expert detailing of the work.

So if you think you've experienced deja vu and have seen that stamp image somewhere else, you probably have!

1980-1983

		Un	U	PB	#	FDC	Q
	Great Americans Issue, Perf. 11x10½						
1843A	1¢ Dorothea Dix, Sept. 23, 1983	.05	.05				
1844	2¢ Igor Stravinsky, Nov. 18, '82	.05	.05	.20		.60	
1847	13¢ Crazy Horse, Jan. 15, '82	.22	.06	1.30		.60	
	1980-1981 continued						
1849	17¢ Rachel Carson, May 28, '81	.28	.05	1.75		.75	
1850	18¢ George Mason, May 7, '81	.30	.05	1.75		.75	
1851	19¢ Sequoyah, Dec. 27, '80	.32	.07	2.00		.80	
1852	20¢ Ralph Bunche, Jan. 12, '82	.33	.05	2.00		.80	
1853	20¢ Thomas Gallaudet, June 10, '83	.33	.05				
1859	35¢ Dr. Charles Drew, June 3, '81	.55	.10	3.50		1.00	
1860	37¢ Robert Millikan, Jan. 26, '82	.60	.07	3.75		1.00	
	Issues of 1981, Perf. 11						
1874	15¢ Everett Dirksen, Jan. 4	.33	.05	1.50		.65	160,155,000
1875	15¢ Whitney Moore Young, Jr.,						
	Jan. 30	.33	.05	1.50		.65	159,505,000
	Flower Issue, April 23						
1876	18¢ Rose	.40	.06			.75	52,658,250
1877	18¢ Camellia	.40	.06			.75	52,658,250
1878	18¢ Dahlia	.40	.06			.75	52,658,250
1879	18¢ Lily	.40	.06			.75	52,658,250
	Block of 4, #1876-1879	1.60	1.10	1.75			
	Wildlife Issue, May 14						
1880	18¢ Bighorned Sheep	.50	.05			.75	
1881	18¢ Puma	.50	.05			.75	
1882	18¢ Harbor Seal	.50	.05			.75	
1883	18¢ Bison	.50	.05			.75	
1884	18¢ Brown Bear	.50	.05			.75	
1885	18¢ Polar Bear	.50	.05			.75	
1886	18¢ Elk (wapiti)	.50	.05			.75	
1887	18¢ Moose	.50	.05			.75	
1888	18¢ White Tailed Deer	.50	.05			.75	
1889	18¢ Prong Horned Antelope	.50	.05			.75	
	Booklet Pane of 10, #1880-1889	4.50					
	Flag Issue, April 24						
1890	18¢ Flag and Anthem, for amber						
	waves of grain	.40	.05	7.50 (20)		.75	
	Perf. 10 Vert.						
1891	18¢ Flag and Anthem, from sea	.40	.05			.75	

Igor Stravinsky USA 2c — 1844

USA 13c Crazy Horse — 1847

Rachel Carson USA 17c — 1849

George Mason USA 18c — 1850

USA 19c Sequoyah — 1851

Ralph Bunche USA 20c — 1852

Charles R Drew MD USA 35c — 1859

Robert Millikan 37c USA — 1860

USA 15c Everett Dirksen — 1874

Whitney Moore Young Black Heritage USA 15c — 1875

Rose USA 18c — 1876 / 1878
Camellia USA 18c
Dahlia USA 18c
Lily USA 18c — 1877 / 1879

1889a

USA 18c ...for amber waves of grain — 1890

USA 18c ...from sea to shining sea — 1891

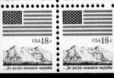

1893a

1894

1895

1896

1897

1897a

1898

1900

1901

1905

1906

1907

1910

1911

1981 continued, Perf. 11	Un	U	PB	#	FDC	Q
1892	6¢ USA Circle of Stars	.35	.12			.75	
1893	18¢ Flag and Anthem, for purple						
	mountains majesties, booklet	.40	.07			.75	
1893a	Booklet Pane of 8,						
	2 #1892, 6 #1893	2.95	—				
1894	20¢ Flag over Supreme Court	.33	.05	8.50 (20)		.75	
	Perf. 10 Vert.						
1895	20¢ Flag over Supreme Court,						
	coil	.33	.05			.75	
	Perf. 11 x 10½						
1896	20¢ Flag over Supreme Court,						
	booklet	.35	.06			.75	
	Transportation Issues Perf. 10 Vert.						
1897	2¢ Locomotive 1870's, May 20	.05	.05			.60	
1897a	4¢ Stagecoach 1890's, Aug. 19	.08	.06			.60	
1898	5.9¢ Bicycle 1870's, Feb. 17	.11	.09			.60	
1900	9.3¢ Mail Wagon	.15	.08			.65	
1901	10.9¢ Hansom Cab 1890's, Mar. 26	.18	.07			.65	
1905	17¢ Electric Auto, June 25	.30	.06			.75	
1906	18¢ Surrey, May 18	.30	.05			.75	
1907	20¢ Fire Pumper	.33	.05			.75	
	Perf. 11x10½						
1910	18¢ American Red Cross, May 1	.40	.05	1.75		.75	165,175,000
	Perf. 11						
1911	18¢ Savings and Loan, May 8	.40	.05	1.75		.75	107,240,000

Emmanuel Leutze

One of the most memorable and widely reproduced paintings of an American historical event is Emmanuel Leutze's "Washington Crossing the Delaware" painted in 1851. The original hangs in the Metropolitan Museum of Art in New York City and is the subject of a Bicentennial souvenir sheet of five 24¢ stamps (#1688).

242

Emmanuel Leutze had another of his paintings depicted on U.S. postage. His "Columbus in Chains" (#242) is the subject of the $2.00 issue of the Columbian Exposition Series of 1893. Mr. Leutze was born in Germany in 1816 and died in Washington, D.C., in 1868. He is known as one of America's finest historical artists.

1981 continued	Un	U	PB #	FDC	Q
Space Achievement Issue, May 21					
1912 18¢ Exploring the Moon	.42	.09		.75	42,227,375
1913 18¢ Benefitting Mankind	.42	.09		.75	42,227,375
1914 18¢ Benefitting Mankind	.42	.09		.75	42,227,375
1915 18¢ Understanding the Sun	.42	.09		.75	42,227,375
1916 18¢ Probing the Planets	.42	.09		.75	42,227,375
1917 18¢ Benefitting Mankind	.42	.09		.75	42,227,375
1918 18¢ Benefitting Mankind	.42	.09		.75	42,227,375
1919 18¢ Comprehending the Universe	.42	.09		.75	42,227,375
Plate Block, #1912-1919	3.15	2.75	3.50 (20)	5.00	
1920 18¢ Professional Management, June 18	.40	.05	1.75	.75	99,420,000
Wildlife Habitat Issue, June 26					
1921 18¢ Wetland Habitats	.40	.06		.75	46,732,500
1922 18¢ Grassland Habitats	.40	.06		.75	46,732,500
1923 18¢ Mountain Habitats	.40	.06		.75	46,732,500
1924 18¢ Woodland Habitats	.40	.06		.75	46,732,500
Plate Block of 4, #1921-1924	1.60	1.10	1.75	2.50	
1925 18¢ International Year of the Disabled, June 29	.40	.05	1.75	.75	100,265,000
1926 18¢ Edna St. Vincent Millay, July 10	.40	.05	1.75	.75	99,615,000
1927 18¢ Alcoholism, Aug. 19	.40	.05	8.00 (20)	.75	97,535,000

Dead Letter Office

When you're waiting for that letter you should've received last week, it might be found in the Dead Letter Office. This office was established in 1825 to receive and investigate undeliverable letters and parcels with no return address on them. The DLO didn't keep records of its operations until 1860 when Congress asked for a report. For that year, there were 2,500,000 undeliverable pieces of mail. And by the early 1930s, the dead letter volume had ballooned to nearly 23,000,000 letters and parcels annually. About 3,500,000 of these were returned to the senders as a result of the evidence that the "returners" staff found inside each piece of mail. So be sure to use a return address, or your mail might meet an untimely death.

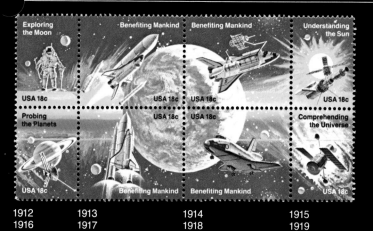

1912 1913 1914 1915
1916 1917 1918 1919

1920

1925

1921 1922
1923 1924

1926

Alcoholism
You can beat it!
USA 18c

1927

Stanford White 1853-1906 NYU Library New York.

Architecture USA 18c

Richard Morris Hunt 1828-1895 Biltmore Asheville NC

Architecture USA 18c

Babe Zaharias

USA 18c

Bobby Jones

USA 18c

1932   1933

Bernard Maybeck 1862-1957 Palace of Arts San Francisco

Architecture USA 18c

Louis Sullivan 1856-1924 Bank Owatonna Minn.

Architecture USA 18c

1928   1929
1930   1931

FREDERIC REMINGTON
American
Sculptor

18c
USA

USA 18c
James Hoban White House Architect

USA 20c
James Hoban White House Architect

1934   1935   1936

1981 continued		Un	U	PB	#	FDC	Q
American Architecture Issue, Aug. 28							
1928	18¢ NYU Library	.40	.06			.75	41,827,000
1929	18¢ Biltmore House	.40	.06			.75	41,827,000
1930	18¢ Palace of the Arts	.40	.06			.75	41,827,000
1931	18¢ National Farmer's Bank	.40	.06			.75	41,827,000
	Plate Block of 4, #1928-1931	1.60	1.10	1.75		2.50	
	Perf. 10½x11						
1932	18¢ Babe Zaharias, Sept. 22	.40	.05	1.75		.75	101,625,000
1933	18¢ Bobby Jones, Sept. 22	.40	.05	1.75		.75	99,170,000
	Perf. 11						
1934	18¢ Remington Sculpture, Oct. 9	.40	.05	1.75		.75	101,155,000
1935	18¢ James Hoban, Oct. 13	.40	.06	1.75		.75	101,200,000
1936	20¢ James Hoban, Oct. 13	.40	.05	2.00		.75	167,360,000
1937	20¢ Yorktown 1781, Oct. 16	.40	.06			.75	81,210,000
1938	20¢ Virginia Capes 1781, Oct. 16	.40	.06			.75	81,210,000
	Pair, #1937-1938	.80	.40	1.75		1.00	
1939	(20¢) Christmas Madonna, Oct. 28	.40	.05	2.00		.75	597,720,000
1940	(20¢) Christmas Child Art, Oct. 28	.40	.05	2.00		.75	792,600,000
1941	20¢ John Hanson, Nov. 5	.40	.05	2.00		.75	167,130,000

U.S. Postage Honors Blacks

For the first 93 years of U.S. philately, there were no stamps issued that commemorated black people. Not until FDR put Booker T. Washington, founder of the Tuskegee Institute, on the 10¢ stamp of the Educator set (#893) for his Famous Americans Series were black people visible on U.S. stamps. Dr. George Washington Carver next received the honor in 1948 (#953) and Booker T. Washington was again honored on a 3¢ stamp in 1956 (#1074).

893

The next 19 years were another dry spell, however, in spite of the many advances made by blacks during the Civil Rights movement. But in 1975, Paul Laurence Dunbar, a popular writer and poet around the turn of the century, was commemorated on a 10¢ stamp (#1554). This seemed to mark a new policy by the Postal Service, because since then blacks have been increasingly used as subjects for U.S. commemoratives. Harriet Tubman (#1744), Dr. Martin Luther King, Jr. (#1771), Benjamin Banneker (#1804), Dr. Charles Drew (#1859), Whitney Moore Young (#1875) and Ralph Bunche (#1852) have been so honored over the last five years. In addition, Jackie Robinson (#2016), the first black baseball player in the Major Leagues, was depicted on the 20¢ commemorative stamp of the 1982 Black Heritage series. Scott Joplin (#2044) is honored on a 1983 issue.

1744

1981-1982		Un	U	PB	#	FDC	Q
U.S. Desert Plants Issue, December 11							
1942	20¢ Barrel Cactus	.40	.06			.75	47,890,000
1943	20¢ Agave	.40	.06			.75	47,890,000
1944	20¢ Beavertail Cactus	.40	.06			.75	47,890,000
1945	20¢ Saguaro	.40	.06			.75	47,890,000
	Plate Block of 4, #1942-1945	1.60	1.20	2.00		1.50	
Perf. 11x10½							
1946	(20¢) "C" Eagle, Oct. 11	.40	.05	2.00		.75	
Perf. 10 Vert.							
1947	(20¢) "C" Eagle, coil, Oct. 11	.40	.05			.75	
1948	(20¢) "C" Eagle, booklet, Oct. 11	.50	.05			.75	
1948a	Booklet Pane of 10	4.50	—				
Issues of 1982, Perf. 11							
1949	20¢ Bighorn, booklet, Jan. 8	.35	.05			.75	
1949a	Booklet Pane of 10	3.25	—				
1950	20¢ Franklin D. Roosevelt, Jan. 3	.40	.05	2.00		.75	163,939,200
1951	20¢ Love, Feb. 1	.40	.05	2.00		.75	
1952	20¢ George Washington, Feb. 22	.40	.05	2.00		.75	180,700,000

USPS 1980 Statistics

The United States Postal Service has become the largest carrier of the written and printed word in the world. In fiscal 1980, the USPS moved more than 106 billion pieces of mail, which is nearly half the postal volume of the western world; this volume could fill 550,000 boxcars stretching from Boston to San Francisco. Along with this, the USPS sold 26.8 billion stamps. A coil of this many stamps would circle the globe 17 times.

Some other USPS statistics…it uses the third largest vehicle fleet in the western world: 190,000 cars and trucks. It also bought nearly $1.3 trillion worth of air, rail, highway and water transportation in fiscal 1980.

- *Rural carriers travel 2 million miles a day.*
- *Our western and southernmost post office is in Pago Pago, Samoa.*
- *The northernmost office is in Barrow, Alaska, and the coldest postal zone is 180 miles north of the Arctic Circle in Wainwright, Alaska.*
- *Hottest postal area is in Death Valley, California.*
- *And there are 275,000 mailboxes worldwide where you can place that letter for pick up by the USPS.*

1946

942

1943
1944

1945

1950

949

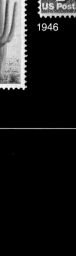

1951

Alabama Yellowhammer & Camellia

Alaska
USA 20c
Willow Ptarmigan &

Arizona
USA 20c
Cactus Wren & Saguaro Cactus Blossom

Arkansas
USA 20c
Mockingbird & Apple Blossom

California
USA 20c
California Quail & California Poppy

1954   1955   1956   1957

Colorado Bunting & Rocky Mountain Columbine

Connecticut
USA 20c
Robin & Mountain Laurel

Delaware
USA 20c
Blue Hen Chicken & Peach Blossom

Florida
USA 20c
Mockingbird & Orange Blossom

Georgia
USA 20c
Brown Thrasher & Cherokee Rose

1959   1960   1961   1962

Hawaii Nene Goose & Hibiscus

Idaho
USA 20c
Mountain Bluebird & Syringa

Illinois
USA 20c
Cardinal & Violet

Indiana
USA 20c
Cardinal & Peony

Iowa
USA 20c
Eastern Goldfinch & Wild Rose

1964   1965   1966   1967

Kansas Meadowlark & Sunflower

Kentucky
USA 20c
Cardinal & Goldenrod

Louisiana
USA 20c
Brown Pelican & Magnolia

Maine
USA 20c
Chickadee & White Pine Cone and Tassel

Maryland
USA 20c
Baltimore Oriole & Black-Eyed Susan

	1982 continued	Un	U	PB	#	FDC	Q
	State Birds & Flowers Issue, Apr. 14, Perf. 10½x11						
1953	20¢ Alabama	.40	.35			.75	13,339,900
1954	20¢ Alaska	.40	.35			.75	13,339,900
1955	20¢ Arizona	.40	.35			.75	13,339,900
1956	20¢ Arkansas	.40	.35			.75	13,339,900
1957	20¢ California	.40	.35			.75	13,339,900
1958	20¢ Colorado	.40	.35			.75	13,339,900
1959	20¢ Connecticut	.40	.35			.75	13,339,900
1960	20¢ Delaware	.40	.35			.75	13,339,900
1961	20¢ Florida	.40	.35			.75	13,339,900
1962	20¢ Georgia	.40	.35			.75	13,339,900
1963	20¢ Hawaii	.40	.35			.75	13,339,900
1964	20¢ Idaho	.40	.35			.75	13,339,900
1965	20¢ Illinois	.40	.35			.75	13,339,900
1966	20¢ Indiana	.40	.35			.75	13,339,900
1967	20¢ Iowa	.40	.35			.75	13,339,900
1968	20¢ Kansas	.40	.35			.75	13,339,900
1969	20¢ Kentucky	.40	.35			.75	13,339,900
1970	20¢ Louisiana	.40	.35			.75	13,339,900
1971	20¢ Maine	.40	.35			.75	13,339,900
1972	20¢ Maryland	.40	.35			.75	13,339,900

Presidential Wives

The wives of three U.S. Presidents have appeared on U.S. postage stamps, beginning with Martha Washington on the 1902 8¢ issue (#306). Mrs. Washington appeared on several other stamps (#556, 585, 601, 636, 662, 673, 805, 840 and 849). Eleanor Roosevelt was portrayed on a 5¢ commemorative in 1963 (#1236) and Dolley Madison was honored in 1980 on a 15¢ issue (#1822). Plans call for a commemorative stamp to be issued in 1984 honoring the 100th anniversary of the birth of Eleanor Roosevelt.

805

1236

	1982 continued	Un	U	PB	#	FDC	Q
1973	20¢ Massachusetts	.40	.35			.75	13,339,900
1974	20¢ Michigan	.40	.35			.75	13,339,900
1975	20¢ Minnesota	.40	.35			.75	13,339,900
1976	20¢ Mississippi	.40	.35			.75	13,339,900
1977	20¢ Missouri	.40	.35			.75	13,339,900
1978	20¢ Montana	.40	.35			.75	13,339,900
1979	20¢ Nebraska	.40	.35			.75	13,339,900
1980	20¢ Nevada	.40	.35			.75	13,339,900
1981	20¢ New Hampshire	.40	.35			.75	13,339,900
1982	20¢ New Jersey	.40	.35			.75	13,339,900
1983	20¢ New Mexico	.40	.35			.75	13,339,900
1984	20¢ New York	.40	.35			.75	13,339,900
1985	20¢ North Carolina	.40	.35			.75	13,339,900
1986	20¢ North Dakota	.40	.35			.75	13,339,900
1987	20¢ Ohio	.40	.35			.75	13,339,900
1988	20¢ Oklahoma	.40	.35			.75	13,339,900
1989	20¢ Oregon	.35	.35			.75	13,339,900
1990	20¢ Pennsylvania	.40	.35			.75	13,339,900
1991	20¢ Rhode Island	.40	.35			.75	13,339,900
1992	20¢ South Carolina	.40	.35			.75	13,339,900

Mutes

Most stamp issuing authorities inscribe on their stamps the country of origin, the stamp's value and the type of service it gives. But it is not always so easy to identify stamps. England issued the first stamps with adhesive on the back and therefore felt no need for the country's name to appear on the stamp. To this day, England still keeps her postage "mute." There are other stamps which not only refuse to tell you where they're from, but also how much they are worth or what they are used for. The Austrian newspaper stamp is a good example.

The U.S. "Eagle" A, B and C stamps say "U.S. Postage" but give no denomination. They are used when postal rates go up and new stamps are not yet available. They can be used only on domestic mail: the A stamp was worth 15¢; B, 18¢; C, 20¢.

There are three other U.S. stamps whose designs are mute, these as to their origin: The Pilgrim Tercentenary stamps of 1920 (#548-550). Nowhere on these stamps will you find the words "U.S. Postage."

Massachusetts USA 20c	Michigan USA 20c	Minnesota USA 20c	Mississippi USA 20c	Missouri USA 20c
Black-Capped Chickadee & Mayflower	Robin & Apple Blossom	Common Loon & Showy Lady Slipper	Mockingbird & Magnolia	Eastern Bluebird & Red Hawthorn
1973	1974	1975	1976	1977

Montana USA 20c	Nebraska USA 20c	Nevada USA 20c	New Hampshire USA 20c	New Jersey USA 20c
Western Meadowlark & Bitterroot	Western Meadowlark & Goldenrod	Mountain Bluebird & Sagebrush	Purple Finch & Lilac	American Goldfinch & Violet
1978	1979	1980	1981	1982

New Mexico USA 20c	New York USA 20c	North Carolina USA 20c	North Dakota USA 20c	Ohio USA 20c
Roadrunner & Yucca Flower	Eastern Bluebird & Rose	Cardinal & Flowering Dogwood	Western Meadowlark & Wild Prairie Rose	Cardinal & Red Carnation
1983	1984	1985	1986	1987

Oklahoma USA 20c	Oregon USA 20c	Pennsylvania USA 20c	Rhode Island USA 20c	South Carolina USA 20c
Scissor-tailed Flycatcher & Mistletoe	Western Meadowlark & Oregon Grape	Ruffed Grouse & Mountain Laurel	Rhode Island Red & Violet	Carolina Wren & Carolina Jessamine
1988	1989	1990	1991	1992

South Dakota
USA 20c
Ring-Necked Pheasant & Pasqueflower

1993

Tennessee
USA 20c
Mockingbird & Iris

1994

Texas
USA 20c
Mockingbird & Bluebonnet

1995

Utah
USA 20c
California Gull & Sego Lily

1996

Vermont
USA 20c
Hermit Thrush & Red Clover

1997

Virginia
USA 20c
Cardinal & Flowering Dogwood

1998

Washington
USA 20c
American Goldfinch & Rhododendron

1999

West Virginia
USA 20c
Cardinal & Rhododendron Maximum

2000

Wisconsin
USA 20c
Robin & Wood Violet

2001

Wyoming
USA 20c
Western Meadowlark & Indian Paintbrush

2002

20c
USA
1782·1982·USA·THE NETHERLANDS

2003

Library of Congress
USA 20c

2004

Wise shoppers
stretch dollars
Consumer
Education
USA 20c

2005

USA 20c
Solar energy Knoxville World's Fair

USA 20c
Synthetic fuels Knoxville World's Fair

USA 20c
Breeder reactor Knoxville World's Fair

USA 20c
Fossil fuels Knoxville World's Fair

2006
2008

2007
2009

Horatio Alger
USA 20c

2010

THE BARRYMORES
Performing Arts USA 20c

2012

Aging
together
USA
20c

	1982 continued	Un	U	PB #	FDC	Q
1993	20¢ South Dakota	.40	.35		.75	13,339,900
1994	20¢ Tennessee	.40	.35		.75	13,339,900
1995	20¢ Texas	.40	.35		.75	13,339,900
1996	20¢ Utah	.40	.35		.75	13,339,900
1997	20¢ Vermont	.40	.35		.75	13,339,900
1998	20¢ Virginia	.40	.35		.75	13,339,900
1999	20¢ Washington	.40	.35		.75 ∗	13,339,900
2000	20¢ West Virginia	.40	.35		.75	13,339,900
2001	20¢ Wisconsin	.40	.35		.75	13,339,900
2002	20¢ Wyoming	.40	.35		.75	13,339,900
	Sheet of 50		20.00			
	Perf. 11					
2003	20¢ USA/Netherlands, Apr. 20	.40	.05	8.50 (20)	.75	109,245,000
2004	20¢ Library of Congress, Apr. 21	.33	.05	2.00	.75	112,535,000
	Perf. 10 Vert.					
2005	20¢ Consumer Education, Apr. 27	.33	.05		.75	
	World's Fair Issue, Apr. 29, Perf. 11					
2006	20¢ Solar Energy	.35	.06		.75	31,160,000
2007	20¢ Synthetic Fuels	.35	.06		.75	31,160,000
2008	20¢ Breeder Reactor	.35	.06		.75	31,160,000
2009	20¢ Fossil Fuels	.35	.06		.75	31,160,000
	Plate Block of 4, (#2006-2009)			2.00		
2010	20¢ Horatio Alger, Apr. 30	.33	.05	2.00	.75	107,605,000
2011	20¢ Aging Together, May 21	.33	.05	2.00	.75	173,160,000
2012	20¢ The Barrymores, June 8	.33	.05	2.00	.75	107,285,000

Mourning vs. Memorial

The first mourning stamp was the 15¢ black postage stamp (#77) of Abraham Lincoln, issued a little over a year after his death, June 17, 1866. Lincoln was also the subject of America's first memorial stamp. The Lincoln 2¢ Memorial (#367) was issued to commemorate the 100th anniversary of his birth on February 12, 1909. A memorial stamp honors a person's life while a mourning stamp marks a death.

77

367

	1982 continued	Un	U	PB #	FDC	Q
2013	20¢ Dr. Mary Walker, June 10	.33	.05	2.00	.75	109,040,000
2014	20¢ International Peace Garden,					
	June 30	.33	.05	2.00	.75	183,270,000
2015	20¢ America's Libraries, July 13	.33	.05	2.00	.75	169,495,000
	Black Heritage Series, Aug. 2, Perf. 11x10½					
2016	20¢ Jackie Robinson	.33	.05	2.00	.75	164,235,000
	Perf. 11					
2017	20¢ Touro Synagogue, Aug. 22	.33	.05	8.50 (20)	.75	110,130,000
2018	20¢ Wolf Trap Farm Park, Sept. 1	.33	.05	2.00	.75	110,995,000
	American Architecture Issue, Sept. 30					
2019	20¢ Fallingwater	.33	.06		.75	41,335,000
2020	20¢ Illinois Institute of Technology	.33	.06		.75	41,335,000
2021	20¢ Gropius House	.33	.06		.75	41,335,000
2022	20¢ Dulles Airport	.33	.06		.75	41,335,000
	Plate Block of 4, (#2019-2022)			2.00		
2023	20¢ Francis of Assisi, Oct. 7	.33	.05	2.00	.75	174,180,000
2024	20¢ Ponce de Leon, Oct. 2	.33	.05	8.50 (20)	.75	110,261,000
2025	13¢ Puppy and Kitten, Nov. 3	.22	.06	1.30	.75	
2026	20¢ Christmas, Madonna					
	and Child—Tiepolo, Oct. 28	.33	.05	8.50 (20)	.75	703,295,000
	Seasons Greetings Issue, Oct. 28					
2027	20¢ Sledding	.33	.06		.75	197,220,000
2028	20¢ Snowman	.33	.06		.75	197,220,000
2029	20¢ Skating	.33	.06		.75	197,220,000
2030	20¢ Tree	.33	.06		.75	197,220,000
	Plate Block of 4, #2027-2030			2.00		

AMA Gets Its Stamp

In February 1947, Postmaster General Hannegan was admitted for treatment to the Boston Memorial Hospital. The treatment he received was evidently more than he expected.

949

Later in that year, the American Medical Association planned to celebrate its centennial in Atlantic City, N.J., and June 8th had been declared Medical Day. The AMA also decided that it was time to commemorate the medical profession on a U.S. postage stamp. Postmaster Hannegan gave his "now or never" approval while still in the hospital so work could begin on a design as soon as possible. "The Doctor" (#949) was issued on June 9, 1947, as a 3¢ commemorative. The picture was from a painting by Sir Luke Fildes, R.A., done in 1891. It shows a physician treating a young boy in his bedroom. Close examination of the patient in the picture shows no resemblance to Postmaster Hannegan.

Dr. Mary Walker
Army Surgeon

Medal of Honor
USA 20c

2013

International Peace Garden

1932
1982
USA 20c

2014

America's
A B C
Libraries
X Y Z
USA 20c
Legacies To Mankind

2015

Jackie R

2016

Touro
Synagogue
Newport, RI 1763

To bigotry,
no sanction.
To persecution,
no assistance.
George Washington

USA 20c

2017

Frank Lloyd Wright 1867-1959 Fallingwater Mill Run PA
Architecture USA 20c

Mies van der Rohe 1886-1969 Illinois Inst Tech Chicago
Architecture USA 20c

USA 20c

Wolf Trap Farm Park
for the performing arts

2018

Walter Gropius 1883-1969 Gropius House Lincoln MA
Architecture USA 20c

Eero Saarinen 1910-1961 Dulles Airport Washington DC
Architecture USA 20c

2019
2021

2020
2022

FRANCIS OF ASSISI 1182-1982 USA 20c

2023

Ponce de León USA 20c

2024

USA

2025

Christmas USA 20c

Tiepolo, National Gallery of Art

2026

Season's Greetings USA 20c

Season's Greetings USA 20c

Season's Greetings USA 20c

Season's Greetings USA 20c

Science & Industry (20¢, #2031)

Type: Commemorative
Date of Issue: January 19, 1983
Place of Issue: Chicago, IL
Designer: Saul Bass
Printing: Offset/Intaglio
Colors: Yellow, Red, Blue, Black

This stamp was issued at Chicago's Museum of Science and Industry, which celebrated its 50th anniversary during 1983. The stamp design explores abstract depictions of the subject matter—science and industry.

Swedish-American Treaty (20¢, #2036)

Type: Commemorative
Date of Issue: March 24, 1983
Place of Issue: Philadelphia, PA
Designer: Dan Jonsson
Printing: Intaglio
Colors: Blue, Black, Maroon

For more information on this issue, please see pages 28 and 29.

Balloons
(20¢, #2032-2035)

Type:
Commemorative
Date of Issue:
March 31, 1983
Place of Issue:
Washington, D.C./
Albuquerque, NM
Designer:
Davis Meltzer
Printing: Offset/Intaglio
Colors: Blue, Green, Red, Yellow, Purple

The vertical stamp at the left depicts the hot air balloon "Intrepid," used by the Union Army for surveillance during the Civil War. The horizontal designs in the center form a se-tenant pair and show modern hot air balloons in flight. The vertical stamp on the right pictures the Explorer II, a balloon used jointly in 1935 by the National Geographic Society and the U.S. Army for research.

Civilian Conservation Corps (20¢, #2037)

Type: Commemorative
Date of Issue: April 5, 1983
Place of Issue: Luray, VA
Designer: David K. Stone
Printing: Gravure
Colors: Blue, Green, Brown

The CCC, established in 1933, was charged with the construction of new roads, irrigation dams, telephone lines, fire towers, campgrounds and trails across the country.

Joseph Priestley (20¢, #2038)

Type: Commemorative
Date of Issue: April 13, 1983
Place of Issue: Northumberland, PA
Designer: Dennis Lyall
Printing: Gravure
Colors: Tan, Yellow, Red, Blue, Brown, Black

This stamp commemorates the 250th birthday anniversary of pioneer chemist Joseph Priestley, who is best known for the discovery of the existence of oxygen in 1774.

Voluntarism (20¢, #2039)

Type: Commemorative
Date of Issue: April 20, 1983
Place of Issue: Washington, D.C.
Designer: Paul Calle
Printing: Intaglio
Colors: Black, Red

Voluntarism honors that very special spirit of helping others.

Concord (20¢, #2040)

Type: Commemorative
Date of Issue: April 29, 1983
Place of Issue: Germantown, PA
Designer: Richard Schlecht
Printing: Intaglio
Colors: Brown

For more information, please see pages 28 and 29.

Transportation Series Stamp

Four subjects were issued in 1983 in the Transportation Series, which now numbers 11 stamps. Begun in 1981, this series features early modes of transportation. The Transportation stamps are issued in coil form only.

Antique Sleigh (5.2¢, #1897D)

Type: Definitive (Transportation Series)
Date of Issue: March 21, 1983
Place of Issue: Memphis, TN
Designer: Walter Brooks
Printing: Intaglio
Colors: Red

Railroad Handcar (3¢, #1897B)

Type: Definitive (Transportation Series)
Date of Issue: March 25, 1983
Place of Issue: Rochester, NY
Designer: Walter Brooks
Printing: Intaglio
Colors: Green

Motorcycle (5¢, #1897C)

Type: Definitive (Transportation Series)
Date of Issue: October 10, 1983
Place of Issue: San Francisco, CA
Designer: Walter Brooks
Printing: Intaglio
Colors: Green

Omnibus (1¢)

Type: Definitive (Transportation)
Date of Issue: August 19, 1983
Place of Issue: Washington, D.C.
Designer: David Stone
Printing: Intaglio
Colors: Purple

Physical Fitness (20¢, #2043)

Type: Commemorative
Date of Issue: May 14, 1983
Place of Issue: Houston, TX
Designer: Donald Moss
Printing: Gravure
Colors: Yellow, Magenta, Cyan, Black

This stamp is intended to draw attention to all forms of exercise. The line behind the runners represents an electrocardiograph tracing.

Brooklyn Bridge (20¢, #2041)

Type: Commemorative
Date of Issue: May 17, 1983
Place of Issue: Brooklyn, NY
Designer: Howard Koslow
Printing: Intaglio
Colors: Blue

This issue marked the 100th anniversary of the opening of the Brooklyn Bridge, the first suspension bridge to use cables made of steel wires and the first to use pneumatic caissons for foundations. The bridge cost $9 million and took 14 years to build.

Tennessee Valley Authority (20¢, #2042)

Type: Commemorative
Date of Issue: May 18, 1983
Place of Issue: Knoxville, TN
Designer: Howard Koslow
Printing: Gravure/Intaglio
Colors: Yellow, Magenta, Cyan, Black (Gravure) and Black (Intaglio)

This stamp was issued to celebrate the 50th anniversary of the founding of TVA, which was created to develop the watershed of the Tennessee River and its tributaries. The TVA is best known for producing and distributing electrical power in this area, but also cooperates with local authorities and citizens in promoting better farming methods, soil conservation, reforestation, control of pollution and energy development.

Scott Joplin (20¢, #2044)

Type: Commemorative (Black Heritage USA Series)
Date of Issue: June 9, 1983
Place of Issue: Sedalia, MO
Designer: Jerry Pinkney
Printing: Gravure
Colors: Yellow, Magenta, Cyan, Brown, Black, Ochre

Composer Scott Joplin is known as the King of Ragtime. While a young man, he played in a honky tonk while attending a black college, taking courses in harmony and composition. Best known for his composition *Maple Leaf Rag,* he also wrote a full-length opera, *Treemonisha.*

Medal of Honor (20¢, #2045)

Type: Commemorative
Date of Issue: June 7, 1983
Place of Issue: Washington D.C.
Designer: Dennis J. Holm
Printing: Offset
Colors: Yellow, Green, Blue, Black

It's the nation's highest award for valor. It is awarded only for "courage above and beyond the call of duty." Only 3,400 Medals of Honor have been awarded to individuals, making it the most precious and coveted of American awards.

Nathaniel Hawthorne (20¢, #2047)

Type: Commemorative (Literary Arts Series)
Date of Issue: July 8, 1983
Place of Issue: Salem, MA
Designer: Bradbury Thompson
Printing: Gravure
Colors: Yellow, Magenta, Cyan, Black

Part of the Literary Arts Series, the stamp honoring Nathaniel Hawthorne was issued at the House of The Seven Gables, site of one of Hawthorne's most famous works. Hawthorne, a nineteenth-century writer, set most of his stories against the somber backdrop of seventeenth-century Puritan New England.

Carl Schurz (4¢, #1845)

Type: Definitive (Great Americans Series)
Date of Issue: June 3, 1983
Place of Issue: Watertown, WI
Designer: Richard Sparks
Printing: Intaglio
Colors: Purple

Carl Schurz (1829-1906) was a noted German-American statesman and journalist.

Pearl Buck (5¢, #1846)

Type: Definitive (Great Americans Series)
Date of Issue: June 25, 1983
Place of Issue: Hillsboro, WV
Designer: Paul Calle
Printing: Intaglio
Colors: Reddish-brown

Pearl Buck (1892-1973) was known as an author and humanitarian.

Thomas Hopkins Gallaudet (20¢, #1853)

Type: Definitive (Great Americans Series)
Date of Issue: June 10, 1983
Place of Issue: West Hartford, CT
Designer: Dennis Lyall
Printing: Intaglio
Colors: Green

Thomas Gallaudet (1787-1851) was a renowned educator of the hearing impaired.

Dorthea Dix (1¢, #1843A)

Type: Definitive (Great Americans Series)
Date of Issue: Sept. 23, 1983
Place of Issue: Hampden, ME
Designer: Bernie Fuchs
Printing: Intaglio
Colors: Black

Dorthea Dix (1802-1887) was a noted social reformer and humanitarian.

Henry Clay (3¢, #1844A)

Type: Definitive (Great Americans Series)
Date of Issue: July 13, 1983
Place of Issue: Washington, D.C.
Designer: Ward Brackett
Printing: Intaglio
Colors: Green

Henry Clay (1777-1852) was known as the Great Compromiser.

1983 ISSUES

Babe Ruth (20¢, #2046)

Type: Commemorative (American Sports Series)
Date of Issue: July 6, 1983
Place of Issue: Chicago, IL
Designer: Richard Gangel
Printing: Intaglio
Colors: Blue

The third in the American Sports Series, the Babe Ruth stamp was issued in conjunction with the 50th anniversary of professional baseball's All-Star Game. Ruth played in the first All-Star Game in Chicago in 1933.

$9.35 Stamp
(#1909 single stamp; #1909a booklet pane of 3)

Type: Definitive (Booklet Pane of 3)
Date of Issue: August 12, 1983
Place of Issue: Kennedy Space Center, FL
Designer: Young & Rubicam
Printing: Gravure
Colors: Yellow, Magenta, Cyan, Black

This special $9.35 stamp is intended for use primarily on Express Mail Next Day Service packages. Can also be used for regular postage.

Civil Service (20¢, #2053)

Type: Commemorative
Date of Issue: September 9, 1983
Place of Issue: Washington, D.C.
Designer: Graphic Design Team of MDB
Communications with the principle
credit to Kathleen Wilmes Herring
Printing: Gravure/Intaglio
Colors: Buff (Gravure)
Red, Blue, (Intaglio)

One hundred years ago, the Pendleton Act was signed into law, creating a federal government job system that was based on merit, rather than political influence.

Metropolitan Opera (20¢, #2054)

Type: Commemorative
Date of Issue: September 14, 1983
Place of Issue: New York, NY
Designer: Ken Davies
Printing: Offset/Intaglio
Colors: Yellow (Offset), Maroon (Intaglio)

Since its first opening night on October 22, 1883, the Metropolitan Opera has entered the lives of countless Americans through its performances in New York, on national tours and through radio and television broadcasts.

American Inventors

(20¢, (4) #2055-58)

Type: Commemorative
Date of Issue:
September 21, 1983
Place of Issue: Washington, D.C.
Designer: Dennis Lyall
Printing: Offset/Intaglio
Colors: Brown (Offset),
Black (Intaglio)

American inventors honored are: Charles Steinmetz (devised many electronic applications and inventions); Edwin Armstrong (invented FM radio); Nikola Tesla (developed the generator and other devices that made a.c. possible); Philo T. Farnsworth (invented all-electronic television system).

Streetcars (20¢, (4) #2059-62)

Type: Commemorative
Date of Issue: October 1, 1983
Place of Issue:
Kennebunkport, ME
Designer: Richard Leech
Printing: Offset/Intaglio
Colors: Yellow, Magenta,
Cyan, Black
(Offset) Black (Intaglio)

This block of four features America's first major form of mass transportation, the streetcar.

Treaty of Paris (20¢, #2052)

Type: Commemorative
Date of Issue: September 2, 1983
Place of Issue: Washington, D.C.
Designer: David Blossom
Printing: Gravure
Colors: Yellow, Magenta, Cyan, Black

The Treaty of Paris, proclaiming that the United States was a free, sovereign and independent nation, was signed on September 3, 1783, thus ending the Revolutionary War.

Christmas Raphael Madonna (20¢, #2063)

Type: Special
Date of Issue: October 28, 1983
Place of Issue: Washington, D.C.
Designer: Bradbury Thompson
Printing: Gravure
Colors: Yellow, Magenta, Cyan, Red, Black

This special Christmas stamp features a painting of the Madonna by Raphael.

Christmas Santa Claus (20¢, #2064)

Type: Special
Date of Issue: October 28, 1983
Place of Issue: Santa Claus, IN
Designer: John Berkey
Printing: Gravure
Colors: Yellow, Magenta, Cyan, Black, Green type

Martin Luther (20¢, #2065)

Type: Commemorative
Date of Issue: November 10, 1983
Place of Issue: Washington, D.C.
Designer: Bradbury Thompson
Printing: Gravure
Colors: Yellow, Red, Blue, Brown, Black

This commemorative celebrates the 500th anniversary of the birth of Martin Luther, whose beliefs brought about the Reformation.

Olympics (40¢, C105-C108)

Type: International Airmail
Date of Issue: April 8, 1983
Place of Issue: Los Angeles, CA
Designer: Bob Peak
Printing: Gravure
Colors: Red, Blue,
Green, Yellow, Purple

Olympics (28¢, C101-C104)

Type: International Airmail
Date of Issue: June 17, 1983
Place of Issue: San Antonio, Texas
Designer: Bob Peak
Printing: Gravure
Colors: Red, Blue,
Green, Yellow, Purple

Olympics (13¢, (4) #2048-2051)

Type: Commemorative
Date of Issue: July 28, 1983
Place of Issue: South Bend, IN
Designer: Bob Peak
Printing: Gravure
Colors: Red, Blue,
Green, Yellow, Purple

Olympics

Type: International Airmail
Date of Issue: November 4, 1983
Place of Issue:
Colorado Springs, CO
Designer: Bob Peak
Printing: Gravure
Colors: Red, Blue,
Green, Yellow, Purple

For more information on the Olympic issues, please see pages 32-43.

237

1918-1935

C1   C2   C3   C3a

C4   C5   C6

C7   C10

C11

C12   C13

C14   C15

C18

C20

Air Post Stamps	Un	U	PB	#	FDC	Q
For prepayment of postage on all mailable matter sent by airmail. All unwatermarked.						
Issue of 1918, Perf. 11						
C1 6¢ Curtiss Jenny	135.00	45.00	1,700.00	(6)	*16,000.00*	3,395,854
C2 16¢ Curtiss Jenny	225.00	55.00	3,500.00	(6)	*16,000.00*	3,793,887
C3 24¢ Curtiss Jenny	210.00	65.00	3,600.00		*19,000.00*	2,134,888
C3a Center Inverted	145,000.00					
Issue of 1923						
C4 8¢ Wooden Propeller and						
Engine Nose	60.00	25.00	825.00	(6)	500.00	6,414,576
C5 16¢ Air Service Emblem	215.00	60.00	5,000.00	(6)	850.00	5,309,275
C6 24¢ De Havilland Biplane	250.00	38.50	6,000.00	(6)	1,000.00	5,285,775
Issue of 1926-27						
C7 10¢ Map of U.S.						
and Two Mail Planes	7.25	.50	85.00	(6)	75.00	42,092,800
C8 15¢ olive brown (C7)	8.50	3.25	100.00	(6)	85.00	15,597,307
C9 20¢ yellow green (C7)	21.50	2.50	250.00	(6)	110.00	17,616,350
Issue of 1927						
C10 10¢ Lindbergh's "Spirit of						
St. Louis", June 18	17.50	3.50	240.00	(6)	25.00	20,379,179
C10a Booklet pane of 3	165.00	*60.00*				
Nos. C1-C10 inclusive were also available for ordinary postage.						
Issue of 1928						
C11 5¢ Beacon on Rocky Mountains,						
July 25	9.00	.65	80.00	(6)	45.00	106,887,675
C12 5¢ Winged Globe, Feb. 10	21.50	.50	275.00	(6)	15.00	97,641,200
Graf Zeppelin Issue, Apr. 19						
C13 65¢ Zeppelin over Atlantic Ocean	560.00	525.00	4,500.00	(6)	2,400.00	93,536
C14 $1.30 Zeppelin between						
Continents	1,175.00	900.00	11,000.00	(6)	1,600.00	72,428
C15 $2.60 Zeppelin Passing Globe	1,900.00	1,450.00	17,000.00	(6)	2,500.00	61,296
Issued for use on mail carried on the first Europe-Pan-American round-trip flight of Graf Zeppelin, May 1930.						
Issues of 1931-32, Perf. 10½x11						
C16 5¢ violet (C12)	10.00	.50	175.00		300.00	57,340,050
C17 8¢ olive bistre (C12)	4.25	.27	65.00		20.00	76,648,803
Issue of 1933, Perf. 11						
C18 50¢ Century of Progress, Oct. 2	165.00	150.00	1,500.00	(6)	300.00	324,070
Issue of 1934, Perf. 10½x11						
C19 6¢ dull orange (C12), July 1	5.50	.11	35.00		*200.00*	302,205,100
Issue of 1935, Perf. 11						
C20 25¢ Transpacific, Nov. 22	3.50	1.75	40.00	(6)	35.00	10,205,400

	Issue of 1937	Un	U	PB	#	FDC	
C21	20¢ The "China Clipper," over the						
	Pacific, Feb. 15	22.50	2.25	225.00	(6)	40.00	12,794,600
C22	50¢ carmine (C21)	22.50	6.75	210.00	(6)	40.00	9,285,300
	Issue of 1938						
C23	6¢ Eagle Holding Shield,						
	Olive Branch, and Arrows, May 14	.70	.09	11.00		20.00	349,946,500
	Issue of 1939						
C24	30¢ Transatlantic, May 16	21.50	1.50	275.00	(6)	50.00	19,768,150
	Issues of 1941-44, Perf. 11x10½						
C25	6¢ Twin-motor Transport Plane,						
	1941	.20	.05	1.00		2.25	4,476,527,700
C25a	Booklet pane of 3	6.00	—				
	Singles No. C25a are imperf. at sides or imperf. at sides and bottom.						
C26	8¢ olive green (C25), 1944	.25	.05	1.50		3.75	1,744,876,650
C27	10¢ violet (C25), 1941	2.25	.15	16.00		7.00	67,117,400
C28	15¢ brown carmine (C25), 1941	5.00	.28	22.00		10.00	78,434,800
C29	20¢ bright green (C25), 1941	3.75	.27	20.00		10.00	42,359,850
C30	30¢ blue (C25), 1941	4.50	.28	21.00		16.50	59,880,850
C31	50¢ orange (C25), 1941	27.50	4.50	150.00		40.00	11,160,600
	Issue of 1946						
C32	5¢ DC-4 Skymaster, Sept. 25	.13	.05	.75		2.00	864,753,100
	Issues of 1947, Perf. 10½x11						
C33	5¢ DC-4 Skymaster, Mar. 26	.13	.05	.75		2.00	971,903,700
	Perf. 11x10½						
C34	10¢ Pan American Union Building,						
	Washington, D.C., Aug. 30	.35	.07	2.50		2.00	207,976,550
C35	15¢ Statue of Liberty/						
	N.Y. Skyline, Aug. 20	.45	.06	2.85		2.75	756,186,350
C36	25¢ Plane over San Francisco-						
	Oakland Bay Bridge, July 30	1.65	.08	7.50		3.50	132,956,100
	Issues of 1948						
	Coil Stamp, Perf. 10 Horizontally						
C37	5¢ carmine (C33), Jan. 15	1.50	1.35			2.00	Unlimited
	Perf. 11x10½						
C38	5¢ New York City, July 31	.15	.14	20.00		1.75	38,449,100
	Issues of 1949						
	Perf. 10½x11						
C39	6¢ carmine (C33), Jan. 18	.17	.05	.85		1.50	5,070,095,200
C39a	Booklet pane of 6	17.50	5.00				
	Perf. 11x10½						
C40	6¢ Alexandria 200th Anniv., May 11	.17	.12	.95		1.25	75,085,000
	Coil Stamp, Perf. 10 Horizontally						
C41	6¢ carmine (C33), Aug. 25	4.50	.06			1.25	Unlimited
	Universal Postal Union Issue, Perf. 11x10½						
C42	10¢ Post Office Dept. Bldg., Nov. 18	.35	.35	3.50		1.75	21,061,300

C21

C23

C24

C25

C32

C33

C34

C35

C36

C38

C40

C42

C43

C44

C45

C46

C47

C48

C49

C51

C53

C54

C55

C56

C57

C58

C59

C60

	1948 continued	Un	U	PB	#	FDC	Q
C43	15¢ Globe and Doves Carrying						
	Messages, Oct. 7	.45	.45	3.00		2.25	36,613,100
C44	25¢ Boeing Stratocruiser						
	and Globe, Nov. 30	.85	.80	11.00		2.75	16,217,100
C45	6¢ Wright Brothers, Dec. 17	.22	.12	1.00		3.75	80,405,000
	Issue of 1952						
C46	80¢ Diamond Head, Honolulu,						
	Hawaii, Mar. 26	15.00	1.25	80.00		17.50	18,876,800
	Issue of 1953						
C47	6¢ Powered Flight, May 29	.17	.13	.85		1.50	78,415,000
	Issue of 1954						
C48	4¢ Eagle in Flight, Sept. 3	.12	.09	5.00		.75	50,483,600
	Issue of 1957						
C49	6¢ Air Force, Aug. 1	.17	.10	1.50		1.75	63,185,000
	Issues of 1958						
C50	5¢ rose red (C48), July 31	.20	.18	5.00		.80	72,480,000
	Perf. 10½x11						
C51	7¢ Silhouette of Jet Liner, July 31	.22	.05	1.30		.75	532,410,300
C51a	Booklet pane of 6	16.50	6.50				1,326,960,000
	Coil Stamp, Perf. 10 Horizontally						
C52	7¢ blue (C51)	3.95	.10			.90	157,035,000
	Issues of 1959, Perf. 11x10½						
C53	7¢ Alaska Statehood, Jan. 3	.20	.09	1.50		.65	90,055,200
	Perf. 11						
C54	7¢ Balloon Jupiter, Aug. 17	.20	.09	1.50		1.10	79,290,000
	Issued for the 100th anniversary of the carrying of mail by the balloon Jupiter from Lafayette to Crawfordsville, Indiana.						
	Perf. 11x10½						
C55	7¢ Hawaii Statehood, Aug. 21	.20	.09	1.50		1.00	84,815,000
	Perf. 11						
C56	10¢ Pan-American Games, Aug. 27	.35	.35	5.00		.90	38,770,000
	Issue of 1959-66						
C57	10¢ Liberty Bell, June 10, 1960	3.00	1.00	15.00		1.50	39,960,000
C58	15¢ Statue of Liberty, Jan. 13, 1961	.70	.10	4.00		1.10	Unlimited
C59	25¢ Abraham Lincoln, Apr. 22, 1960	.70	.06	4.00		1.50	Unlimited
	Issue of 1960, Perf. 10½x11						
C60	7¢ Jet Airliner (C51), Aug. 12	.22	.05	1.50		.70	289,460,000
C60a	Booklet pane of 6	19.50	7.00				
	Coil Stamp, Perf. 10 Horizontally						
C61	7¢ carmine (C60), Oct. 22	7.25	.25			1.00	87,140,000

	Issue of 1961, Perf. 11	Un	U	PB	#	FDC	
C62	13¢ Liberty Bell, June 28, 1961	.65	.10	7.00		.80	Unlimited
C63	15¢ Statue of Liberty, Jan. 13, 1961	.40	.06	2.25		1.00	Unlimited
	No. C63 has a gutter between the two parts of the design; No. C58 does not.						
	Issue of 1962, Perf. 10½x11						
C64	8¢ Jetliner over Capitol, Dec. 5	.23	.05	1.10		.60	Unlimited
	Booklet pane of 5 + label	2.75	1.25				
	Coil Stamp, Perf. 10 Horizontally						
C65	8¢ carmine (C64), Dec. 5	.45	.06			.80	Unlimited
	Issue of 1963, Perf. 11						
C66	15¢ Montgomery Blair, May 3	1.30	.85	11.00		1.35	42,245,000
	Issues of 1963-64, Perf. 11x10½						
C67	6¢ Bald Eagle, July 12, 1963	.22	.14	4.00		.50	Unlimited
	Perf. 11						
C68	8¢ Amelia Earhart, July 24, 1963	.35	.12	4.50		2.50	63,890,000
C69	8¢ Robert H. Goddad, Oct. 5, 1964	1.00	.12	7.50		2.75	65,170,000
	Issues of 1967						
C70	8¢ Alaska Purchase, Mar. 30	.45	.20	7.00		.70	64,710,000
C71	20¢ "Columbia Jays" by Audubon,						
	Apr. 26	1.75	.09	10.00		2.00	165,430,000
	Issues of 1968, Perf. 11x10½						
C72	10¢ 50-Star Runway, Jan. 5	.33	.05	2.25		.60	Unlimited
C72b	Booklet pane of 8	3.50	.75				
C72c	Booklet pane of 5 + label	5.50	.75				
C73	10¢ carmine (C72), Coil, Perf. 10	.45	.05			.60	Unlimited
	Air Mail Service Issue, Perf. 11						
C74	10¢ Curtiss Jenny, May 15	.50	.14	8.00		1.50	74,180,000
C75	20¢ U.S.A. and Jet, Nov. 22	1.00	.08	6.50		1.10	Unlimited
	Issue of 1969						
C76	10¢ Moon Landing, Sept. 9	.28	.18	3.50		3.50	152,364,800
	Issues of 1971-73, Perf. 10½x11, 11x10½						
C77	9¢ Plane, May 15, 1971	.23	.20	3.00		.50	Unlimited
C78	11¢ Silhouette of Jet, May 7, 1971	.30	.05	1.35		.50	Unlimited
C78a	Booklet pane of 4 + 2 labels	1.50	.10				
C79	13¢ Winged Airmail Envelope,						
	Nov. 16, 1973	.32	.05	1.65		.55	Unlimited
C79a	Booklet pane of 5 + label,						
	Dec. 27, 1973	1.75	.10				
	Perf. 11						
C80	17¢ Statue of Liberty, July 13, 1971	.50	.12	2.75		.60	Unlimited
	Perf. 11x10½						
C81	21¢ red, blue and black (C75)						
	May 21, 1971	.50	.08	2.75		.75	Unlimited

C62

C63

C64

C66

C67

C68

C69

C70

C71

C72

C74

C75

C76

C77

C78

C79

C80

C81

C84

C85

C86

C87

C88

C89

C90

C91
C92

C93
C94

C95
C96

C97

C98

C99

C100

CE1

CE2

		Un	U	PB	#	FDC	Q
	Coil Stamps, Perf. 10 Vertically						
C82	11¢ Silhouette of Jet (C78),						Unlimited
	May 7, 1971	.35	.05			.50	
C83	13¢ red (C79), Dec. 27, 1973	.40	.05			.50	
	Issues of 1972, Perf. 11						
C84	11¢ City of Refuge, May 3	.28	.12	2.25		.65	78,210,000
	Perf. 11x10½						
C85	11¢ Skiing and Olympic Rings,						
	Aug. 17	.28	.12	3.50 (10)		.50	96,240,000
	Issue of 1973						
C86	11¢ De Forest Audions, July 10	.28	.12	1.75		.50	58,705,000
	Issues of 1974, Perf. 11						
C87	18¢ Statue of Liberty, Jan. 11	.45	.45	2.50		.65	Unlimited
C88	26¢ Mt. Rushmore National						
	Memorial, Jan. 2	.65	.10	2.85		.85	Unlimited
	Issue of 1976						
C89	25¢ Plane & Globes, Jan. 2	.65	.15	2.50		.85	
C90	31¢ Plane, Globes & Flag, Jan. 2	.75	.08	3.10		1.10	
	Issues of 1978, Wright Brothers Issue, Sept. 23						
C91	31¢ Orville & Wilbur Wright	.85	.15			1.15	
C92	31¢ Orville & Wilbur Wright	.85	.15			1.15	
	Pair, #C91-C92	1.65	1.10	3.10			
	Issues of 1979, Octave Chanute Issue, March 29						
C93	21¢ Octave Chanute	.60	.30			1.00	
C94	21¢ Octave Chanute	.60	.30			1.00	
	Pair, #C93-C94	1.10	.70	2.10			
	Wiley Post Issue, Nov. 20						
C95	25¢ Wiley Post	.70	.30			1.00	
C96	25¢ Wiley Post	.70	.30			1.00	
	Pair, #C95-C96	1.30	.90	2.50			
	Olympic Games Issue						
C97	31¢ High Jump	.90	.30	8.75		1.15	4,720,000
	Issues of 1980						
C98	40¢ Philip Mazzei, Oct. 13	.80	.18	11.00		1.35	
C99	28¢ Blanche Stuart Scott, Dec. 30	.55	.20	7.75 (12)		1.10	
C100	35¢ Glenn Curtiss, Dec. 30	.70	.20	10.00 (12)		1.25	
	Air Post Special Delivery Stamps						
	Issue of 1934, Perf. 11						
CE1	16¢ dark blue (CE2)	1.10	1.10	30.00 (6)		25.00	
	For imperforate variety see No. 771.						
	Issue of 1936						
CE2	16¢ Great Seal of United States	.70	.30	12.00		17.50	

		Un	U	PB	#	FDC
	Special Delivery Stamps.					
	Unwmkd., Issue of 1885, Perf. 12					
E1	10¢ Messenger Running	365.00	37.50	15,000.00	(8)	8,000.00
	Issue of 1888					
E2	10¢ blue (E3)	365.00	9.50	15,000.00	(8)	
	Issue of 1893					
E3	10¢ Messenger Running	250.00	17.50	9,000.00	(8)	
	Issue of 1894, Line under "Ten Cents"					
E4	10¢ Messenger Running	850.00	18.75	16,500.00	(6)	
	Issue of 1895, Wmkd. (191)					
E5	10¢ blue (E4)	170.00	3.00	5,500.00	(6)	
	Issue of 1902					
E6	10¢ Messenger on Bicycle	125.00	3.25	3,250.00	(6)	
	Issue of 1908					
E7	10¢ Mercury Helmet and					
	Olive Branch	90.00	30.00	1,200.00	(6)	
	Issue of 1911, Wmdk. (190)					
E8	10¢ ultramarine (E6)	125.00	5.00	3,000.00	(6)	
	Issue of 1914, Perf. 10					
E9	10¢ ultramarine (E6)	250.00	6.50	5,750.00	(6)	
	Unwmkd., Issue of 1916					
E10	10¢ ultramarine (E6)	425.00	20.00	7,500.00	(6)	
	Issue of 1917, Perf. 11					
E11	10¢ ultramarine (E6)	21.50	.40	350.00	(6)	
	Issue of 1922					
E12	10¢ Postman and Motorcycle	37.50	.15	525.00	(6)	
	Issue of 1925					
E13	15¢ Postman and Motorcycle	27.50	1.00	325.00	(6)	
E14	20¢ Post Office Truck	4.00	2.00	50.00	(6)	
	Issue of 1927, Perf. 11x10½					
E15	10¢ Postman and Motorcycle	1.00	.08	6.50		100.00
	Issue of 1931					
E16	15¢ orange (E12)	1.00	.10	6.50		135.00
	Issue of 1944					
E17	13¢ Postman and Motorcycle	.80	.09	5.00		12.00
E18	17¢ Postman and Motorcycle	7.00	2.75	30.00		12.00
	Issue of 1951					
E19	20¢ black (E14)	3.75	.11	12.00		5.00
	Issue of 1954-57					
E20	20¢ Delivery of Letter	.75	.07	4.50		3.00
E21	30¢ Delivery of Letter	.85	.05	5.25		2.25
	Issue of 1969-71, Perf. 11					
E22	45¢ Arrows	2.00	.20	14.50		3.50
E23	60¢ Arrows	1.25	.10	6.00		3.50

E1

E3

E4

E6

E7

E12

E13

E14

E15

E17

E18

E20

E21

E22

E23

1879-1959

F1

FA1

JQ1

JQ2

J2

J19

J25

J33

J69

J78

J88

J98

J101

	Un	U	PB	#	FDC	Q
Registration Stamp						
Issued for the prepayment of registry; not usable for postage. Sale discontinued May 28, 1913.						
Issue of 1911, Perf. 12, Wmkd. USPS (190)						
F1 10¢ Bald Eagle	115.00	5.00	*2,100.00*	(6)	*9,000.00*	9,000.00
Certified Mail Stamp						
For use on first-class mail for which no indemnity value is claimed, but for which proof of mailing and proof of delivery are available at less cost than registered mail.						
Issue of 1955, Perf. 10½x11						
FA1 15¢ Letter Carrier	.55	.40	6.25		3.25	54,460,300

	Un	U
Postage Due Stamps		
For affixing by a postal clerk to any mail to denote amount to be collected from addressee because of insufficient prepayment of postage.		
Printed by American Bank Note Company Issue of 1879, Design of J2, Perf. 12, Unwmd.		
J1 1¢ brown	25.00	5.00
J2 2¢ Figure of Value	165.00	5.00
J3 3¢ brown	19.50	2.50
J4 5¢ brown	250.00	20.00
J5 10¢ brown	335.00	8.75
J6 30¢ brown	140.00	16.50
J7 50¢ brown	210.00	33.50
Special Printing		
J8 1¢ deep brown	*4,850.00*	—
J9 2¢ deep brown	*3,000.00*	—
J10 3¢ deep brown	*2,750.00*	—
J11 5¢ deep brown	*2,250.00*	—
J12 10¢ deep brown	*1,350.00*	—
J13 30¢ deep brown	*1,350.00*	—
J14 50¢ deep brown	*1,350.00*	

	Un	U
Regular Issue of 1884-89, Design of J19		
J15 1¢ red brown	27.50	2.95
J16 2¢ red brown	35.00	2.95
J17 3¢ red brown	415.00	80.00
J18 5¢ red brown	195.00	8.00
J19 10¢ Figure of Value	160.00	4.50
J20 30¢ red brown	100.00	18.75
J21 50¢ red brown	1,000.00	120.00
Issue of 1891-93, Design of J25		
J22 1¢ bright claret	8.50	.55
J23 2¢ bright claret	10.75	.50
J24 3¢ bright claret	21.00	3.00
J25 5¢ Figure of Value	25.00	3.00
J26 10¢ bright claret	50.00	7.00
J27 30¢ bright claret	225.00	75.00
J28 50¢ bright claret	250.00	80.00
Printed by the Bureau of Engraving and Printing, Issue of 1894, Design of J33, Perf. 12		
J29 1¢ vermillion	415.00	65.00
J30 2¢ vermillion	195.00	30.00

Parcel Post Postage Due Stamps

For affixing by a postal clerk to any parcel post package to denote the amount to be collected from the addressee because of insufficient prepayment of postage.

Beginning July 1, 1913, these stamps were valid for use as regular postage due stamps.

	Un	U
Issue of 1912, Design of JQ1 and JQ5, Perf. 12		
JQ1 1¢ Figure of Value	13.50	3.75
JQ2 2¢ dark green	110.00	18.50
JQ3 5¢ dark green	16.50	4.50
JQ4 10¢ dark green	200.00	42.50
JQ5 25¢ Figure of Value	115.00	4.50

		Un	U	PB	#	FDC	Q
J31	1¢ deep claret	18.00	3.25		(6)		
J32	2¢ deep claret	15.00	2.00		(6)		
J33	3¢ Figure of Value	50.00	16.50		(6)		
J34	5¢ deep claret	55.00	19.50		(6)		
J35	10¢ deep rose	50.00	9.00		(6)		
J36	30¢ deep claret	195.00	45.00				
J37	50¢	375.00	90.00				
	Issue of 1895, Design of J33, Wmkd. (191)						
J38	1¢ deep claret	4.25	.30		(6)		
J39	2¢ deep claret	4.25	.22		(6)		
J40	3¢ deep claret	27.50	1.25		(6)		
J41	5¢ deep claret	27.50	1.20		(6)		
J42	10¢ deep claret	31.00	1.95		(6)		
J43	30¢ deep claret	250.00	18.00		(6)		
J44	50¢ deep claret	155.00	21.00		(6)		
	Issue of 1910-12, Design of J33, Wmkd. (190)						
J45	1¢ deep claret	18.00	2.00	400.00	(6)		
J46	2¢ deep claret	17.50	.17	350.00	(6)		
J47	3¢ deep claret	295.00	12.00	3,850.00	(6)		
J48	5¢ deep claret	46.50	2.75	600.00	(6)		
J49	10¢ deep claret	50.00	7.00	1,150.00	(6)		
J50	50¢ deep claret	575.00	65.00	6,500.00	(6)		
	Issue of 1914-15, Design of J33, Perf. 10						
J52	1¢ carmine lake	37.50	6.25	550.00	(6)		
J53	2¢ carmine lake	22.50	.20	350.00	(6)		
J54	3¢ carmine lake	365.00	9.00	4,500.00	(6)		
J55	5¢ carmine lake	18.50	1.50	285.00	(6)		
J56	10¢ carmine lake	30.00	1.00	675.00	(6)		
J57	30¢ carmine lake	140.00	13.00	2,350.00	(6)		
J58	50¢ carmine lake	4,250.00	335.00	30,000.00	(6)		
	Issue of 1916, Design of J33, Unwmkd.						
J59	1¢ rose	800.00	130.00	7,250.00	(6)		
J60	2¢ rose	75.00	3.00	800.00	(6)		
	Issue of 1917, Design of J33, Perf. 11						
J61	1¢ carmine rose	1.65	.12	40.00	(6)		
J62	2¢ carmine rose	1.35	.08	35.00	(6)		
J63	3¢ carmine rose	7.50	.11	85.00	(6)		
J64	5¢ carmine	7.50	.13	85.00	(6)		
J65	10¢ carmine rose	10.00	.13	125.00	(6)		
J66	30¢ carmine rose	50.00	.50	575.00	(6)		
J67	50¢ carmine rose	60.00	.13	750.00	(6)		

		Un	U	PB	#	FDC	Q
	Issue of 1925, Design of J33						
J68	½¢ dull red	.90	.10	11.00	(6)		
	Issue of 1930-31, Design of J69						
J69	½¢ Figure of Value	3.50	.85	35.00	(6)		
J70	1¢ carmine	2.75	.18	27.50	(6)		
J71	2¢ carmine	3.75	.20	40.00	(6)		
J72	3¢ carmine	20.00	1.00	240.00	(6)		
J73	5¢ carmine	20.00	1.50	225.00	(6)		
J74	10¢ carmine	32.50	.60	400.00	(6)		
J75	30¢ carmine	120.00	1.15	1,000.00	(6)		
J76	50¢ carmine	135.00	.30	1,150.00	(6)		
	Design of J78						
J77	$1 carmine	30.00	.10	275.00	(6)		
J78	$5 "FIVE" on $	52.50	.18	375.00	(6)		
	Issue of 1931-56, Design of J69, Perf 11x10½						
J79	½¢ dull carmine	1.10	.10	22.50			
J80	1¢ dull carmine	.15	.08	2.00			
J81	2¢ dull carmine	.15	.08	2.00			
J82	3¢ dull carmine	.25	.08	3.00			
J83	5¢ dull carmine	.45	.08	4.00			
J84	10¢ dull carmine	1.10	.08	8.50			
J85	30¢ dull carmine	8.00	.10	45.00			
J86	50¢ dull carmine	9.50	.09	57.50			
	Perf. 10½x11						
J87	$1 scarlet, same design as J78	37.50	.20	325.00			
	Issue of 1959, Perf. 11x10½, Design of J88 and J98						
J88	½¢ Figure of Value	1.50	1.00	125.00			
J89	1¢ carmine rose	.05	.05	.50			
J90	2¢ carmine rose	.06	.05	.60			
J91	3¢ carmine rose	.07	.05	.70			
J92	4¢ carmine rose	.08	.05	1.25			
J93	5¢ carmine rose	.10	.05	.75			
J94	6¢ carmine rose	.12	.07	1.40			
J95	7¢ carmine rose	.14	.08	1.60			
J96	8¢ carmine rose	.16	.06	1.75			
J97	10¢ carmine rose	.20	.05	1.25			
J98	30¢ Figure of Value	.55	.06	5.50			
J99	50¢ carmine rose	.90	.06	6.50			
	Design of J101						
J100	$1 carmine rose	1.75	.06	10.00			
J101	$5 Outline Figure of Value	8.75	.14	40.00			
	Design of J88						
J102	11¢ carmine rose	.22	.07	1.10			
J103	13¢ carmine rose	.25	.07	1.30			

1873-1911

O7   O14   O18   O34   O44

O52   O57   O76   O91

O71

O93   O95   O101   O114   O121

Official Stamps

The franking privilege having been abolished, as of July 1, 1873, these stamps were provided for each of the departments of Government for the prepayment on official matter.

These stamps were supplanted on May 1, 1879 by penalty envelopes and on July 5, 1884 were declared obsolete.

Designs are as follows: Post Office officials, figures of value and department name; all other departments, various portraits and department names.

Issues of 1873
Printed by the Continental Bank Note Co. Thin Hard Paper
Dept. of Agriculture: Yellow

		Un	U
O1	1¢ Franklin	52.50	27.50
O2	2¢ Jackson	37.50	14.00
O3	3¢ Washington	30.00	4.00
O4	6¢ Lincoln	40.00	13.50
O5	10¢ Jefferson	95.00	45.00
O6	12¢ Clay	150.00	75.00
O7	15¢ Webster	85.00	45.00
O8	24¢ Winfield Scott	110.00	57.50
O9	30¢ Hamilton	140.00	75.00

Executive Dept.

		Un	U
O10	1¢ carmine, Franklin	210.00	95.00
O11	2¢ Jackson	150.00	80.00
O12	3¢ carmine, Washington	160.00	65.00
O13	6¢ carmine, Lincoln	275.00	150.00
O14	10¢ Jefferson	230.00	150.00

Dept. of the Interior: Vermilion

		Un	U
O15	1¢ Franklin	13.50	2.50
O16	2¢ Jackson	11.00	1.75
O17	3¢ Washington	18.50	1.80
O18	6¢ Lincoln	13.50	1.80
O19	10¢ Jefferson	10.75	4.50
O20	12¢ Clay	17.50	2.75
O21	15¢ Webster	33.50	8.50
O22	24¢ W. Scott	27.50	6.50
O23	30¢ Hamilton	35.00	9.50
O24	90¢ Perry	85.00	15.00

Dept. of Justice: Purple

		Un	U
O25	1¢ Franklin	30.00	17.50
O26	2¢ Jackson	53.50	21.50
O27	3¢ Washington	57.50	7.50
O28	6¢ Lincoln	52.50	11.00
O29	10¢ Jefferson	55.00	25.00

		Un	U
O30	12¢ Clay	32.50	12.50
O31	15¢ Webster	95.00	50.00
O32	24¢ W. Scott	285.00	125.00
O33	30¢ Hamilton	250.00	90.00
O34	90¢ Perry	375.00	195.00

Navy Dept: Ultramarine

		Un	U
O35	1¢ Franklin	26.50	11.00
O36	2¢ Jackson	17.50	8.75
O37	3¢ Washington	22.50	3.50
O38	6¢ Lincoln	18.50	5.00
O39	7¢ Stanton	145.00	65.00
O40	10¢ Jefferson	25.00	11.50
O41	12¢ Clay	35.00	9.00
O42	15¢ Webster	65.00	25.00
O43	24¢ W. Scott	65.00	31.50
O44	30¢ Hamilton	52.50	13.00
O45	90¢ Perry	275.00	95.00

Post Office Dept.: Black

		Un	U
O47	1¢ Figure of Value	7.75	3.25
O48	2¢ Figure of Value	7.50	3.00
O49	3¢ Figure of Value	2.75	.95
O50	6¢ Figure of Value	7.50	1.85
O51	10¢ Figure of Value	35.00	18.50
O52	12¢ Figure of Value	14.50	4.75
O53	15¢ Figure of Value	18.00	7.50
O54	24¢ Figure of Value	22.50	10.00
O55	30¢ Figure of Value	22.50	7.75
O56	90¢ Figure of Value	36.50	10.75

Dept. of State

		Un	U
O57	1¢ dark green Franklin	32.50	12.00
O58	2¢ dark green Jackson	82.50	27.50
O59	3¢ bright green Washington	27.50	8.50
O60	6¢ bright green Lincoln	25.00	8.00
O61	7¢ dark green Stanton	52.50	16.00
O62	10¢ dark green Jefferson	33.50	14.50
O63	12¢ dark green Clay	63.50	30.00
O64	15¢ dark green Webster	46.50	16.50
O65	24¢ dark green W. Scott	150.00	80.00
O66	30¢ Hamilton	135.00	65.00

		Un	U
	1873 continued		
O67	90¢ dark green Perry	300.00	120.00
O68	$2 green and black		
	Seward	550.00	250.00
O69	$5 green and black		
	Seward	4,250.00	2,250.00
O70	$10 green and black		
	Seward	2,650.00	1,400.00
O71	$20 Seward	2,250.00	1,200.00
	Treasury Dept.: Brown		
O72	1¢ Franklin	11.00	1.95
O73	2¢ Jackson	16.50	1.95
O74	3¢ Washington	8.75	1.20
O75	6¢ Lincoln	17.50	1.20
O76	7¢ Stanton	32.50	11.50
O77	10¢ Jefferson	32.50	4.75
O78	12¢ Clay	31.50	1.65
O79	15¢ Webster	35.00	3.85
O80	24¢ W. Scott	165.00	55.00
O81	30¢ Hamilton	42.50	4.00
O82	90¢ Perry	53.50	3.75
	War Dept.: Rose		
O83	1¢ Franklin	50.00	3.50
O84	2¢ Jackson	50.00	5.75
O85	3¢ Washington	47.50	1.10
O86	6¢ Lincoln	180.00	2.85
O87	7¢ Stanton	43.50	27.00
O88	10¢ Jefferson	12.75	3.50
O89	12¢ Clay	38.50	2.50
O90	15¢ Webster	9.75	1.30
O91	24¢ W. Scott	11.00	2.00
O92	30¢ Hamilton	11.00	1.60
O93	90¢ Perry	32.50	10.75
	Issues of 1879 **Printed by the American Bank Note Co. Soft, Porous Paper, Dept. of Agriculture: Yellow**		
O94	1¢ Franklin, issued		
	without gum	1,350.00	—
O95	3¢ Washington	165.00	27.50
	Dept. of the Interior: Vermilion		
O96	1¢ Franklin	110.00	65.00
O97	2¢ Jackson	2.75	.80
O98	3¢ Washington	2.15	.75

		Un	U
O99	6¢ Lincoln	3.15	1.10
O100	10¢ Jefferson	30.00	20.00
O101	12¢ Clay	43.50	32.50
O102	15¢ Webster	105.00	62.50
O103	24¢ W. Scott	1,075.00	—
	Dept. of Justice: Bluish Purple		
O106	3¢ Washington	45.00	18.50
O107	6¢ Lincoln	110.00	65.00
	Post Office Dept.: Black		
O108	3¢ Figure of Value	5.00	1.50
	Treasury Dept.: Brown		
O109	3¢ Washington	18.75	3.00
O110	6¢ Lincoln	40.00	16.50
O111	10¢ Jefferson	55.00	15.00
O112	30¢ Hamilton	750.00	150.00
O113	90¢ Perry	750.00	150.00
	War Dept.: Rose Red		
O114	1¢ Franklin	1.90	.95
O115	2¢ Jackson	3.00	1.10
O116	3¢ Washington	2.95	.80
O117	6¢ Lincoln	2.75	.85
O118	10¢ Jefferson	12.75	7.25
O119	12¢ Clay	10.75	1.85
O120	30¢ Hamilton	32.50	27.50

Official Postal Savings Mail, Perf. 12

These stamps were used to prepay postage on official correspondence of the Postal Savings Division of the Post Office Department.

Discontinued Sept. 23, 1914

		Un	U
	Issues of 1911, Wmkd. (191)		
O121	2¢ Official Postal		
	Savings	9.50	1.15
O122	50¢ Official Postal		
	Savings	110.00	40.00
O123	$1 Official Postal		
	Savings	105.00	12.50
	Wmkd. (190)		
O124	1¢ Official Postal		
	Savings	4.25	1.10
O125	2¢ Official Postal		
	Savings	33.50	4.35
O126	10¢ Official Postal		
	Savings	8.75	1.20

1861-1863

1
    2
    3
    6

5

8
    9
    13
    14

11

		Un	U
	General Issues, All Imperf. **Issue of 1861: Lithographed,** **Unwatermarked**		
1	5¢ Jefferson Davis	165.00	95.00
2	10¢ Thomas Jefferson	215.00	150.00
	Issue of 1862		
3	2¢ Andrew Jackson	550.00	675.00
4	5¢ blue J. Davis (6)	100.00	87.50
5	10¢ Thomas Jefferson	850.00	550.00
	Typographed		
6	5¢ J. Davis		
	(London print)	11.00	12.00
7	5¢ blue (6) (local print)	15.00	16.50
	Issues of 1863, Engraved		
8	2¢ Andrew Jackson	60.00	225.00

	Thick or Thin Paper		
9	10¢ Jefferson Davis	750.00	575.00
10	10¢ blue (9), (with		
	rectangular frame)	3,000.00	1,800.00
	Prices of No. 10 are for copies showing parts of lines on at least two sides of frame.		
11	10¢ Jefferson Davis,		
	die A	12.00	14.00
12	10¢ blue J. Davis,		
	die B (11)	13.50	16.00
	Dies A and B differ in that B has an extra line outside its corner ornaments.		
13	20¢ George Washington	41.50	225.00
	Issue of 1862, Typographed		
14	1¢ John C. Calhoun		
	(This stamp was never		
	put in use.)	125.00	—

1865-1880

PR1   PR2   PR3

	Un	U

Newspaper Stamps
Perf. 12, Issues of 1865
Printed by the National Bank Note Co.,
Thin, Hard Paper, No Gum, Unwmkd.,
Colored Borders

		Un	U
PR1	5¢ Washington	125.00	—
PR2	10¢ Franklin	60.00	—
PR3	25¢ Lincoln	60.00	—

White Border, Yellowish Paper

		Un	U
PR4	5¢ light blue (PR1)	30.00	25.00

Reprints of 1875
Printed by the Continental Bank Note Co.,
Hard, White Paper, No Gum

		Un	U
PR5	5¢ dull blue (PR1),		
	white border	50.00	—
PR6	10¢ dark bluish green,		
	(PR2), colored border	32.50	—
PR7	25¢ dark carmine		
	(PR3), colored border	60.00	—

Issue of 1880
Printed by the American Bank Note Co.,
Soft, Porous Paper, White Border

		Un	U
PR8	5¢ dark blue (PR1)	100.00	—

Issue of 1875
Printed by the Continental Bank Note Co.,
Thin, Hard Paper

PR9-PR15; "Statue of Freedom" (PR15)

		Un	U
PR9	2¢ black	6.50	6.50
PR10	3¢ black	9.00	9.00
PR11	4¢ black	8.00	8.00
PR12	6¢ black	10.00	10.00
PR13	8¢ black	15.00	15.00
PR14	9¢ black	30.00	30.00
PR15	10¢ Statue of Freedom	15.00	12.00

PR16-PR23: "Justice" (PR18)

		Un	U
PR16	12¢ rose	32.00	25.00
PR17	24¢ rose	45.00	35.00
PR22	84¢ rose	135.00	95.00
PR23	96¢ rose	100.00	85.00
PR24	$1.92 Ceres	120.00	90.00
PR25	$3 "Victory"	160.00	110.00
PR26	$6 Clio	300.00	145.00
PR27	$9 Minerva	385.00	180.00
PR28	$12 Vesta	450.00	235.00
PR29	$24 "Peace"	450.00	260.00

		Un	U
PR30	$36 "Commerce"	500.00	300.00
PR31	$48 red brown Hebe		
	(PR78)	650.00	425.00
PR32	$60 violet Indian		
	Maiden (PR79)	650.00	375.00

Special Printing, Hard, White Paper,
Without Gum

PR33-PR39: Statue of Freedom (PR15)

		Un	U
PR33	2¢ gray black	60.00	—
PR34	3¢ gray black	65.00	—
PR35	4¢ gray black	80.00	—
PR36	6¢ gray black	110.00	—
PR37	8¢ gray black	120.00	—
PR38	9¢ gray black	135.00	—
PR39	10¢ gray black	165.00	—

PR40-PR47: "Justice" (PR18)

		Un	U
PR40	12¢ pale rose	190.00	—
PR41	24¢ pale rose	225.00	—
PR42	36¢ pale rose	325.00	—
PR43	48¢ pale rose	375.00	—
PR44	60¢ pale rose	450.00	—
PR45	72¢ pale rose	600.00	—
PR46	84¢ pale rose	625.00	—
PR47	96¢ pale rose	775.00	—
PR48	$1.92 dark brown		
	Ceres (PR24)	2,000.00	—
PR49	$3 vermilion "Victory"		
	(PR25)	4,500.00	—
PR50	$6 ultra. Clio (PR26)	5,000.00	—
PR51	$9 yel. Minerva		
	(PR27)	7,500.00	—
PR52	$12 bl. grn. Vesta		
	(PR28)	10,000.00	—
PR53	$24 dark gray violet		
	"Peace" (PR29)	—	—
PR54	$36 brown rose		
	"Commerce" (PR30)	—	—
PR55	$48 red brown Hebe		
	(PR78)	—	—
PR56	$60 violet Indian		
	Maiden (PR79)	—	—

All values of this issue Nos. PR33 to PR56 exist
imperforate but were not regularly issued.

		Un	U
	Issue of 1879, Printed by the American Bank Note Co., Soft, Porous Paper		
	PR57-PR62: Statue of Freedom (PR15)		
PR57	2¢ black	4.00	3.50
PR58	3¢ black	5.00	4.50
PR59	4¢ black	6.00	6.00
PR60	6¢ black	10.50	9.00
PR61	8¢ black	10.50	9.00
PR62	10¢ black	10.50	9.00
	PR63-PR70: "Justice" (PR18)		
PR63	12¢ red	30.00	20.00
PR64	24¢ red	30.00	18.50
PR65	36¢ red	110.00	85.00
PR66	48¢ red	80.00	50.00
PR67	60¢ red	60.00	50.00
PR68	72¢ red	145.00	90.00
PR69	84¢ red	110.00	75.00
PR70	96¢ red	80.00	55.00
PR71	$1.92 pale brown		
	Ceres (PR24)	60.00	50.00
PR72	$3 red vermilion		
	"Victory" (PR25)	60.00	50.00
PR73	$6 blue Clio (PR26)	110.00	75.00
PR74	$9 org. Minerva (PR27)	70.00	50.00
PR75	$12 yellow green		
	Vesta (PR28)	110.00	70.00
PR76	$24 dark violet		
	"Peace" (PR29)	145.00	100.00
PR77	$36 Indian red		
	"Commerce" (PR30)	185.00	120.00
PR78	$48 Hebe	250.00	140.00
PR79	$60 Indian Maiden	275.00	140.00

All values of the 1879 issue except Nos. PR63 to PR66 and PR68 to PR70 exist imperforate but were not regularly issued.

	Issue of 1883 Special Printing		
PR80	2¢ intense black Statue		
	of Freedom (PR15)	130.00	—

		Un	U
	Regular Issue of 1885		
PR81	1¢ black Statue of		
	Freedom (PR15)	4.50	2.50
	PR82-PR89: "Justice" (PR18)		
PR82	12¢ carmine	12.50	7.50
PR83	24¢ carmine	15.00	11.00
PR84	36¢ carmine	22.50	12.50
PR85	48¢ carmine	30.00	22.50
PR86	60¢ carmine	45.00	30.00
PR87	72¢ carmine	55.00	35.00
PR88	84¢ carmine	115.00	75.00
PR89	96¢ carmine	80.00	60.00

All values of the 1885 issue exist imperforate but were not regularly issued.

	Issue of 1894 Printed by the Bureau of Engraving and Printing, Soft Wove Paper		
	PR90-PR94: Statue of Freedom (PR90)		
PR90	1¢ Statue of Freedom	21.00	—
PR91	2¢ intense black	22.50	—
PR92	4¢ intense black	30.00	—
PR93	6¢ intense black	750.00	—
PR94	10¢ intense black	45.00	—
	PR95-PR99: "Justice" (PR18)		
PR95	12¢ pink	235.00	—
PR96	24¢ pink	210.00	—
PR97	36¢ pink	1,450.00	—
PR98	60¢ pink	1,450.00	—
PR99	96¢ pink	2,250.00	—
PR100	$3 sclt. "Victory" (PR25)	3,600.00	—
PR101	$6 pl. blue Clio (PR26)	4,250.00	2,250.00
	Issue of 1895, Unwmkd. PR102-PR105: Statue of Freedom (PR116)		
PR102	1¢ black	15.00	4.00
PR103	2¢ black	17.50	4.50
PR104	5¢ black	23.00	7.00
PR105	10¢ black	45.00	20.00
PR106	25¢ cme. "Justice" (PR118)	60.00	20.00
PR107	50¢ cme. "Justice" (PR119)	150.00	65.00
PR108	$2 sclt. "Victory" (PR120)	175.00	40.00
PR109	$5 ultra Clio (PR121)	300.00	135.00

PR15

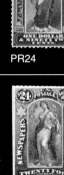
PR18

PR24

PR25

PR26

PR27

PR28

PR29

PR30

PR78

PR79

PR90

PR116

PR118

PR119

PR120

PR121

PR122

PR123

PR124

PR125

Q1

Q2

Q3

Q4

Q5

Q6

Q7

Q8

Q9

Q10

Q11

Q12

QE1

QE2

QE3

QE4

	Un	U
PR110	$10 green Vesta		
	(PR122)	285.00	140.00
PR111	$20 slate "Peace"		
	(PR123)	525.00	250.00
PR112	$50 dull rose		
	"Commerce" (PR124)	525.00	250.00
PR113	$100 purple Indian		
	Maiden (PR125)	625.00	300.00

Issue of 1895-97
Wmkd. (191), Yellowish Gum

PR114-PR117: Statue of Freedom (PR116)

	Un	U
PR114	1¢ black	2.50	2.00
PR115	2¢ black	2.50	1.50
PR116	5¢ black	4.00	3.00
PR117	10¢ black	2.50	2.00
PR118	25¢ "Justice"	4.00	3.75
PR119	50¢ "Justice"	4.25	3.50
PR120	$2 "Victory"	7.50	8.50
PR121	$5 Clio	15.00	20.00
PR122	$10 Vesta	12.50	18.50
PR123	$20 "Peace"	14.00	21.00
PR124	$50 "Commerce"	15.00	21.00
PR125	$100 Indian Maiden	18.50	30.00

In 1899, the Government sold 26,989 sets of these stamps, but, as the stock of the high values was not sufficient to make up the required number, the $5, $10, $20, $50 and $100 were reprinted. These are virtually indistinguishable from earlier printings.

Parcel Post Stamps

Issued for the prepayment of postage on parcel post packages only.

Beginning July 1, 1913, these stamps were valid for all postal purposes.

Issue of 1912-13, Perf. 12

		Un	U
Q1	1¢ Post Office Clerk	5.00	1.10
Q2	2¢ City Carrier	5.75	.75
Q3	3¢ Railway Postal Clerk	15.00	6.75
Q4	4¢ Rural Carrier	35.00	2.15
Q5	5¢ Mail Train	32.50	1.60
Q6	10¢ Steamship and		
	Mail Tender	55.00	1.85
Q7	15¢ Automobile		
	Service	85.00	9.50
Q8	20¢ Airplane Carrying		
	Mail	175.00	16.50
Q9	25¢ Manufacturing	90.00	5.25
Q10	50¢ Dairying	275.00	40.00
Q11	75¢ Harvesting	95.00	30.00
Q12	$1 Fruit Growing	475.00	25.00

Special Handling Stamps

For use on parcel post packages to secure the same expeditious handling accorded to first class mail matter.

Issue of 1925-29, Design of QE3, Perf. 11

		Un	U
QE1	10¢ Special Handling	2.25	.95
QE2	15¢ Special Handling	2.50	.95
QE3	20¢ Special Handling	4.50	1.85
QE4	25¢ Special Handling	32.50	8.00

SOUVENIR PAGES

With First Day Cancellations

The Postal Service offers Souvenir Pages for new stamps. The series began with a page for the Yellowstone Park Centennial stamp issued March 1, 1972. The pages feature one or more stamps tied by the first day cancel, technical data and information on the subject of the issue. More than just collectors' items, Souvenir Pages make wonderful show and conversation pieces. Souvenir Pages are issued in limited editions. For information on becoming a subscriber, see the postal card following page 272.

1972

1	Yellowstone Park,	$75.00
1A	Family Planning (sold only with FD cancellation by USPS at ASDA show in NYC),	$200.00
2	Cape Hatteras,	$75.00
3	Fiorello La Guardia,	$75.00
4	City of Refuge,	$75.00
5	Wolf Trap Farm,	$25.00
6	Colonial Craftsman, (4),	$25.00
7	Mount McKinley,	$25.00
8	Olympic Games, (4),	$15.00
9	Parent Teachers Association,	$12.00
10	Wildlife Conservation, (4),	$12.00
11	Mail Order,	$12.00
12	Osteopathic Medicine,	$9.00
13	Tom Sawyer,	$9.00
14	Benjamin Franklin,	$9.00
15	Christmas, (2),	$9.00
16	Pharmacy,	$8.00
17	Stamp Collecting,	$8.00

1973

18	Eugene O'Neill Coil,	$15.00
19	Love,	$8.00
20	Pamphleteer,	$8.00
21	George Gershwin,	$8.00
22	Posting Broadside,	$6.00
23	Copernicus,	$6.00
24	Postal Service Employees, (10),	$10.00
25	Harry S. Truman,	$6.00
26	Postrider,	$6.00
27	Giannini,	$6.00
28	Boston Tea Party, (4),	$10.00
29	Progress in Electronics, (4),	$8.00
30	Robinson Jeffers,	$6.00
31	Lyndon B. Johnson,	$6.00
32	Henry O. Tanner,	$6.00
33	Willa Cather,	$6.00
34	Colonial Drummer,	$6.00
35	Angus Cattle,	$6.00
36	Christmas, (2),	$8.00
37	13¢ Airmail sheet stamp,	$5.00
38	10¢ Crossed Flags,	$5.00
39	Jefferson Memorial,	$5.00
40	13¢ Airmail Coil,	$5.00

1974

41	Mount Rushmore,	$5.00
42	ZIP Code,	$5.00
43	Statue of Liberty,	$5.00
44	Elizabeth Blackwell,	$5.00
45	Veterans of Foreign Wars,	$4.50
46	Robert Frost,	$4.50
47	EXPO '74,	$4.50
48	Horse Racing,	$4.50
49	Skylab,	$6.00
50	Universal Postal Union, (8),	$8.00
51	Mineral Heritage, (4),	$5.00
52	Fort Harrod,	$4.50
53	Continental Congress, (4),	$5.00
54	Chautauqua,	$4.50
55	Kansas Wheat,	$4.50
56	Energy Conservation,	$4.50
57	6.3¢ Bulk Rate, (2),	$4.50
58	Sleepy Hollow,	$4.50
59	Retarded Children,	$4.50
60	Christmas, (3),	$5.00

1975

61	Benjamin West,	$4.50
62	Pioneer,	$6.00
63	Collective Bargaining,	$4.50
64	Sybil Ludington,	$4.50
65	Salem Poor,	$4.50
66	Haym Salomon,	$4.50
67	Peter Francisco,	$4.50
68	Mariner,	$6.00
69	Lexington & Concord,	$5.00
70	Paul Laurence Dunbar,	$4.50
71	D.W. Griffith,	$4.50
72	Bunker Hill,	$4.50
73	Military Uniforms, (4),	$6.00
74	Apollo Soyuz, (2),	$7.00
75	International Women's Year,	$4.50
76	Postal Bicentennial, (4),	$6.00
77	World Peace Through Law,	$4.50
78	Banking & Commerce, (2),	$4.50
79	Christmas, (2),	$4.50
80	Francis Parkman,	$3.50
81	Freedom of the Press,	$3.50
82	Old North Church,	$3.50
83	Flag & Independence Hall,	$3.50

84	Freedom to Assemble,	$3.50
85	Liberty Bell Coil,	$3.50
86	American Eagle & Shield,	$3.50

1976

87	Spirit of '76, (3),	$6.00
88	25¢ & 31¢ Airmails, (2),	$4.50
89	Interphil,	$3.50
90	Fifty State Flag Series,	$50.00
91	Freedom to Assemble Coil,	$3.50
92	Telephone Centennial,	$3.50
93	Commercial Aviation,	$3.50
94	Chemistry,	$3.50
95	7.9¢ Bulk Rate,	$3.50
96	Benjamin Franklin,	$3.50
97	Bicentennial SS,	$50.00
98	Declaration of Independence, (4),	$6.00
99	Olympics, (4),	$6.00
100	Clara Maass,	$3.50
101	Adolph S. Ochs,	$3.50
102	Christmas, (3),	$4.00
103	7.7¢ Bulk Rate,	$3.50

1977

104	Washington at Princeton,	$3.50
105	$1 Vending Machine Booklet Pane, perf. 10,	$30.00
106	Sound Recording,	$3.50
107	Pueblo Art, (4),	$4.00
108	Lindbergh Flight,	$3.50
109	Colorado Centennial,	$3.50
110	Butterflies, (4),	$4.00
111	Lafayette,	$3.50
112	Skilled Hands, (4),	$4.00
113	Peace Bridge,	$3.50
114	Herkimer at Oriskany,	$3.50
115	Alta, California,	$3.50
116	Articles of Confederation,	$3.50
117	Talking Pictures,	$3.50
118	Surrender at Saratoga,	$3.50
119	Energy, (2),	$3.50
120	Christmas Mailbox,	$3.50
121	Christmas, Valley Forge,	$3.50
122	Petition for Redress Coil, (2),	$3.00
123	Petition for Redress sheet stamp,	$3.00

Issue Date: March 31, 1983
First Day City: Albuquerque, New Mexico
Washington, D. C.
Designer: Davis Meltzer
Royers Ford, Pennsylvania
Modeler: Ronald C. Sharpe
Press: Gravure
Colors: Yellow, magenta, cyan, blue and black

Image Area: .84 x 1.83 inches or
21.33 x 46.46 millimeters
Plate Numbers: One group
Stamps Per Pane: 40
Selvage: U. S. Postal Service 1982 ©
* Use Correct ZIP Code
* Mr. ZIP (standing position)

Balloon Commemorative Stamps

A block of four commemorative stamps honoring the 200th anniversary of the sport of ballooning was issued March 31 in both Washington, D. C., and Albuquerque, New Mexico.

The design of the stamps was unveiled on October 2, 1982, during opening ceremonies of the International Balloon Fiesta in Albuquerque, New Mexico. The perforation pattern for the block of four stamps is the same one used for the Desert Plants issue of 1981. The two designs in the center of the block of four are horizontal, with a vertical design on either side.

The still vertical stamp features the gas balloon, "Intrepid," which was used for aerial surveillance by the Union Army during the Civil War. Thaddeus Lowe manned the balloon, making progress reports to President Abraham Lincoln at 15-minute intervals.

The two horizontal stamps in the center of the block form a ne-tenant pair. Both stamps depict multicolored modern-day hot air balloons in flight.

The right vertical stamp depicts the Explorer II, a balloon used jointly by the National Geographic Society and the U. S. Army in 1935 to perform scientific research. The helium-filled balloon, piloted by Captains Albert W. Stevens and Orvila A. Anderson, was used to study cosmic rays, atmospheric conditions and the survivability of living spores at high altitudes.

Issue Date: May 17, 1983
First Day City: Brooklyn, New York
Designer: Howard Koslow
East Norwich, New York
Modeler: Esther Porter
Engravers: Edward P. Archer (vignette)
Robert G. Culin, Sr. (lettering and numerals)

Press: Intaglio
Color: Blue
Image Area: .84 x 1.44 inches or
21.3 x 36.5 millimeters
Plate Number: One
Stamps per Pane: 50
Selvage: U. S. Postal Service 1983 ©
* Use Correct ZIP Code
* Mr. ZIP (standing position)

Brooklyn Bridge Commemorative Stamp

A 20-cent commemorative stamp marking the 100th anniversary year of the opening of the Brooklyn Bridge was issued May 17 in Brooklyn, New York. The first day of issue ceremony was held at the Brooklyn Borough Hall. The design of the stamp was unveiled March 2 in ceremonies at Manhattan City Hall to officially begin the anniversary celebration.

The Brooklyn Bridge was the first suspension bridge to use cables made of steel wire and was one of the first to use pneumatic caissons for foundations. When the bridge was opened for service on May 24, 1883, it had the longest span in the world. Built over the East River between Brooklyn and Manhattan, it has a main span of 1,595 feet and it features two massive granite masonry towers and two main suspension cables augmented by vertical suspender cables as well as 400 extra-strong stay cables that radiate diagonally from the towers.

The Brooklyn Bridge was designed by John A. Roebling (1806-1869), who was appointed chief engineer of the project in 1867. He died two years later as a result of an accident while supervising the final surveys of the bridge. His son, Washington A. Roebling (1837-1926), served as chief engineer and supervisor of the construction work until 1883. His duties involved spending hours inside the bridge's pneumatic caissons and two years' exposure to compressed air destroyed his health. Reduced to his limits, he supervised the construction from his room overlooking the span. The bridge which cost nine million dollars to build, was completed in 1883, some 14 years after it was begun. It was designated a national landmark in 1965.

Issue Date: May 18, 1983
First Day City: Knoxville, Tennessee
Designer: Howard Koslow
East Norwich, New York
Modeler: Clarence Holbert
Engraver: Gary J. Slaght (lettering and numerals)
Press: Gravure/Intaglio

Colors: Yellow, magenta, cyan, black (gravure)
Black (intaglio)
Image Area: .84 x 1.44 inches or
21.33 x 36.57 millimeters
Plate Numbers: One group
Stamps per Pane: 50
Selvage: U. S. Postal Service 1983 ©
* Mr. ZIP (standing position)

Tennessee Valley Authority Commemorative Stamp

A 20-cent commemorative stamp marking the 50th anniversary of the Tennessee Valley Authority was issued May 18 in Knoxville, Tennessee. The first day of issue ceremony was held at the Tennessee Valley Authority Headquarters.

The Tennessee Valley Authority (TVA) was created by the federal government in 1933, to develop the watershed of the Tennessee River and its tributaries. The area was subject to periodic flooding. On May 18, 1933, President Franklin D. Roosevelt approved the act which was designed to help the economically distressed region covering 40,910 square-miles and encompassing parts of seven states. This was to be accomplished by developing the natural resources of the area, creating industry and jobs.

The greatest success of the TVA over the last 50 years has been as a producer and distributor of its expanded electric power system. That has made it possible for the residents of the Valley to enjoy a system of dams and locks which were built to harness the Tennessee River for flood control and to provide a 650-mile inland waterway for navigation. No major power source of the valley since the major dams were built, thus, saving millions of dollars in cumbustible block damage and providing a decreased economy to flourish.

The TVA has cooperated with local authorities and citizen groups in promoting better farming methods, soil conservation techniques, aforestation, the control of air and water pollution and energy conservation. During World War II, the TVA provided large amounts of electric power for the nation's defense, and later turned an idle government munitions plant into a national fertilizer development center providing farmers a tool to increase their output and their incomes. TVA also has sponsored libraries, educational programs, research into the creation of the Lake Between the Lakes project—a variety of recreational and environmental education facilities open to the public.

Issue Date: January 19, 1983
First Day City: Chicago, Illinois
Designer: Saul Bass
Los Angeles, California
Modeler: Ronald C. Sharpe
Engraver: Robert G. Culin, Sr. (lettering and intaglio shape)
Press: Offset/Intaglio

Image Area: .84 x 1.44 inches or
21.33 x 36.57 millimeters
Colors: Yellow, red, blue (Offset)
Black (Intaglio)
Plate Numbers: Two groups
Stamps per Pane: 50
Selvage: U. S. Postal Service 1982 ©
* Use Correct ZIP Code
* Mr. ZIP (standing position)

Science and Industry Commemorative Stamp

The first 1983 commemorative stamp was issued January 19, in Chicago, Illinois. The stamp called attention to the significance of science and industry to U. S. growth and development.

The first day of issue ceremony was held at the Museum of Science and Industry, which is celebrating its 50th anniversary this year. Founded by merchant-philanthropist Julius Rosenwald in 1933, the museum attracts approximately four million visitors annually. The museum is housed in the reconstructed Palace of Fine Arts from the World's Columbian Exposition of 1893 located in Jackson Park on Chicago's south side.

The Science and Industry stamp was designed by Saul Bass, an internationally-known graphic designer and film maker, who heads the California design firm of Saul Bass/Herb Yeager and Associates in Los Angeles. Bass' design depicts the merger of industry and modern technology through the superimposing of symbols and forms in a computer-like grid. When viewed together, the design suggests a modern high-technology industrial complex. The symbols are tubular, square, cubic and globular.

124	1¢, 2¢, 3¢, 4¢	
	Americana,	$3.00
1978		
125	Carl Sandburg,	$3.00
126	Indian Head Penny,	$4.00
127	Captain Cook,	
	Anchorage,	$4.00
128	Captain Cook,	
	Honolulu,	$4.00
129	Harriet Tubman,	$3.00
130	American Quilts, (4),	$4.00
131	16¢ Statue of Liberty,	$3.00
132	Sandy Hook	
	Lighthouse,	$3.00
133	American Dance, (4),	$4.00
134	French Alliance,	$3.00
135	Dr. Papanicolaou,	$3.00
136	"A" Stamp, (2),	$3.00
137	Jimmie Rodgers,	$3.00
138	CAPEX '78, (SS),	$6.00
139	Oliver Wendell Holmes,	$3.00
140	Photography,	$3.00
141	Fort McHenry Flag,	
	(2),	$3.00
142	George M. Cohan,	$3.00
143	Rose Booklet single,	$3.00
144	8.4¢ Bulk Rate,	$3.00
145	Viking Missions,	$5.00
146	Remote Outpost,	$4.00
147	American Owls, (4),	$4.00
148	Wright Brothers, (2),	$3.00
149	American Trees,	$4.00
150	Hobby Horse,	$3.00
151	Andrea della Robbia,	$3.00
152	$2 Kerosene Lamp,	$8.00
1979		
153	Robert F. Kennedy,	$3.00
154	Martin Luther King, Jr.,	$3.00
155	International Year of	
	the Child,	$3.00
156	John Steinbeck,	$3.00
157	Albert Einstein,	$3.00
158	Octave Chanute, (2),	$4.00
159	Pennsylvania	
	Toleware, (4),	$4.00
160	American	
	Architecture, (4),	$4.00
161	Endangered Flora, (4),	$4.00
162	Seeing Eye Dogs,	$3.00
163	$1 Americana,	$6.00
164	Special Olympics,	$3.00
165	$5 Americana,	$20.00
166	30¢ Americana,	$4.00
167	Olympics,	$4.00
168	50¢ Americana,	$4.00
169	John Paul Jones,	$3.00
170	15¢ Olympic, (4),	$5.00
171	Gerard David	
	Madonna,	$3.00
172	Santa Claus,	$3.00
173	3.1¢ Coil,	$3.00
174	31¢ Olympic,	$4.50
175	Will Rogers,	$3.00
176	Vietnam Veterans,	$3.00
177	Wiley Post,	$4.00
1980		
178	W. C. Fields,	$3.00
179	Winter Olympics, (4),	$5.00
180	Windmills Booklet,	$5.00
181	Benjamin Banneker,	$3.00
182	Letter Writing, (6),	$4.00
183	1¢ Quill Pen Coil,	$3.00

184	Frances Perkins,	$3.00
185	Dolley Madison,	$3.00
186	Emily Bissell,	$3.00
187	3.5¢ Non-Profit Bulk	
	Rate Coil,	$3.00
188	Helen Keller/	
	Anne Sullivan,	$3.00
189	Veterans	
	Administration,	$3.00
190	General Bernardo de	
	Galvez,	$3.00
191	Coral Reefs, (4),	$4.00
192	Organized Labor,	$3.00
193	Edith Wharton,	$3.00
194	American Education,	$3.00
195	Northwest Indian	
	Masks, (4),	$4.00
196	Architecture, (4),	$4.00
197	Phillip Mazzei,	$3.00
198	Stained Glass	
	Window,	$3.00
199	Antique Toys,	$3.00
200	19¢ Sequoyah,	$3.00
201	28¢ Scott A/M,	$3.50
202	35¢ Curtiss A/M,	$3.50
1981		
203	Everett Dirksen,	$2.50
204	Whitney M. Young,	$2.50
205	"B" Sheet & Coil,	$3.50
206	"B" Booklet Pane,	$5.00
207	12¢ Americana S & C,	$3.50
208	Flowers Block, (4),	$3.50
209	18¢ Flag Sheet & Coil,	$3.50
210	18¢ Flag Booklet	
	Pane,	$5.00
211	American Red Cross,	$2.50
212	George Mason,	$2.50
213	Savings & Loan,	$2.50
214	Animals Booklet Pane,	$6.00
215	18¢ Surrey Coil,	$3.00
216	Space	
	Achievement, (8),	$10.00
217	17¢ Rachel Carson,	$2.50
218	35¢ Dr. Charles Drew,	$3.00
219	Professional	
	Management,	$2.50
220	17¢ Electric Car Coil,	$3.00
221	Wildlife Habitat, (4),	$3.50
222	International Year	
	Disabled,	$2.50
223	Edna St. Vincent	
	Millay,	$2.50
224	Alcoholism,	$2.50
225	Architecture, (4),	$3.50
226	Zaharis,	$2.50
227	Bobby Jones,	$2.50
228	Frederic Remington,	$2.50
229	"C" Sheet/Coil,	$3.50
230	"C" Booklet,	$5.00
231	18¢/20¢ Hoban, (2),	$3.00
232	Yorktown, (2),	$3.00
233	Teddybear-Christmas,	$2.50
234	Art-Christmas '81,	$2.50
235	John Hanson,	$2.50
236	20¢ Pumper, (2),	$3.00
237	Desert Plant, (4),	$4.00
238	9.3¢ Wagon, (3),	$3.00
239	20¢ Reg + Coil,	$3.50
240	20¢ Booklet,	$4.50
1982		
241	Sheep Booklet,	$5.00
242	20¢ Ralph Bunche,	$2.50
243	13¢ Crazy Horse,	$2.50

244	37¢ Millikan,	$3.00
245	Roosevelt, FD.,	$2.50
246	20¢ LOVE,	$2.50
247	5.9¢ Bicycle, (4),	$2.50
248	20¢ Washington,	$2.50
249	10.9¢ Cab Coil, (2),	$2.50
250	Birds & Flowers,	$30.00
251	Netherlands,	$2.50
252	Library of Congress,	$2.50
253	20¢ Consumer Coil,	$2.50
254	World's Fair, (4),	$3.00
255	Horatio Alger,	$2.50
256	2¢ Locomotive Coil,	$2.50
257	20¢ Aging,	$2.50
258	20¢ Barrymores,	$2.50
259	Mary Walker,	$2.50
260	Peace Garden,	$2.50
261	America's Libraries,	$2.50
262	Jackie Robinson,	$2.50
263	Stagecoach,	$2.50
264	Touro Synagogue,	$2.50
265	Wolf Trap,	$2.50
266	Architecture, (4),	$3.00
267	Francis of Assisi,	$3.00
268	Ponce de Leon,	$2.50
269	Snow Scenes, (4),	$3.00
270	Art-Christmas,	$2.50
271	Kitten & Puppy,	$2.50
272	Igor Stravinsky,	$2.50
1983*		
273	Officials	
	(7 stamps-3 pgs),	$22.50
274	Science,	$2.50
275	Sleigh Coil,	$2.50
276	Sweden,	$2.50
277	Handcar Coil,	$2.50
278	Ballooning Block,	$3.00
279	Civilian Conservation	
	Corps,	$2.50
280	40¢ Olympics Block,	$5.00
281	Priestley,	$2.50
282	Voluntarism,	$2.50
283	German Immigrants,	$2.50
284	Physical Fitness,	$2.50
285	Brooklyn Bridge,	$2.50
286	Tennessee Valley	
	Authority,	$2.50
287	Carl Schurz,	$2.50
288	Medal of Honor,	$2.50
289	Scott Joplin,	$2.50
290	Thomas H. Gallaudet,	$2.50
291	28¢ Olympics Block,	$3.50
292	Pearl S. Buck,	$2.50
293	Babe Ruth,	$2.50
294	Nathaniel Hawthorne,	$2.50
295	13¢ Olympics Block,	$3.00
296	Henry Clay,	$2.50
297	Dorothea Dix,	$2.50
298	Treaty of Paris,	$2.50
299	Civil Service,	$2.50
300	Metropolitan Opera,	$2.50
301	Inventors Block,	$3.00
302	Streetcars Block,	$3.00
303	Motorcycle Coil,	$2.50
304	Contemporary	
	Christmas,	$2.50
305	Art Masterpiece	
	Christmas,	$2.50
306	Olympic Block,	$4.50
307	Martin Luther,	$2.50
308	Omnibus,	$2.50

*Numbers for 1983 subject
to change.

The Postal Service offers American Commemorative Panels for each new commemorative stamp and special Christmas stamp issued. The series first began September 20, 1972, with the issuance of the Wild Life Commemorative Panel and will total over 200 panels by the end of 1983. The panels feature stamps in mint condition complemented by reproductions of steel line engravings and stories behind the commemorated subject. For further information, please see page 279.

1972
1	Wildlife,	$14.50
2	Mail Order,	$14.50
3	Osteopathic Medicine,	$14.50
4	Tom Sawyer,	$14.50
5	Pharmacy,	$14.50
6	Christmas 1972,	$18.00
7	'Twas the Night Before Christmas,	$18.00
8	Stamp Collecting,	$14.50

1973
9	Love,	$14.50
10	Pamphleteers,	$18.00
11	George Gershwin,	$18.00
12	Posting Broadside,	$18.00
13	Copernicus,	$14.50
14	Postal People,	$18.00
15	Harry S. Truman,	$21.50
16	Post Rider,	$24.00

17	Boston Tea Party,	$48.00
18	Electronics,	$14.50
19	Robinson Jeffers,	$14.50
20	Lyndon B. Johnson,	$21.50
21	Henry O. Tanner,	$14.50
22	Willa Cather,	$14.50
23	Drummer,	$24.00
24	Angus Cattle,	$14.50
25	Christmas 1973,	$18.00
26	Christmas Needlepoint,	$18.00

1974
27	Veterans of Foreign Wars,	$14.50
28	Robert Frost,	$14.50
29	EXPO '74,	$18.00
30	Horse Racing,	$14.50
31	Skylab,	$18.00
32	Universal Postal Union,	$21.50

33	Mineral Heritage,	$14.50
34	Fort Harrod,	$14.50
35	Continental Congress,	$14.50
36	Chautauqua,	$14.50
37	Kansas Wheat,	$14.50
38	Energy Conservation,	$14.50
39	Sleepy Hollow,	$14.50
40	Retarded Children,	$14.50
41	Christmas "The Road-Winter",	$18.00
42	Christmas Angel Altarpiece,	$18.00

1975
43	Benjamin West,	$14.50
44	Pioneer,	$18.00
45	Collective Bargaining,	$14.50
46	Contributors to the Cause,	$18.00

47	Mariner,	$18.00
48	Lexington & Concord,	$18.00
49	Paul Laurence Dunbar,	$14.50
50	D. W. Griffith,	$14.50
51	Bunker Hill,	$18.00
52	Military Services,	$18.00
53	Apollo Soyuz,	$18.00
54	World Peace Through Law,	$14.50
55	International Women's Year,	$14.50
56	Postal Bicentennial,	$18.00
57	Banking and Commerce,	$14.50
58	Early Christmas Card,	$18.00
59	Christmas Madonna,	$18.00

1976

60	Spirit of '76,	$18.00
61	Interphil 76,	$18.00
62	State Flags,	$30.00
63	Telephone Centennial,	$14.50
64	Commercial Aviation,	$14.50
65	Chemistry,	$14.50
66	Benjamin Franklin,	$20.00
67	Declaration of Independence,	$18.00
68	Olympics,	$18.00
69	Clara Maas,	$18.00
70	Adolph S. Ochs,	$14.50
71	Currier Winter Pastime,	$18.00
72	Copley Nativity,	$18.00

1977

73	Washington at Princeton,	$21.50
74	Sound Recording,	$26.50
75	Pueblo Art,	$120.00
76	Lindbergh Flight,	$120.00
77	Colorado Centennial,	$26.50
78	Butterflies,	$30.00
79	Lafayette,	$26.50
80	Skilled Hands,	$26.50
81	Peace Bridge,	$26.50
82	Herkimer at Oriskany,	$26.50
83	Alta, California,	$26.50
84	Articles of Confederation,	$26.50
85	Talking Pictures,	$26.50
86	Surrender at Saratoga,	$26.50
87	Energy Conservation & Development,	$26.50
88	Christmas, Washington at Valley Forge,	$30.00
89	Christmas, Rural Mailbox,	$30.00

1978

90	Carl Sandburg,	$18.00
91	Captain Cook,	$30.00
92	Harriet Tubman,	$18.00
93	American Quilts,	$26.50
94	American Dance,	$18.00
95	French Alliance,	$25.00
96	Dr. Papanicolaou,	$18.00

97	Jimmie Rodgers,	$18.00
98	Photography,	$18.00
99	George M. Cohan,	$18.00
100	Viking Missions,	$30.00
101	American Owls,	$26.50
102	American Trees,	$26.50
103	Madonna and Child,	$18.00
104	Christmas Hobby Horse,	$18.00

1979

105	Robert F. Kennedy,	$18.00
106	Martin Luther King, Jr.	$18.00
107	Year of the Child,	$18.00
108	John Steinbeck,	$18.00
109	Albert Einstein,	$25.00
110	Pennsylvania Toleware,	$18.00
111	American Architecture,	$18.00
112	Endangered Flora,	$18.00
113	Seeing Eye Dogs,	$18.00
114	Special Olympics,	$18.00
115	John Paul Jones,	$30.00
116	15¢ Olympic Games,	$24.00
117	Virgin and Child,	$18.00
118	Santa Claus,	$18.00
119	Will Rogers,	$18.00
120	Vietnam Veterans,	$21.50
121	10¢, 31¢ Olympic Games,	$24.00

1980

122	W.C. Fields,	$18.00
123	Winter Olympics,	$24.00
124	Benjamin Banneker,	$18.00
125	Frances Perkins,	$18.00
126	Emily Bissell,	$18.00
127	Helen Keller/ Anne Sullivan,	$18.00
128	Veterans Administration,	$18.00
129	General Bernardo de Galvez,	$18.00
130	Coral Reefs,	$18.00
131	Organized Labor,	$18.00
132	Edith Wharton,	$18.00
133	American Education,	$18.00
134	Northwest Indian Masks,	$22.50
135	American Architecture,	$18.00
136	Christmas Stained Glass Window,	$18.00
137	Christmas Antique Toys,	$18.00

1981

138	Everett Dirksen,	$14.50
139	Whitney Moore Young,	$14.50
140	American Flowers,	$18.00
141	American Red Cross,	$14.50
142	Savings & Loan,	$14.50
143	Space Achievement,	$18.00
144	Professional Management,	$14.50
145	Wildlife Habitats,	$25.00
146	Int'l. Year Disabled Persons,	$18.00
147	Edna St. Vincent Millay,	$14.50

148	American Architecture,	$18.00
149	Bobby Jones/Babe Zaharias,	$18.00
150	James Hoban,	$18.00
151	Frederic Remington,	$14.50
152	Battle of Yorktown/ Va. Capes,	$14.50
153	Christmas "Teddy Bear",	$18.00
154	Christmas Madonna & Child,	$18.00
155	John Hansen,	$14.50
156	U. S. Desert Plants,	$18.00

1982

157	Roosevelt,	$32.50
158	Love,	$32.50
159	G. Washington,	$32.50
160	State Birds & Flowers,	$35.00
161	Netherlands,	$32.50
162	Library of Congress,	$32.50
163	World's Fair,	$32.50
164	Horatio Alger,	$32.50
165	Aging,	$32.50
166	Barrymores,	$32.50
167	Dr. Mary Walker,	$32.50
168	International Peace Garden,	$35.00
169	America's Libraries,	$32.50
170	Jackie Robinson,	$35.00
171	Touro Synagogue,	$32.50
172	American Architecture,	$32.50
173	Wolf Trap,	$32.50
174	Francis of Assisi,	$32.50
175	Ponce de Leon,	$32.50
176	Christmas Tiepolo Art,	$32.50
177	Christmas Snow Scene,	$32.50
178	Kitten & Puppy,	$32.50

1983*

179	Science and Industry
180	Sweden/USA Treaty
181	Balloons Block
182	Civilian Conservation Corps
183	Olympics (40¢) Block
184	Joseph Priestley
185	Voluntarism
186	The Concord
187	Physical Fitness
188	Brooklyn Bridge
189	Tennessee Valley Authority
190	Medal of Honor
191	Scott Joplin
192	Olympics (28¢) Block
193	Babe Ruth
194	Nathaniel Hawthorne
195	Olympics (13¢) Block
196	Treaty of Paris
197	Civil Service
198	Metropolitan Opera
199	American Inventors Block
200	Streetcars Block
201	Christmas Traditional
202	Christmas Contemporary
203	Olympics
204	Martin Luther

*Numbers for 1983 subject to change.

269

These cards were issued as souvenirs of the philatelic gatherings at which they were distributed by the United States Postal Service, its predecessor the United States Post Office Department, or the Bureau of Engraving and Printing. They were not valid for postage.

Most of the cards bear reproductions of United States stamps with the design enlarged or altered. The U.S. reproductions are engraved except stamps Nos. 914, 1396, 1460-1462 and C85. The cards are not perforated.

For information regarding current availability of souvenir cards, send postal card following page 272.

A forerunner of the souvenir cards is the 1938 Philatelic Truck souvenir sheet which the Post Office Department issued and distributed in various cities visited by the Philatelic Truck. It shows the White House, printed in blue on white paper. Issued with and without gum. Price with gum, $80, without gum, $10.

**United States Post Office
& United States Postal Service**

1960 Barcelona, 1st International Philatelic Congress, Mar. 26-Apr. 5. Enlarged vignette, Landing of Columbus from No. 231. Printed in black. 400.00

1968 EFIMEX, International Philatelic Exhibition, Nov. 1-9, Mexico City. Card of 1. No. 292, inscribed in Spanish. 6.00

1970 PHILYMPIA, London International Stamp Exhibition, Sept. 18-26. Card of 3. Nos. 548-550. 4.50

1971 EXFILIMA 71, 3rd Inter-American Philatelic Exhibition, Nov. 6-14, Lima, Peru. Card of 3. Nos. 1111 and 1126, Peru No. 360. Card inscribed in Spanish. 3.50

1972 BELGICA 72, Brussels International Philatelic Exhibition, June 24-July 9. Brussels, Belgium. Card of 3. Nos. 914, 1026 and 1104. Card inscribed in Flemish and French. 3.50
OLYMPIA PHILATELIC MÜNCHEN 72, Aug. 18-Sept. 10. Munich, Germany. Card of 4. Nos. 1460-1462 and C85. Card inscribed in German. 3.75
EXFILBRA 72, 4th Inter-American Philatelic Exhibition, Aug. 26-Sept. 2, Rio de Janeiro, Brazil. Card of 3. No. C14, Brazil Nos. C18-C19. Card inscribed in Portuguese. 3.50
NATIONAL POSTAL FORUM VI, Aug. 28-30, Washington, D.C. Card of 4. No. 1396. 3.50

1973 IBRA 73 Internationale Briefmarken Ausstellung, May 11-20, Munich, Germany. With one No. C13. 4.00
APEX 73, International Airmail Exhibition, July 4-7, Manchester, England. Card of 3. Newfoundland No. C4, U.S. No. C3a and Honduras No. C12. 3.50
POLSKA 73, Swiatowa Wystawa Filatelistyczna, Aug. 19-Sept. 2, Poznan, Poland. Card of 3. No. 1488 and Poland Nos. 1944-1945. Card inscribed in Polish. 4.00
POSTAL PEOPLE CARD, Card of 10 (#1489-1498) distributed to Postal Service employees. Not available to public. 14x11". $75.00 (est.)

1974 HOBBY, The Hobby Industry Association of America Convention and Trade Show, February 3-6, Chicago, Illinois. Card of 4. Nos. 1456-1459. 4.00
INTERNABA, International Philatelic Exhibition, June 7-16, Basel, Switzerland. Card of 8, strip of five. Nos. 1530-1537. Card inscribed in 4 languages. 4.00
STOCKHOLMIA 74, International frimarksustallning, September 21-29, Stockholm, Sweden. Card of 3. No. 836, Sweden Nos. 300 and 765. Card inscribed in Swedish. 4.50
EXFILMEX 74 UPU, Philatelic Exposition Inter-Americana, October 26-November 3, Mexico City, Mexico. Card of 2. No. 1157 and Mexico No. 910. Card inscribed in Spanish and English. 4.50

1975 ESPANA 75, World Stamp Exhibition, Apr. 4-13, Madrid, Spain. Card of 3. Nos. 233, 1271 and Spain No. 1312. Card inscribed in Spanish. 4.00
ARPHILA 75, June 6-16, Paris, France. Card of 3. Nos. 1187, 1207 and France No. 1117. Card inscribed in French. 3.50

1976 WERABA 76, Third International Space Stamp Exhibition, April 1-4, Zurich, Switzerland. Card of 2. Nos. 1434 and 1435 se-tenant. 4.00
BICENTENNIAL EXPOSITION on Science and Technology, May 30-Sept. 6. Kennedy Space Center, Fla. Card of 1. No. C76. 5.50
COLORADO STATEHOOD CENTENNIAL, August 1, Card of 3. Nos. 743, 288 and 1670. 5.00
HAFNIA 76, International Stamp Exhibition, Aug. 20-29, Copenhagen, Denmark. Card of 2. No. 5 and Denmark No. 2. Card inscribed in Danish and English. 5.00
ITALIA 76, International Philatelic Exhibition, Oct. 14-24, Milan, Italy. Card of 3. No. 1168 and Italy Nos. 578 and 601. Card inscribed in Italian. 4.00
NORDPOSTA 76, North German Stamp Exhibition, Oct. 30-31, Hamburg, Germany. Card of 3. No. 689 and Germany Nos. B366 and B417. Card inscribed in German. 4.00

TEMBAL 83

Basel, Schweiz   21. - 29. Mai 1983

UNITED
STATES
AIR
MAIL

Audubon 1785 - 1851

20c

Mit der Herausgabe dieser Erinnerungs-Postkarte mochte die amerikanische Postverwaltung auf die in Basel statt-findende "Internationale Motivbriefmarkenausstellung Tembal 83" aufmerksam machen.

Seit jeher gelten Vogel als Sinnbild der schnellen und speditiven Postbeforderung. Um nun den symbolische und kunstlerische Bedeutung von Vogelmotiven auf Postwert-zeichen entsprechend zu wurdigen, sind zwei bekannte Marken dieses Typs fur die Erinnerungskarte ausgewahlt worden.

Rechts figuriert das moglicherweise erste Postwertzeichen dieser Art; es ist hier deshalb wiedergegeben, weil die wichtige philatelistische Veranstaltung in der Heimatstadt der beruhmten "Basler-Taube" abgehalten wird.

Die amerikanische Marke (links) wurde 1967 fur den interna-tionalen Briefpostverkehr nach Europa entworfen; als Vorlage dazu diente das Werk "Columbia Jays" des amerikanischen Kunstlers John James Audubon.

W F Bolger

William F. Bolger
Postmaster General

STADT-POST BASEL

Idaho
USA 20c

JOINT STAMP ISSUES • SWEDEN AND UNITED STATES OF AMERICA
MARCH 24, 1983

Det amerikanska postverket gladjer sig at att genom gemensam utgivning av frimarken fa forena sig med det svenska postverket i 200-arsfirandet av undertecknanden av traktaten for vanskap och handel, det forsta avtal som tecknades mellan Forenta Staterna och ett neutralt land.

Frimarkena har samma motiv med undantag av landsnamnet och valor. Bada markena har graverats av Czeslaw Slania, hovgravor i Sverige och en av de mest kanda frimarks-gravorena i varlden. Markena har utformats av den svenske konstnaren Dan Jonsson. Frimarkena visar ett portratt av Benjamin Franklin och det svenska riksssigillet. Signaturena av traktatens undertecknare, Benjamin Franklin for Forenta Staterna och Gustaf Philip Creutz for Sverige, avbildas ocksa pa frimarkena.

Bada frimarkena avbildas pa kortet tillsammans med en reproduktion av en amerikansk frimarksgravyr fran 1948 till minne av 100-arsjubileet av svensk immigration till Mellanvastern.

Stjarnorna pa var sida om frimarket representerar de 12 stater i Mellanvastern dar svenska immigranter bosatte sig 1848. De tre markena minner om den bestaende omsesidiga vanskapen mellan Sverige och Forenta Staterna.

SVERIGE

VANSKAPS-
OCH HANDELSTRAKTAT
MELLAN SVERIGE
OCH USA 1783

2.70

D JONSSON

SWEDISH PIONEER CENTENNIAL

5¢

1848   1948

UNITED STATES POSTAGE

TREATY OF AMITY
AND COMMERCE
BETWEEN USA AND
SWEDEN 1783

20c

USA

The U. S. Postal Service is happy to join with the Postal Administration of Sweden in celebrating the 200th anniversary of the signing of the Treaty of Amity and Commerce, the first treaty between the United States and a neutral country, through the joint issuance of postage stamps. The stamps are similar in motif except for national identification and denomination. Both stamps were engraved by Czeslaw Slania, the court engraver of Sweden and one of the most prolific stamp engravers in the world. They were designed by Swedish artist, Dan Jonsson. The design of the stamps features a portrait of Benjamin Franklin and the Great Seal of Sweden. The signatures of the signers of the treaty, Benjamin Franklin for the United States and Gustav Philip Creutz for Sweden, also are featured on the stamps.

Reproductions of both of these stamps are depicted on this souvenir card along with the engraved reproduction of a U. S. stamp from 1948 commemorating the 100th anniversary of Swedish pioneers moving to the midwest. The 12 stars on each side of the stamp design represent 12 midwestern states settled by Swedish immigrants during 1848. All three stamps commemorate the enduring mutual friendship between Sweden and the United States.

W F Bolger

William F. Bolger
Postmaster General

JOINT STAMP ISSUES
FEDERAL REPUBLIC OF GERMANY AND UNITED STATES OF AMERICA
APRIL 29, 1983

Die Postverwaltungen der Vereinigten Staaten von Amerika und der Bundesrepublik Deutschland würdigen die 300-Jahrfeier des Beginns der deutschen Einwanderung in die Vereinigten Staaten durch die gleichzeitige Herausgabe je einer Sonderbriefmarke, die das Segelschiff "Concord" zeigt.

Im Jahre 1683 verließ die "Concord" London. An Bord befanden sich 13 Familien, die auf der Suche nach religiöser Freiheit von Krefeld, einer Stadt im heutigen Nordrhein-Westfalen, den Weg in die Neue Welt angetreten hatten. Die Einwanderer waren am 24. Juli 1683 in London aufgebrochen und landeten am 6. Oktober 1683 in Philadelphia. Sie kauften Land in Pennsylvania und gründeten die Stadt Germantown, die heute ein Stadtteil von Philadelphia ist.

Die Herausgabe dieser Briefmarke ehrt den Mut, die Ausdauer und die Zielstrebigkeit jener ersten Einwanderer und all derer, die ihnen folgen sollten. Die amerikanische und die deutsche Briefmarke wurden beide von Richard Schlecht, einem Amerikaner deutscher Abstammung aus Arlington, Virginia, entworfen. Da kein Bild der "Concord" aufzufinden war, beruht der Entwurf der Marke auf vorhandenen Beschreibungen des Schiffes.

The United States Postal Service and the Postal Administration of the Federal Republic of Germany are commemorating the tricentennial of German immigration to the United States by the joint issuance of postage stamps featuring the **Concord**.

In 1683, the **Concord** sailed from London, carrying 13 families making their way to the New World from Krefeld, which is now in North-Rhine Westphalia, in search of religious freedom. The immigrants sailed on July 24, 1683, and landed in Philadelphia on October 6, 1683. They purchased land in Pennsylvania to build the community of Germantown, which today is part of Philadelphia.

The issuance of these stamps salutes the courage, stamina and motivation of those first immigrants and all who followed in their footsteps. Both the U. S. and German stamps were designed by Richard Schlecht of Arlington, Virginia, who is an American of German descent. Since a picture of the **Concord** was not available, his design is based upon written descriptions of the ship.

W.F.Bolger

William F. Bolger
Postmaster General

1977 AMPHILEX 77, International Philatelic Exhibition, May 26-June 5, Amsterdam, Netherlands. Card of 3. No. 1027 and Netherlands Nos. 41 and 294. Card inscribed in Dutch. 4.50

SAN MARINO 77, International Philatelic Exhibition, Aug. 28-Sept. 4, San Marino, Card of 3. Nos. 1-2 and San Marino No. 1. Card inscribed in Italian. 5.00

1978 ROCPEX 78, International Philatelic Exhibition, Mar. 20-29, Taipei, Taiwan. Card of 6. Nos. 1706-1709 and Taiwan Nos. 1812 and 1816. Card inscribed in Chinese. 4.00

NAPOSTA 78, Philatelic Exhibition, May 20-25, Frankfurt, Germany. Card of 3. Nos. 555, 563 and Germany No. 1216. Card inscribed in German. 4.00

1979 BRASILIANA 79, International Philatelic Exhibition, Sept. 15-23, Rio de Janeiro, Brazil. Card of 3. Nos. C91—C92 (C92a) and Brazil No. A704. Card inscribed in Portuguese. 4.00

JAPEX 79, International Philatelic Exhibition, Nov. 2-4, Tokyo, Japan. Card of 2. Nos. 1158 and Japan No. A674. Card inscribed in Japanese. 4.00

1980 LONDON 80—IPEX, May 6-14, London, England. Card of 1. U.S. 2¢ 1907 No. 329. Card inscribed in English. 4.00

NORWEX 80—IPEX, June 13-22, Oslo, Norway. 1975 Norway stamp and two 1925 Nos. 620-621 (Norse-American issue). Card inscribed in Norwegian. 4.00

ESSEN 80—IPEX, Nov. 15-19, Essen, West Germany. Card of 2. 1954 West German and No. 1014 Gutenberg Bible. Card inscribed in German. 4.00

1981 WIPA 81, May 22-31, Vienna, Austria. Card of 2. 1967 Austria and No. 1252 American Music. NSCM, National Stamp Collecting Month, Oct. 1981. Issued to call attention to special month for stamp collectors. Card of 2. Nos. 245 and 1918. Card inscribed in English. 4.00

PHILATOKYO 81, International Philatelic Exhibition, Oct. 9-18, Tokyo, Japan. Card of 2. Nos. 1531 and Japan No. 800. Card inscribed in Japanese. 4.00

NORDPOSTA 81, North German Stamp Exhibition, Nov. 7-8, Hamburg, Germany. Card of 2. Nos. 923 and Germany 9NB133. Card inscribed in German. 4.00

1982 CANADA 82 International Philatelic Youth Exhibition, May 20-24, Toronto, Ontario, Canada. Card of 2: 1869 U.S. Eagle and Shield and 1859 Canadian Beaver. 4.00

PHILEXFRANCE 82, June 11-21, Paris, France. Card of 2: 1978 U.S. French Alliance and 1976 French commemoration of American Bicentennial. 4.00

ESPAMER 82, Oct. 12-17, San Juan, Puerto Rico. Card of 3: Nos. 810 and 1437 and the U.S. Ponce de Leon 1982 issue. 4.00

NSCM National Stamp Collecting Month, October. Issued to call attention to special month for stamp collectors. Card of 1: No. C3a. 4.00

1983 Sweden/U.S., March 24, Philadelphia, PA. Card of 3, U.S. Nos. 958 and 2036. Sweden No. 1453. 4.00

German/U.S., April 29, Germantown, PA. Card of 2, U.S. No. 2040 and German No. 1397. 4.00

TEMBAL '83, May 21-29, Basil, Switzerland. Card of 2, in German. U.S. No. C71 and Switzerland No. 3L1. 4.00

BRASILIANA '83, July 29-August 7, Rio de Janeiro, Brazil. Card of 2, in Portuguese. U.S. No. 1 and Brazil No. 1. 4.00

BANGKOK '83, August 4-13, Bangkok, Thailand. Card of 2, in Thai. U.S. No. 210 and Thailand No. 1. 4.00

NSCM—National Stamp Collecting Month. Card of 1, U.S. No. 293. 4.00

1954 POSTAGE STAMP DESIGN EXHIBITION, National Philatelic Museum, Mar. 13. Philadelphia. Card of 4. Monochrome views of Washington, D.C. Inscribed: "Souvenir sheet designed, engraved and printed by members, Bureau, Engraving and Printing./Reissued by popular request". 625.00

1966 SIPEX, 6th International Philatelic Exhibition, May 21-30, Washington, D.C. Card of 3. Multicolored views of Washington, D.C. Inscribed "Sixth International Philatelic Exhibition/Washington, D.C./Designed, Engraved, and Printed by Union Members of Bureau of Engraving and Printing". 210.00

1969 SANDIPEX, San Diego Philatelic Exhibition, July 16-20, San Diego, Cal. Card of 3. Multicolored views of Washington, D.C. Inscribed: "Sandipex—San Diego 200th Anniversary—1769-1969". 80.00
ASDA National Postage Stamp Show, Nov. 21-23, 1969, New York. Card of 4. No. E4. 30.00

1970 INTERPEX, Mar. 13-15, New York. Card of 4. Nos. 1027, 1035, C35 and C38. 65.00
COMPEX, Combined Philatelic Exhibition of Chicagoland, May 29-31, Chicago. Card of 4. No. C18. 20.00
HAPEX, American Philatelic Society Convention, Nov. 5-8, Honolulu, Hawaii. Card of 3. Nos. 799, C46 and C55. 25.00

1971 INTERPEX, Mar. 12-14, New York. Card of 4. No. 1193. Background includes Nos. 1331-1332, 1371 and C76. 5.00
WESTPEX, Western Philatelic Exhibition, Apr. 23-25, San Francisco. Card of 4. Nos. 740, 852, 966 and 997. 4.50
NAPEX 71, National Philatelic Exhibition, May 21-23, Washington, D.C. Card of 3. Nos. 990, 991, 992. 4.50
TEXANEX 71, Texas Philatelic Association and American Philatelic Society conventions, Aug. 26-29, San Antonio, Tex. Card of 3. Nos. 938, 1043 and 1242. 4.50
ASDA National Postage Stamp Show, Nov. 19-21, New York. Card of 3. Nos. C13-C15. 4.50
ANPHILEX '71, Anniversary Philatelic Exhibition, Nov. 26-Dec. 1, New York. Card of 2. Nos. 1-2. 4.50

1972 INTERPEX, Mar. 17-19, New York. Card of 4. No. 1173. Background includes Nos. 976, 1434-1435 and C69. 4.00
NOPEX, Apr. 6-9, New Orleans. Card of 4. No. 1020. Background includes Nos. 323-327. 3.50
SEPAD 72, Oct. 20-22, Philadelphia. Card of 4. No. 1044. 3.50
ASDA National Postage Stamp Show, Nov. 17-19, New York. Card of 4. Nos. 883, 863, 868 and 888. 3.00
STAMP EXPO, Nov. 24-26, San Francisco. Card of 4. No. C36. 3.00

1973 INTERPEX, March 9-11, New York. Card of 4. No. 976. 4.00
COMPEX 73, May 25-27, Chicago. Card of 4. No. 245. 4.00
NAPEX 73, Sept. 14-16, Washington, D.C. Card of 4. No. C3. Background includes Nos. C4-C6. 3.50
ASDA National Postage Stamp Show. Nov. 16-18, New York. Card of 4. No. 908. Foreground includes Nos. 1139-1144. 4.00
STAMP EXPO NORTH, Dec. 7-9, San Francisco. Card of 4. No. C20. 4.00

1974 MILCOPEX, March 8-10, Milwaukee, Wisconsin. Card of 4. No. C43. Background depicts U.P.U. monument at Berne, Switzerland. 5.00

1975 NAPEX 75, May 9-11, Washington, D.C. Card of 4. No. 708. 14.00
INTERNATIONAL WOMEN'S YEAR. Card of 3. Nos. 872, 878 and 959. Reproduction of 1886 dollar bill. 35.00
ASDA National Postage Stamp Show, Nov. 21-23, New York. Bicentennial series. Card of 4. No. 1003. "...and maintain the liberty which we have derived from our ancestors." 57.50

1976 INTERPHIL 76, Seventh International Philatelic Exhibition, May 29-June 6, Philadelphia. Bicentennial series. Card of 4. No. 120. "that all men are created equal." 9.50
STAMP EXPO 76, June 11-13, Los Angeles. Bicentennial series. Card of 4. Nos. 1351, 1352, 1345 and 1348 se-tenant vertically. "when we assumed the soldier, we did not lay aside the citizen". 6.50

1977 MILCOPEX, Milwaukee Philatelic Society, Mar. 4-6, Milwaukee. Card of 2. Nos. 733 and 1128. 5.00
ROMPEX 77, Rocky Mountain Philatelic Exhibition, May 20-22, Denver. Card of 4. No. 1001. 4.00
PURIPEX 77, Silver Anniversary Philatelic Exhibit, Sept. 2-5, San Juan, Puerto Rico. Card of 4. No. 801. 5.00
ASDA National Postage Stamp Show, Nov. 15-20, New York. Card of 4. No. C45. 4.50

1978 CENJEX 78, Federated Stamp Clubs of New Jersey, 30th annual exhibition, June 23-25, Freehold, N.J. Card of 9. Nos. 646, 680, 689, 1086, 1716 and 4 No. 785. 5.00

1980 NAPEX 80, July 4-6, Washington, D.C. Card of 4. No. 573. 5.00
ASDA National Postage Stamp Show, Sept. 25-28, New York. Card of 4. No. 962. 5.00

1981 STAMP EXPO 81, South International Stamp Collectors Society, Mar. 20-22, Anaheim, Cal. Card of 4. No. 1287. 5.00

1982 MILCOPEX, March 5-7, Milwaukee, Wisconsin. Card of 4. No. 1136. 5.00
ESPAMER 82, Oct. 12-17, San Juan, Puerto Rico. Card of 1. No. 244. 5.00

1983 TEXANEX-TOPEX 83, June 17-19, San Antonio, Texas. Card of 2. Nos. 776 and 1660. 5.00
NORTHEASTERN 83, Oct. 21-23, Boston, Mass. Card of 2, Nos. 718 and 719. 5.00

VALUES FOR OTHER USPS PRODUCTS

Over the years, the U.S. Postal Service has published a number of limited edition philatelic products issued to commemorate various philatelic and other events. These current market values were determined through various dealers who carry these products.

Commemorative Mint Sets	Original Price	Current Market Value
1968	$ 2.50	$22.50
1969	2.50	28.50
1970	2.50	14.95
1971	2.50	7.95
1972	3.00	7.95
1973	3.00	7.95
1974	3.50	7.95
1975	3.50	7.95
1976	3.50	7.95
1977	4.50	7.95
Bicentennial Mint Set With Souvenir Sheets	$11.80	$25.00
Without Souvenir Sheets	7.50	9.95
1980 Olympics Mint Set	6.50	9.95
Prominent Americans Series Mint Set	12.00	22.50
Women's Mint Set	3.00	6.00
Americana Series Mint Set	14.00	19.50
Fifty Birds and Flowers Mint Set Hardbound	17.00	17.00
Softbound	11.00	11.00
American Wildlife Album	3.50	3.50

Birds and Flowers of the Fifty States
A Collection of United States Commemorative Stamps

American Wildlife
A Collection of U.S. Mint Stamps

For The Complete Collector

A relative newcomer to the world of stamps, the Definitive Mint Set was first offered in 1980 and has, in that short period of time, become a philatelic article of considerable importance and in great demand. With its introduction, collectors now have the special opportunity to acquire one of every postal item issued by the USPS during the year. Then, too, the Set is issued in a limited edition printing of 350,000 (compared to a production of 1.2 million for the Commemorative Mint Set), which offers added appeal to many collector enthusiasts.

For 1982, the Definitive Set is particularly impressive: a 16-page, four-color album contains 13 regular stamp issues and nine stationery items, each to be mounted in plastic protectors and accompanied by illustrations, photographs and articles relevant to the featured topic.

The 1982 Definitive Mint Set is available for $7.50 at more than 15,000 Post Offices nationwide, through all Philatelic Centers, and by mail order from the Postal Service's Philatelic Sales Division, Washington, D.C. 20265-9997. For additional information, send the postal card following page 272.

Philatelic Societies

American Air Mail Society
102 Arbor Rd.
Cinnaminson, NJ 08077-3859
Specializes in aerophilately, and periodically presents the Conrath Award to a member of the society in the name of Walter Conrath, one of its founders.

American First Day Cover Society
Mrs. Monte Eiserman
Membership Chairman
14359 Chadbourne
Houston, TX 77079-6611

American Philatelic Society
Box 8000
State College, PA 16801-8000
A full complement of services and resources for the philatelist. Membership offers: American Philatelic Research Library; expertizing service; estate advisory service; translation services; a stamp theft committee which functions as a clearing house for stamp theft information; a speakers' bureau and a monthly journal, "The American Philatelist," sent to all members.

American Stamp Dealer's Association
5 Dakota Dr.
Suite 102
Lake Success, NY 11042-1109
Association of dealers engaged in every facet of philately, with eleven regional chapters nation wide. Sponsors national and local shows, seminars for member and non-member dealers, credit information service, monthly newsletter and ASDA membership directory.

American Topical Association
3306 No. 50th Street
Milwaukee, WI 53216-3299
A service organization concentrating on the specialty of topical collecting. Offers handbooks on specific topics; an exhibition award; *Topical Time,* a bi-monthly publication dealing with topical interest areas; a slide and film loan service; information, translation, biography and sales services; and an heirs' estate service.

Black American Philatelic Society
% Walt Robinson
9101 Taylor Street
Landover, MD 20785-2554
For collectors interested in the study of black Americans on postage stamps.

Bureau Issues Association
Box 1125
Falls Church, VA 22041-0125

Collectors Club, Inc.
22 East 35th Street
New York, NY 10016-3806
Regular services include library and reading rooms, a publication and lectures on philatelic subjects. The group also honors a great American collector annually and actively supports national and international exhibitions.

Council of Philatelic Organizations
P.O. Box 3492
North New Hyde Park Station
New Hyde Park, NY 11040-0801
A non-profit organization comprised of more than 200 national, regional and local stamp clubs, organizations, societies and philatelic business firms. The objective of COPO is to promote and encourage the hobby of stamp collecting. Membership is open only to organizations; COPO uses a variety of methods to promote stamp collecting including an on-going publicity campaign, a quarterly newsletter and joint sponsorship (with the USPS) of National Stamp Collecting Month. For more information on COPO send a stamped, self-addressed envelope requesting a copy of "COPO is Everyone."

Junior Philatelists of America
Box 195
Minetto, NY 13115-0195
Provides an auction department, library service, tape and slide service, stamp identification and translation services. Publishes a bi-monthly, illustrated publication titled the *Philatelic Observer.*

Maximum Card Study Club
Bill Kelleher
Box 375
Bedford, MA 01730-0375

Mobile Post Office Society
5030 Aspen Drive
Omaha, NE 68157-2267
A non-profit organization concentrating on transit markings and the history of postal transit routes. The Society is engaged in documenting and recording transit postal history by publishing books, catalogs and monographs, as well as a semi-monthly journal.

Modern Postal History Association
% Psychology Department
Pace University
Pleasantville, NY 10570-2799

National Association of Precancel Collectors
5121 Park Blvd.
Wildwood, NJ 08260-1454

The Perfin Club
10550 Western Ave.
Stanton, CA 90680-2254

Philatelic Foundation
270 Madison Ave.
New York, NY 10016-0656
A non-profit organization known for its excellent expertization service. The Foundation's broad resources, including extensive reference collections, 5,000-volume library and Expert Committee, provide collectors with comprehensive consumer protection. It also publishes educational information. Slide and cassette programs are available on such subjects as the Pony Express, Provisionals, Confederate Postal History and special programs for beginning collectors. A directory of these programs is available upon request. The Foundation is also the publisher of Bogg's *Foundations of Philately* and R.H. White's *Color in Philately.*

ate Block Collector Club
Box 937
Homestead, FL 33090-0937

Plate Number Society
9600 Colesville Rd.
Silver Spring, MD 20901-3144

Postal History Society
Box 20
Bayside, NY 11361-0020

Post Mark Collectors Club
Wilma Hinrichs
4200 SE. Indianola Rd.
Des Moines, IA 50320-1555

Precancel Stamp Society
David A. Coates, Secretary
2500 Wisconsin Avenue, N.W. #829
Washington, D.C. 20007-4561

Society of Philatelic Americans
Box 9041
Wilmington, DE 19809-0041
    An organization with members from all over the
world, the Society publishes a monthly magazine, "The
SPA Journal," provides sales circuits, and services in
exchange, expertization, insurance, publications and
slide films. It also sponsors numerous philatelic
awards.

Souvenir Card Collectors Society
Box 7116
Rochester, MN 55903-7116

United Postal Stationery Society
Mrs. J. Thomas
Box 48
Redlands, CA 92373-0601

**The United States Possessions
Philatelic Society**
141 Lyford Drive
Tiburon, CA 94920-1652

The Universal Ship Cancellation Society
P.O. Box 13
New Britain, CT 06050-0013

Catalogs

Brookman Price List of U.S. Stamps
91 South 9th Street
Minneapolis, MN 55402-3295
    Brookman's values are used for used and unused
single stamp pricing in The Postal Service Guide to
U.S. Stamps.

Catalogue of United States Souvenir Cards
The Washington Press
2 Vreeland Rd.
Florham Park, NJ 07932-1587

First Day Cover Catalogue (U.S.-U.N.)
The Washington Press
2 Vreeland Rd.
Florham Park, NJ 07932-1587

Perfins of the World
9801 Dewey Drive
Garden Grove, CA 92641-1344

Souvenir Pages Price List
(Please send self-addressed stamped envelope
to receive current listings.)
Charles D. Simmons
P.O. Box 6238
Buena Park, CA 90622-6238

Stamps of the World 1982 Catalogue
Stanley Gibbons Publications. Available through
dealers only. All the stamps of the world from 1840 to
date. Over 1,900 pages feature more than 200,000
stamps (47,900 illustrations) from over 200 issuing
countries.

Commemorative Panel Price List
(Please send self-addressed stamped envelope
to receive current listings.)
Frank Riolo
P.O. Box 1540
Delray Beach, FL 33447-1540

Fleetwoods Standard First Day Cover Catalog
Unicover Corporation
Cheyenne, WY 82008-0001

Harris Illustrated Postage Stamp Catalog
H.E. Harris & Co., Inc.
Boston, MA 02117-0810

Minkus New World Wide Stamp Catalogue
116 West 32nd Street
New York, NY 10001-3284

American Air Mail Catalogue
American Air Mail Society
Cinnaminson, NJ 08077-3859

Scott Standard Postage Stamp Catalogue
3 East 57th St.
New York, NY 10022-2562

Magazines and Newspapers

Linn's Stamp News
Box 29
Sidney, OH 45365-0029

Mekeel's Weekly Stamp News
Box 1660
Portland, ME 04104-1660

Minkus Stamp Journal
41 West 25th Street
New York, NY 10010-2021

Scott's Monthly Stamp Journal
3 East 57th St.
New York, NY 10022-2562

Stamps
153 Waverly Place
New York, NY 10014-3849

Stamp Collector
Box 10
Albany, OR 97321-0006

Stamp Review
1839 Palmer Ave.
Larchmont, NY 10538-3099

Stamp World
P.O. Box 601
Sidney, OH 45365-0601
    Monthly publication directed to informational and
feature articles on stamp subjects, stamp designs
and other general topics.

Philatelic Literature

Blume, Marshall E., editor. Encyclopedia of
Investments Warren, Gorham & Lamont, Inc., $47.50.

Brookman, Lester G., The 19th Century Postage
Stamps of the United States, (3 volumes), NY, 1968.

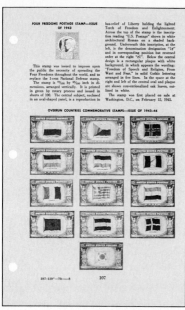

*Selected pages from the USPS
Publication 9 covering U.S. stamps.*

Browning, Peter. *The Directory of Stamp-Auction Houses* Frederick Pell Publishing, NY, $24.95.

Chase, Carroll C., *The 3¢ Stamps of the United States, 1942.*

Johl, Max G., *The United States Commemorative Stamps of the Twentieth Century, 1947.*

Linn's World Stamp Almanac, latest edition.

Patrick, Douglas and Mary, *The Musson Stamp Dictionary, 1972.*

D.G. Phillips Publ. Co., *The American Stampless Cover Catalog, 1978.*

Scheele, Carl H., *A Short History of the Mail Service, 1970.*

Sutton, R.J., *Stamp Collector's Encyclopedia.*

Topical Stamp Publications List, 1982-83, American Topical Association.

Thorp, Prescott H., *Stamped Envelopes and Wrappers of the United States.*

United Postal Stationery Society. *United States Postal Card Catalog, 1980.*

United States Postal Service, United States Postage Stamps, Pub. 9.
   A popular reference book compiled and produced by the United States Postal Service's Stamps Division. Includes illustrations, background data and technical information (designers, engravers, etc.) on all U.S. postage stamps complete through 1980. Basic book and latest update supplements available through the Superintendent of Documents, Government Printing Office, Washington, D.C. 20402.

American Air Mail Catalogue, 4 volumes.

Brookman, L., *Bank Note Issues of U.S. Stamps, 1870-1893,* 1981.

Fletcher, H.G. Leslie, *Postal Forgeries of the World,* 1977.

French, Loran C., *Encyclopedia of Plate Varieties on U.S. Bureau-printed Postage Stamps,* 1979.

Gobie, H., *The Speedy, A History of U.S. Special Delivery Service,* 1976.

Gobie, H., *U.S. Parcel Post,* 1979.

Hargest, George, E., *History of Letter Post Communication between the U.S. and Europe, 1845-1875,* revised 1975.

Herst & Sampson, *19th Century United States Fancy Cancellations,* 4th edition, 1972.

Hooper, R. Malcolm, *A Historical Survey of Precancels,* 1979.

Schmid, Paul W., *How to Detect Damaged, Altered & Repaired Stamps,* 1979.

Skinner, H.C. & Amos Eno, *United States Cancellations, 1845-1869,* 1980.

Staff, Frank, *The Picture Postcard and its Origin,* reprinted 1979.

Turner, George T., *Sloane's Column,* 2nd printing, 1980.

Turner, George T. and Thomas Stanton, *Pat Paragraphs,* 1981.

A Treasured Tradition

In 1972, the Postal Service inaugurated a great philatelic tradition: the limited edition of American Commemorative Panels. Since that time, the panels have been offered annually to honor each new commemorative issue for that year. First in the continuing series was the famous Wildlife Commemorative Panel.

Commemorative Panels represent the highest standards of stamp art and the engraver's craft. Each one highlights newly issued, mint condition stamps on an 8½" x 11¼" page. Then, the stamps are enhanced by intaglio-printed reproductions of historical engravings (many over 100 years old) and are accompanied by carefully researched, informative articles on the commemorative subject. The finished display is a work of art in itself— worthy of framing, exhibiting and sharing. As gifts or awards, perhaps as a simple gesture of appreciation, the Commemorative Panels are in a class of their own.

Beginning in 1982, complete annual sets of the Commemorative Panel series, produced as a limited edition, were made available on an advance subscription basis only. Subscriptions are for a full year beginning each January. For additional information write the Philatelic Sales Division, Commemorative Panel Program, Washington, D.C. 20265-9993.

The year was 1938. The President was Franklin D. Roosevelt, then in his second term. He was an avowed and enthusiastic stamp collector. His Postmaster General, James Farley, was resourceful and diligent about his boss' ideas. Roosevelt thought up appropriate subjects for stamps; sketched out philatelic themes; and anxiously watched their course through the Bureau of Design. With such a powerful push from the top, an idea was maturing within the Post Office Department to sponsor a special "motorized postage stamp display car" that would tour the country.

This traveling stamp exhibition was to be directed to the young collector, to boys and girls of school age. The idea was to stimulate interest in collecting among the youth of this country. The truck would carry a display of U.S. stamps from the first two issues of 1847 down to the present time. And, it would travel to rural areas and sparsely settled communities.

The Philatelic Truck was specially designed on a 1931 truck chassis. It was about the size of a small bus, approximately 24 feet in overall length, and had a double rear door as well as two side exits near the front. When the complete collection of U.S. stamps was installed, the Truck and its contents became exceedingly valuable; estimates ranged up to a million dollars. It had to be guarded day and night. When the show hit the road, this problem got bigger.

Inside the Truck, official and ordinary Post Office stamps series, commemoratives and airmails were displayed on side panels, which were surrounded by 24 pictures of government buildings. In glass cases along the walls, there were photographs of stamp designs, books, stamp coils and brochures. Weather permitting, two display cases could be mounted outside on the front bumpers of the Truck, showing Airmail and the 1938 Presidential stamp series. Additionally, a miniature Stickney press (1/8th scale, designed and built by the Bureau of Engraving and Printing) was displayed inside the truck.

The Philatelic Truck made its grand debut on the White House grounds on May 9, 1939, with Postmaster General Farley and President Roosevelt in attendance. After a few days in Washington, it started on its remarkable odyssey of 2½ years which took it into 490 cities, towns and villages over a distance of 20,750 miles. (It must be remembered that in this period, there were virtually no superhighways.) Nearly half a million people visited the Truck to view the exhibits.

Postmaster General James Farley gives the Philatelic Truck an official send-off.

SOUVENIR
DISTRIBUTED ON THE OCCASION OF THE VISIT OF THE PHILATELIC TRUCK

ISSUED BY THE
★ UNITED STATES POST OFFICE DEPARTMENT ★

The "Souvenir Poster Stamps" were issued for visitors to the Philatelic Truck.

The first route of the Truck was from Washington to Maine and then back to Florida. Then, twice in a series of four giant zig-zag sweeps, it went from the Gulf of Mexico to the Great Lakes and back. Lastly, it trekked west from Galveston, Texas, and came to a final halt in San Diego just a few days after Pearl Harbor ushered in World War II on December 7, 1941. The original plan of covering every state in the Union was left unfulfilled, for with the onset of the war there was an official call to conserve gas and rubber; and it was also felt that there would be no drivers to man the traveling exhibit.

But before the Truck came to journey's end, who were the people who manned the Philatelic Truck—drove from point to point; set up the displays; greeted local dignitaries; explained the contents to 200, 400, 600, 1,000, (and in Pittsburgh) 5,000 daily visitors; then packed up and immediately pushed on to yet another destination?

Three clerks in the Division of Stamps were originally detailed as crew. None of them had volunteered and it is easy to see why. Ralph A. Davis, a stamp fan and expert, was put in charge of the Truck, and was the only one to see it through its tour of duty. Others came on board and were replaced as the strain of the job took its toll. The assignment was grueling: seats were stiff and roads often rough. For security reasons, Davis bunked on the display cases to guard the truck's contents throughout the night. The crew was away from home for months and sometimes a wife or entire family tagged along in a follow-up car. With their gypsy schedule, they often worried about getting their pay checks while on the road. Then in 1941 they had another worry—the army draft.

The Philatelic Truck was an ambitious, popular and successful project, but it over-estimated what mortals could accomplish. After 2½ years, fully one-half of the U.S. had never been visited.

But the positive effects of this "Stamp Crusade" remain. The souvenir card idea has grown and prospered; First Day ceremonies received an impetus; philatelic press releases and philatelic windows appeared in post offices; the public has become far more involved—and critical; young people have been brought in. Most of all, the hobby has flourished mightily, thanks to this brainchild of Roosevelt and Farley—the one and only Philatelic Truck!

(The basis for this article is The Philatelic Truck *by James H. Bruns, published by the Bureau Issues Association, Inc.)*

STAMP COLLECTING KITS

Discover the "Hobby of a Lifetime"

Stamp collecting! It's educational, exciting, challenging…and fun! You've heard about it and you're eager to join the ranks of 20,000,000 Americans who enjoy the world's most popular hobby. But where and how do you start? With the U.S. Postal Service Stamp Collecting Kits. Available at your local post office, these Kits offer an inexpensive introduction to the world of stamps.

Every USPS Kit contains four essential tools: a color-illustrated album with background information and display space for each stamp; a selection of genuine, colorful stamps ready for mounting; a convenient packet of mounting hinges; and *The Introduction to Stamp Collecting,* a 32-page booklet.

Your local post office may have additional Stamp Collecting Kits beyond those shown here. Be sure to ask. Since availability may vary, you may also wish to check more than one post office.

USPS Stamp Collecting Kits to be issued during the next few months include these interesting topics: Conquest of Air, Ships, Creatures of the Sea and the Winter Olympics.

And in early 1984...the 1984 U.S. Commemorative Stamp Collecting Kit will be available at your local post office. A preview of 1984 stamps—the great Roberto Clemente and the legendary Jim Thorpe, Vietnam Veterans Memorial stamp, Smokey Bear, the Roanoke Voyages, Eleanor Roosevelt and much more.

1983 United States Commemorative Stamp Collecting Kit is now available at your local post office. It contains five 1983 U.S. commemorative stamps, a full-color album describing all 1983 U.S. commemoratives, stamp mounts and the booklet *Introduction to Stamp Collecting.* $3.00.

A Tour of Two New Homes

The new Virginia Administrative Center receives mail orders for philatelic materials from all over the country.

As a stamp collector and correspondent with the Philatelic Sales Division, you may have often wondered what this government agency looks like and what goes on there. Until recently, all Philatelic Sales operations were housed in a 39,000 square foot facility in the Waterside Mall, a complex near the Postal Service Headquarters in Washington, D.C. But space was limited and ever-increasing prohibitive rents indicated a move was necessary. And so it was decided to establish two separate divisions in two different locations of the country. The Administrative Center packed off to Merrifield, Virginia, while the Fulfillment Branch went west to Kansas City, Missouri.

Although the two new facilities are half a continent apart, they operate and coordinate as efficiently as if they were housed under the same roof. Mail orders from around the country are received at Merrifield, entered into the computers, then transferred to the Kansas City facility for processing and shipment. The entire cycle takes only six working days or less to process philatelic mail orders between the two centers (up to two in Merrifield, and up to four in Kansas City). According to one official, "The moves to Merrifield and Kansas City have provided greater work space and improved customer service by reducing the time it takes to process philatelic orders."

In addition to handling order-entry operations, the Virginia Administrative Center is also headquarters for the accounting offices and First Day Cancellation unit of the Philatelic Sales Division. The Merrifield facility consists of 48,300 square feet of space in a new two-story building and has approximately 95 employees.

Some 1,000 miles to the west of Merrifield, the Fulfillment Branch has taken up residence in a former limestone mine on the outskirts of Kansas City, Missouri. But any image you may have of workers descending by elevator into dank subterranean passages is quickly dispelled by a Division director: "The mine is a horizontal excavation into a hill, only about 150 feet underground. The entrance and all 141,200 feet of office, storage and work space are at ground level." The section that the USPS has leased for 15 years is part of a 140-acre industrial park known as The Great Midwest Underground Center.

It is at the Fulfillment Center where stamps are stored and dispatched to mail order customers throughout the country. Presently, the staff numbers 38 strong, but, depending on the growth of the mail order sales, it could easily expand to 100 or 150 in the next five years.

The subterranean space offers many advantages for the Fulfillment Center: The underground temperature stays within a constant range of 58 to 62 degrees Fahrenheit. Not only is this an ideal climate for stamp storage but it greatly reduces the cost of air conditioning and heating. Then, too, humidity is easy to control. The facility is highly secure and the solid limestone floor can support heavy cartons of stamps. Also, the geographical location is another bonus for this branch of the Philatelic Sales Division: situated near the center of the United States, Kansas City is a focal point for all kinds of transportation —rail, air and highway—making it ideal for the Division's mail order business.

The U.S. Postal Service Philatelic Sales Division, with two new facilities, is like two hearts that beat as one. Commenting on this dual arrangement, one observer noted: "With the improved tandem service promised—and so far provided—by the Merrifield-Kansas City connection, philatelists' pleasure and satisfaction with the improved order-fulfillment system will no doubt be reflected by the number of positive 'votes of confidence.'"

The Fulfillment Branch is now located in a mine which is a horizontal excavation into a Missouri hill.

Lasting Value for All Collectors

U.S. Postal Service Commemorative Mint Sets are more than just a collection of all commemorative stamps issued in one year—the sets are fun, informative and valuable (see page 274 for current values of past Commemorative Mint Sets). Each year's complete set of commemoratives includes protection sleeves or individual plastic mounts to help preserve and display your stamps. The attractive folders feature concise background on the subjects of commemoration, the stamp artists and other philatelic information. Mint Sets launch the new collector in an absorbing, often lifelong, avocation. Experienced enthusiasts also value the Sets as adjuncts to their own collecting efforts. Commemorative Mint Sets are available at your local post office.

1982's Mint Set—28 stamps comprising 20 issues—highlights the World's Fair, American Architecture, and Christmas (contemporary) in three separate blocks of four. It also incorporates a random single from the 50 State Birds and Flowers pane and stamps honoring the International Peace Garden, Wolf Trap, and America's Libraries, among others. $6.50.

The mint set pictured is the 1982 edition.

Energy
This block of four stamps served a dual purpose, calling attention to the World's Fair in Knoxville, Tennessee (the theme of which is "Energy"), and to the continuing need to both conserve available energy resources and develop new ones. Based on original acrylic paintings, the stamp designs are colorful and imaginative. The vignette of the solar energy stamp depicts the sun against a multicolored background. The design of the synthetic fuels stamp depicts symbolic representations of devices used in laboratories. The central feature of the "Breeder reactor" design is a representation of the core from a nuclear breeder reactor. Fossil fuels are represented by decaying matter below the surface of the earth.
Designer: Charles Harper
Issued: Knoxville, Tennessee
April 29

Horatio Alger (1832-1899)
The design of this stamp, honoring the American author of more than 100 stories, is based on the frontispiece from the Ragged Dick series of six books, which first brought Alger national prominence in 1867 and 1868. He influenced generations of readers with stories that featured the theme, "strive and succeed."
Designer: Robert Hallock
Issued: Willow Grove, Pennsylvania
April 30

International Peace Garden
The International Peace Garden, spanning the border between North Dakota and the province of Manitoba, Canada, symbolizes the harmony in which two nations live along the longest unfortified boundary in the world. It is a positive, living example of more than 150 years of peace and friendship between the U.S. and Canada.
Designer: Gyo Fujikawa
Issued: Dunseith, North Dakota
June 30

The Barrymores
Students of theatrical arts around the world know that the Barrymores—Lionel (1878-1954), Ethel (1879-1959) and John (1882-1942)—left a legacy of exquisite moments on film and the stage, radio and in the theatre. Over the years the telecast marks the centennial anniversary of the Actors' Fund, the oldest ongoing theatrical charity in the world.
Designer: Jim Sharpe
Issued: New York

Aging Together
The Aging Together stamp was intended to bring to the American people an awareness that older people are highly valued for their contributions to society. They bring a wealth of experience and creative energies to an endless variety of endeavors. Issuance of this stamp was intended

Dr. Mary Walker (1832-1919)
This stamp was issued to honor Dr. Mary Walker, the first woman to have been awarded the Congressional Medal of Honor. The second

Wolf Trap Farm Park
Wolf Tr

1983's Commemorative Mint Set, 26 issues totaling 47 separate stamps, marks the beginning of the Postal Service salute to the 1984 Olympic Games. The tribute includes 16 stamps that encompass a variety of Olympic events. Also notable in 1983: two joint issues, one with the government of Sweden, the other with the Federal Republic of Germany (see pages 28 and 29), new issues in the American Inventors, Black Heritage and American Sports Series, and the celebration of several American anniversaries.

In addition to the more than 15,000 postal facilities authorized to sell philatelic products, the U.S. Postal Service also maintains more than 330 Philatelic Centers located in major population centers throughout the country.

These Philatelic Centers have been developed to serve stamp collectors and make it convenient for them to acquire an extensive range of all current postage stamps, postal stationery and philatelic products issued by the Postal Service.

All Centers listed here are located at the Main Post Office unless otherwise indicated.

Alabama

351 North 24th Street
Birmingham, AL 35203

101 Holmes N.W.
Huntsville, AL 35804

250 St. Joseph
Mobile, Al 36601

Downtown Station
135 Catoma Street
Montgomery, AL 31604

1313 22nd Avenue
Tuscaloosa, AL 35401

Alaska

College Branch
3350 College Road
Fairbanks, AK 99708

Downtown Station
3rd & C Street
Anchorage, AK 99510

Arizona

Osborn Station
3905 North 7th Avenue
Phoenix, AZ 85013

1501 South Cherrybell
Tucson, AZ 85726

Arkansas

South 6th & Rogers Ave.
Fort Smith, AR 72901

100 Reserve
Hot Springs National
Park, AR 71901

310 East Street
Jonesboro, AR 72401

600 West Capitol
Little Rock, AR 72201

California

Downtown Station
135 East Olive Street
Burbank, CA 91502

315 G. Street
Davis, CA 95616

8111 East Firestone
Downey, CA 90241

Cutten Station
3901 Walnut Drive
Eureka, CA 95501

1900 E Street
Fresno, CA 93706

313 E. Broadway
Glendale, CA 91209

Hillcrest Station
303 E. Hillcrest
Inglewood, CA 90311

300 Long Beach Blvd.
Long Beach, CA 90801

300 N. Los Angeles St.
Los Angeles, CA 90012

Terminal Annex
900 N. Alameda
Los Angeles, CA 90052

Village Station
11000 Wilshire Blvd.
Los Angeles, CA 90024

El Viejo Station
1125 I Street
Modesto, CA 95354

Civic Center Annex
201 13th Street
Oakland, CA 94612

281 E. Colorado Blvd.
Pasadena, CA 91109

1647 Yuba St.
Redding, CA 96001

1201 North Catalina
Redondo Beach, CA
90277

Downtown Station
3890 Orange St.
Riverside, CA 92501

2000 Royal Oaks Drive
Sacramento, CA 95813

Base Line Station
1164 North E Street
San Bernardino, CA
92410

2535 Midway Drive
San Diego, CA 92199

7th and Mission Sts.
San Francisco, CA 94101

1750 Meridian Drive
San Jose, CA 95101

Spurgeon Station
615 North Bush
Santa Ana, CA 92701

836 Anacada Street
Santa Barbara, CA
93102

4245 West Lane
Stockton, CA 95208

15701 Sherman Way
Van Nuys, CA 91408

396 South California St.
West Covina, CA 91790

Colorado

1905 15th St.
Boulder, CO 80302

201 E. Pikes Peak
Colorado Springs, CO
80901

241 N. 4th St.
Grand Junction, CO
81501

1823 Stout Street
Denver, CO 80202

421 N. Main Street
Pueblo, CO 81003

Connecticut

141 Weston Street
Hartford, CT 06101

11 Silver Street
Middletown, CT 06457

141 Church Street
New Haven, CT 06510

27 Masonic Street
New London, CT 06320

421 Atlantic Street
Stamford, CT 06904

135 Grand Street
Waterbury, CT 06701

Delaware

55 The Plaza
Dover, DE 19801

Federal Station
110 E. Main St.
Newark, DE 19711

11th and Market Streets
Wilmington, DE 19801

District of Columbia

L'Enfant Plaza Philatelic
Center
U.S. Postal Service
Headquarters
475 L'Enfant Plaza
West, SW
Washington, DC 20260

Harriet Tubman
Philatelic Center
North Capitol Street and
Massachusetts Avenue
Washington, DC 20013

National Visitors Center
Union Station
50 Massachusetts
Ave., N.E.
Washington, DC 20002

Headsville Station
National Museum of
American History
Smithsonian Institution
Washington, DC 20560

Florida

824 Manatee Ave. West
Bradenton, FL 33506

100 South Belcher Road
Clearwater, FL 33515

1900 West Oakland Park
Boulevard
Fort Lauderdale, FL
33310

401 S.E. 1st Avenue
Gainesville, FL 32601

1801 Polk Street
Hollywood, FL 33022

1110 Kings Road
Jacksonville, FL 32201

210 North Missouri Ave.
Lakeland, FL 33802

118 North Bay Drive
Largo, FL 33540

2200 NW 72nd Avenue
Miami, FL 33101

1200 Goodlette Rd. North
Naples, FL 33940

400 Southwest First Ave.
Ocala, FL 32678

46 East Robinson Street
Orlando, FL 32801

1400 West Jordan Street
Pensacola, FL 32501

3135 First Avenue North
Saint Petersburg, FL
33730

Open Air Station
76 4th St. N.
Saint Petersburg, FL
33701

1661 Ringland Blvd.
Sarasota, FL 33578

5201 Spruce Street
Tampa, FL 33602

npa Bay Postique
mpa, FL 33630

801 Clematis Street
West Palm Beach, FL
33401

Georgia
115 Hancock Avenue
Athens, GA 30601

Downtown Station
101 Marietta Street
Atlanta, GA 30304

1-285 & Ashford-
Dunwoody Rd.
Perimeter Mall Shopping
Center
Atlanta, GA 30346

General Mail Facility
3916 Milgen Road
Columbus, GA 31908

364 Green Street
Gainesville, GA 30501

451 College Street
Macon, GA 31201

2 North Fahm Street
Savannah, GA 31401

Hawaii
3600 Aolele Street
Honolulu, HI 96819

Idaho
770 South 13th Street
Boise, ID 83708

Illinois
909 West Euclid Avenue
Arlington Heights, IL
60004

Moraine Valley Station
7401 100th Place
Bridgeview, IL 60455

433 West Van Buren St.
Chicago, IL 60607

Loop Station
211 South Clark Street
Chicago, IL 60604

1000 East Oakton
Des Plaines, IL 60018

2350 Madison Ave.
Granite City, IL 62040

2000 McDonough St.
Joliet, IL 60436

901 Lake Street
Oak Park, IL 60301

123 Indianwood
Park Forest, IL 60466

211-19th Street
Rock Island, IL 61201

Schaumburg Station
450 W. Roselle Road
Roselle, IL 60194

2105 E. Cook St.
Springfield, IL 62703

Edison Square Station
1520 Washington
Waukegan, IL 60085

Indiana
North Park Branch
44923 1st Avenue
Evansville, IN 47710

Fort Wayne Postal
Facility
1501 S. Clinton Street
Fort Wayne, IN 46802

5530 Sohl Street
Hammond, IN 46320

125 West South Street
Indianapolis, IN 46206

2719 South Webster
Kokomo, IN 46901

3450 State Road 26. E
Lafayette, IN 47901

424 South Michigan
South Bend, IN 46624

30 N. 7th Street
Terre Haute, IN 47808

Iowa
615 6th Avenue
Cedar Rapids, IA 52401

1165 Second Avenue
Des Moines, IA 50318

320 6th Street
Sioux City, IA 51101

Kansas
1021 Pacific
Kansas City, KS 66110

434 Kansas Avenue
Topeka, KS 66603

Downtown Station
401 North Market
Wichita, KS 67202

Kentucky
1088 Nadino Blvd.
Lexington, KY 40511

St. Mathews Station
4600 Shelbyville Road
Louisville, KY 40207

Louisiana
1724 Bank Drive
Alexandria, LA 71301

1715 Odom St.
Alexandria, LA 71301

750 Florida Street
Baton Rouge, LA 70821

1105 Moss Street
Lafayette, LA 70501

3301 17th Street
Metairie, LA 70004

501 Sterlington Road
Monroe, LA 71201

701 Loyola Avenue
New Orleans, LA 70113

Vieux Carre Station
1022 Iberville Street
New Orleans, LA 70112

2400 Texas Avenue
Shreveport, LA 71102

Maine
40 Western Avenue
Augusta, ME 04330

202 Harlow Street
Bangor, ME 04401

125 Forest Avenue
Portland, ME 04101

Maryland
900 E. Fayette Street
Baltimore, MD 21233

201 East Patrick Street
Frederick, MD 21701

6411 Baltimore Avenue
Riverdale, MD 20840

U.S. Route 50 and
Naylor Road
Salisbury, MD 21801

Massachusetts
Post Office and
Courthouse Bldg.
Boston, MA 02109

120 Commercial Street
Brockton, MA 02401

7 Bedford Street
Burlington, MA 01803

330 Cocituate Road
Framingham, MA 01701

385 Main Street
Hyannis, MA 02601

Post Office Square
Lowell, MA 01853

212 Fenn Street
Pittsfield, MA 01201

Long Pond Road
Plymouth, MA 02360

Quincy Branch
47 Washington Street
Quincy, MA 02169

2 Margin Street
Salem, MA 01970

74 Elm Street
West Springfield, MA
01089

462 Washington St.
Woburn, MA 01888

4 East Central Street
Worcester, MA 01603

Michigan
2075 W. Stadium Blvd.
Ann Arbor, MI 48106

26200 Ford Road
Dearborn Heights, MI
48127

1401 West Fort Street
Detroit, MI 48233

250 East Boulevard Dr.
Flint, MI 48502

225 Michigan Avenue
Grand Rapids, MI 49501

200 South Otsego
Jackson, MI 49201

Downtown Station
315 West Allegan
Lansing, MI 48901

200 West 2nd Street
Royal Oak, MI 48068

30550 Gratiot Street
Roseville, MI 48066

1233 South Washington
Saginaw, MI 48605

Minnesota
2800 West Michigan
Duluth, MN 55806

1st and Marquette Ave.
Minneapolis, MN 55401

The Pioneer Postal
Emporium
133 Endicott Arcade
St. Paul, MN 55101

Mississippi
2421-13th Street
Gulfport, MS 39501

245 East Capitol
Jackson, MS 32905

500 West Miln Street
Tupelo, MS 38801

Missouri
315 Pershing Road
Kansas City, MO 64108

Northwest Plaza Station
500 Northwest Plaza
St. Ann, MO 63074

8th and Edmond
St. Joseph, MO 64501

Clayton Branch
7750 Maryland
St. Louis, MO 63105

H.S. Jewell Station
870 Boonville Ave.
Springfield, MO 65801

Montana
841 South 26th
Billings, MT 59101

Nebraska
700 R Street
Lincoln, NE 68501

204 W. South Front St.
Grand Island, NE 68801

1124 Pacific
Omaha, NE 68108

Nevada
1001 Circus Circus Dr.
Las Vegas, NV 89114

200 Vassar Street
Reno, NV 89510

New Hampshire
South Main Street
Hanover, NH 03755

80 Daniel Street
Portsmouth, NH 03801

955 Goffs Falls Road
Manchester, NH 03103

New Jersey
1701 Pacific Avenue
Atlantic City, NJ 08401

3 Miln Street
Cranford, NJ 07016

Belimawr Branch
Haag Ave. & Benigno
Boulevard
Gloucester, NJ 08031

Route 35 & Hazlet Ave.
Hazlet, NJ 07730

150 Ridgedale
Morristown, NJ 07960

Federal Square
Newark, NJ 07102

86 Bayard Street
New Brunswick, NJ
08901

194 Ward Street
Paterson, NJ 07510

171 Broad Street
Red Bank, NJ 07701

757 Broad Ave.
Ridgefield, NJ 07657

76 Huyler Street
South Hackensack, NJ
07606

680 Highway #130
Trenton, NJ 08650

155 Clinton Road
West Caldwell, NJ 07006

41 Greenwood Avenue
Wykoff, NJ 07481

New Mexico

Main Post Office
1135 Broadway NE
Albuquerque, NM 87101

200 E. Las Cruces Ave.
Las Cruces, NM 88001

New York

General Mail Facility
30 Old Karner Road
Albany, NY 12212

Empire State Plaza
Station
Albany, NY 12220

115 Henry Street
Binghampton, NY 13902

Bronx General Post
Office
149th Street & Grand
Concourse
Bronx, NY 10401

Parkchester Station
1449 West Avenue
Bronx, NY 10462

Riverdale Station
5951 Riverdale Avenue
Bronx, NY 10471

Throggs Neck Station
3630 East Tremont Ave.
Bronx, NY 10465

Wakefield Station
4165 White Plains Rd.
Bronx, NY 10466

Bayridge Station
5501 7th Avenue
Brooklyn, NY 11229

Brooklyn General
Post Office
271 Cadman Plaza East
Brooklyn, NY 11201

Greenpoint Station
66 Meserole Avenue
Brooklyn, NY 11222

Homecrest Station
2002 Avenue U
Brooklyn, NY 11229

Kensington Station
421 McDonald Avenue
Brooklyn, NY 11218

1200 William Street
Buffalo, NY 14240

Downtown Station
255 Clemens Ave.
Elmira, NY 14901

Rte. 9
Clifton Park, NY 12065

1836 Mott Avenue
Far Rockaway, NY 11691

41-65 Main Street
Flushing, NY 11351

Ridgewood Station
869 Cypress Avenue
Flushing, NY 11385

Old Glenham Road
Glenham, NY 12527

16 Hudson Avenue
Glens Falls, NY 12801

185 West John Street
Hicksville, NY 11802

88-40 164th Street
Jamaica, NY 11431

Ansonia Station
1980 Broadway
New York, NY 10004

Bowling Green Station
25 Broadway
New York, NY 10004

Church Street Station
90 Church Street
New York, NY 10007

Empire State Station
350 Fifth Avenue
New York, NY 10001

F.D.R. Station
909 Third Avenue
New York, NY 10022

Grand Central Station
45th St. & Lexington Ave.
New York, NY 10017

Madison Square Station
149 East 23rd Street
New York, NY 10010

New York General
Post Office
33rd and 8th Avenue
New York, NY 10001

Rockefeller Center
Station
610 Fifth Avenue
New York, NY 10020

Times Square Station
340 West 42nd Street
New York, NY 10036

Franklin & S. Main Sts.
Pearl River, NY 10965

55 Mansion Street
Poughkeepsie, NY 12601

1335 Jefferson Road
Rochester, NY 14692

Rockville Centre Main
Post Office
250 Merrick Road
Rockville Centre, NY
11570

25 Route 11
Smithtown, NY 11787

550 Manor Road
Staten Island, NY 10314

New Springville Station
2843 Richmond Ave.
Staten Island, NY 10314

5640 East Taft Road
Syracuse, NY 13220

10 Broad Street
Utica, NY 13503

143 Grand Street
White Plains, NY 10602

North Carolina

West Asheville Station
1300 Patton Avenue
Asheville, NC 28806

Eastway Station
3065 Eastway Drive
Charlotte, NC 28205

301 Green Street
Fayetteville, NC 28302

310 New Bern Avenue
Raleigh, NC 27611

North Dakota

657 2nd Avenue North
Fargo, ND 58102

Ohio

675 Wolf Ledges Pkwy.
Akron, OH 44309

2650 N. Cleveland Ave.
Canton, OH 44701

Fountain Square Station
5th and Walnut Street
Cincinnati, OH 45202

301 W. Prospect Ave.
Cleveland, OH 44101

850 Twin Rivers Drive
Columbus, OH 43216

1111 East 5th Street
Dayton, OH 45401

200 North Diamond St.
Mansfield, OH 44901

200 North 4th Street
Steubenville, OH 43952

435 S. St. Clair Street
Toledo, OH 46301

99 South Walnut Street
Youngstown, OH 44503

Oklahoma

101 East First
Edmond, OK 73034

115 West Broadway
Enid, OK 73701

102 South 5th
Lawton, OK 73501

525 West Okmulgee
Muskogee, OK 74401

129 West Gray
Norman, OK 73069

76320 SW 5th
Oklahoma City, OK
73125

333 West 4th
Tulsa, OK 74101

12 South 5th
Yukon, OK 73099

Oregon

520 Willamette Street
Eugene, OR 97401

751 N.W. Hoyt
Portland, OR 97208

Pennsylvania

Lehigh Valley Branch
Airport Rd. & Route 22
Bethlehem, PA 18001

535 Wood St.
Bethlehem, PA 18016

Main Post Office
Beaver Drive Industrial
Park
Dubois, PA 15801

442-456 Hamilton St.
Allentown, PA 18101

Griswold Plaza
Erie, PA 16501

238 S. Pennsylvania Ave.
Greensburg, PA 15601

10th and Markets Sts.
Harrisburg, PA 17105

111 Franklin Street
Johnstown, PA 15901

Downtown Station
48-50 W. Chestnut St.
Lancaster, PA 17603

1 W. Washington Street
Kennedy Square
New Castle, PA 16101

30th and Market Sts.
Philadelphia, PA 19104

B. Free Franklin Station
316 Market Street
Philadelphia, PA 19106

William Penn Annex
Station
9th and Chestnut Sts.
Philadelphia, PA 19107

Seventh Avenue &
Grant Street
Pittsburgh, PA 15219

450 N. Center Street
Pottsville, PA 17901

59 North 5th Street
Reading, PA 19603

North Washington Ave.
& Linden St.
Scranton, PA 18503

237 South Frazer Street
State College, PA 16801

300 S. Main St.
Wilkes Barre, PA 18701

200 S. George Street
York, PA 17405

Puerto Rico

San Juan General
Post Office
Roosevelt Avenue
San Juan, PR 00936

Plaza Las Americas
Station
San Juan, PR 00938

Rhode Island

24 Corliss Street
Providence, RI 02904

uth Carolina
4290 Daley Avenue
Charleston, SC 29411

1601 Assembly Street
Columbia, SC 29201

600 West Washington
Greenville, SC 29602

South Dakota
500 East Boulevard
Rapid City, SD 57701

320 S. 2nd Avenue
Sioux Falls, SD 57101

Tennessee
General Mail Facility
6050 Shallowford Road
Chattanooga, TN 37422

9th and Georgia
Chattanooga, TN 37401

Tom Murray Station
133 Tucker Street
Jackson, TN 38301

501 West Main Avenue
Knoxville, TN 37901

Colonial Finance Unit
4695 Southern Avenue
Memphis, TN 38124

555 South Third
Memphis, TN 38101

Crosstown Finance Unit
1520 Union Street
Memphis, TN 38104

901 Broadway
Nashville, TN 37202

Texas
2300 South Ross
Amarillo, TX 79105

300 East South Street
Arlington, TX 76010

300 East 9th
Austin, TX 78710

300 Willow
Beaumont, TX 77704

809 Nueces Bay
Corpus Christi, TX 78408

Bryan & Ervay Streets
Dallas, TX 75221

5300 East Paisano Dr.
El Paso, TX 79910

Jennings & Lancaster
Streets
Fort Worth, TX 76101

408 Main Street
Hereford, TX 79045

401 Franklin Avenue
Houston, TX 77201

411 "L" Avenue
Lubbock, TX 79408

601 E. Pecan
McAllen, TX 78501

100 East Wall
Midland, TX 79702

10410 Perrin Beitel Road
San Antonio, TX 78284

615 East Houston
San Antonio, TX 78205

2211 North Robinson
Texarkana, TX 75501

221 West Ferguson
Tyler, TX 75702

800 Franklin
Waco, TX 76701

1000 Lamar Street
Wichita Falls, TX 76307

Utah
1760 West 2100 South
Salt Lake City, UT 84119

Vermont
1 Elmwood Avenue
Burlington, VT 05401

151 West Street
Rutland, VT 05701

Virginia
1155 Seminole Trail
Charlottesville, VA 22906

1425 Battlefield Blvd.,
North
Chesapeake, VA 23320

Merrified Branch
8409 Lee Highway
Fairfax, VA 22116

600 Granby Street
Norfolk, VA 23501

Tyson's Corner Branch
Tyson's Corner Shopping
Center
McLean, VA 22102

Thomas Corner Station
6274 East Virginia Beach
Blvd.
Norfolk, VA 23502

1801 Brook Road
Richmond, VA 23232

419 Rutherford Ave. NE
Roanoke, VA 24022

London Bridge Station
550 1st Colonial Road
Virginia Beach, VA 23454

Washington
Crossroads Station
15800 N.E. 8th
Bellevue, WA 98008

315 Prospect St.
Bellingham, WA 98225

301 Union Street
Seattle, WA 98101

West 904 Riverside
Spokane, WA 99210

1102 A Street
Tacoma, WA 98402

205 West Washington
Ave.
Yakima, WA 98903

West Virginia
301 North Street
Bluefield, WV 24701

Lee and Dickinson St.
Charleston, WV 25301

500 West Pike Street
Clarksburg, WV 26301

1000 Virginia Street
Huntington, WV 25704

217 King Street
Martinsburg, WV 25401

Wisconsin
325 East Walnut
Green Bay, WI 54301

345 West St. Paul Ave.
Milwaukee, WI 53203

Wyoming
2120 Capitol Avenue
Cheyenne, WY 82001

INDEX

This Index covers all issues from the 1893 Columbian Exposition issues (#230) through 1982. Listings in italic typeface refer to Definitive or Regular issues. Airmail issues not included.

INDEX

INDEX

INDEX